The
Rediscovery
of
Lost
America

Arlington Mallery and a Mallery bridge, one of first all-
steel riveted bridges. January 1953. (Photograph by
Leland Puttcamp.)

The Rediscovery of Lost America

Arlington Mallery
and
Mary Roberts Harrison

A Dutton Paperback
E. P. Dutton / New York

For information contact:
E.P. Dutton, 2 Park Avenue,
New York, N.Y. 10016

Library of Congress Cataloging in Publication Data

Mallery, Arlington Humphrey.
The rediscovery of lost America.

A revision of the author's Lost America.
Includes bibliographical references.
1. America—Discovery and exploration—Pre-
Columbian. 2. America—Discovery and exploration—
Norse. 3. Iroquois Indians. I. Harrison, Mary Roberts,
joint author. II. Title.
E103.M32 1979   970.01'3   78-11319

ISBN: 0-525-47545-1

Published simultaneously in Canada by Clarke, Irwin & Company
Limited, Toronto and Vancouver

Designed by Mary Beth Bosco

10 9 8 7 6 5 4 3 2 1

First Edition

To Paul and Hal
with love and gratitude
for their encouragement
and professional assistance

Contents

Author's Note

This is, of course, Arlington Mallery's book. Its principal value as history is in his two major historic breakthroughs: his discovery of the remains of an ancient Iron Age civilization in Ohio and Virginia and his analysis of the Piri Re'is map. Its value as literature is mainly in his eloquent and poetic accounts of the Vinland voyages and other historic events. These passages have been retained much as he wrote them for the first edition of his findings, called *Lost America*. Following the advice of authorities in prehistory to have his research findings copyrighted immediately, Mallery rushed that book, on which he and I were collaborating, into print before our job of assembling material and preparing it for publication was completed. I have rewritten the original book, adding several new chapters, including Chapter 23, "My 'Discovery' of the Piri Re'is Map," based on Mallery's notes and our conversations. Besides these chapters, I have added sections of chapters and two complete chapters, "The Clash of Theories" and "The Ancient Worldwide Signary," based on my own research. Mallery is not responsible for either of these chapters, except for several references to his thinking reported in them. They were written after his death.

Professor Jere Fleck, Department of Germanic and Slavic Languages and Literatures, University of Maryland, assisted me with the Old Norse linguistic materials. Donal Buchanan, past president of the Northern Virginia Chapter of the Archaeological Society of Virginia, has worked with me on the chapter on the ancient signary. Rollin W. Gillespie, space scientist who is writing a book on world history, has clarified technical factors for me relating to cartography and epigraphy and has contributed ideas based on his research on prehistory.

MARY ROBERTS HARRISON

Introduction
to the
Original Edition
of
Mallery's
Lost America

by
Matthew W. Stirling
Director, Bureau of American Ethnology
Smithsonian Institution

This is a book that is so bold in concept and so startling in its implications that it will produce widespread skepticism among scholars. This is all the more likely because many of the ideas set forth have been advanced before and rejected because of insufficient or badly selected supporting data. Nevertheless it is a thought-provoking book. Specialists in cartography, linguistics, metallurgy, climatology, archaeology, and early European history will no doubt find many things to criticize. The author is a student of all these things without being a specialist in any unless it be cartography. As a student he is well aware of the orthodox ideas held in these matters. The value of his book lies in the fact that he has not allowed himself to adhere to orthodox ideas when the evidence seems to him to lead to other conclusions. It is the broad approach which, though often liable to error, is most likely to produce important new ideas. Botanists, astronomers, and physicists have been responsible for producing many of the most recent advances in archaeology.

Captain Mallery is an engineer by profession. He is a skilled navigator who has sailed ships over the seas of which he writes. He knows charts and ships and ocean currents from years of practical experience. He has an intimate understanding of the problems and equipment of the early navigators and the capacities and limitations of their vessels. As an engineer he approaches all technological problems from the practical viewpoint.

A number of previously rejected items and theories have been reexamined and given new validity. When the evidence is meager or inferential such things are difficult to evaluate. It was not long ago when no archaeologist of repute would admit that man was once contemporary with the mammoth in this continent, and it is only recently that the question of pre-Columbian trans-Pacific voyages to America has become a respectable subject for discussion among anthropologists.

That the Norse visited the mainland of North America centuries before Columbus is now a virtually undisputed fact. In his descriptions of the classic Norse voyages the author gives a number of new interpretations as to the routes followed, but it is in his conclusions as to the extent and impact of these voyages plus the viewpoint that still earlier North Europeans had extensive contacts with the New World that he deviates most widely from present accepted theories.

Historical information is fairly detailed for Southern Europe and the Eastern Mediterranean because of the early development of writing in this area. On the other hand, we know much less of the accomplishments of the illiterate and semiliterate peoples of North Europe. We know that they were expert navigators and made long voyages of which, in early times, no records were kept. In view of the long period during which there were permanent settlements in Iceland and Greenland, it would be strange if there were not more voyages to the North American mainland than those few to which such scant reference was made. If it is true, as geological, archaeological, and climatological evidence seems to show, that the Arctic Coast formerly had a considerably warmer climate, there is no reason why this region should not have been visited by early navigators.

It will be difficult to convince American archaeologists that there was a pre-Columbian Iron Age in America. This startling item, however, is one that should not long remain in doubt. The detailed studies of metallurgists and the new carbon-14 dating method should be sufficient to give a definite answer on this point. To this writer, the possible Norse connections with the Great Lakes copper culture seem more convincing in the light of present evidence.

This introduction is by no means intended as an endorsement of all the theories presented in the book. This writer suggests that the reader make his own evaluation of the evidence presented, and draw his own conclusions.

The book deals with one of the most fascinating and at the same time tantalizing subjects with which historians have had to deal. The author should have the readers' full admiration for the scholarly manner in which he has handled so controversial a subject, and for the way in which he has followed his evidence no matter how far it leads him from conventional points of view.

1

Spruce Hill

Spruce Hill is a flat-top mountain towering above the Scioto Valley in south-central Ohio. Since the time of the earliest modern settlements nearby, this lofty land bulge intruding upon the horizon near the hamlet of Bourneville has been host to professional archaeologists and to local antiquity buffs. They have come in search of vestiges of a long-vanished civilization. Through many decades they have struggled up the precipitous, often muddy, slopes of the hill, always hoping to find among the many relics at the top answers to questions Ohioans have been asking for nearly two centuries. Who were the people who built the many man-made earthworks standing out so boldly on our picturesque landscape or hiding in the shelter of our primeval forests? Who were the people whose novel artifacts are scattered around our countryside and so regularly exposed by farmers' plows? When did they live here? And what was their culture like?

Among the many residents of the area in the early 1800s speculating on the origin of the ancient fort lying in ruins on the crest of the hill was James Foster, a local newspaper editor. Foster has left a description of Spruce Hill as it was then—more than 150 years ago. In 1811, before leaving for service in the War of 1812, he climbed up the

Fig. 1-1. Spruce Hill terrain. (Photograph by Marcus T. Orr.)

hill to examine the controversial ruins, and later wrote a letter describing the remains of the fort. His letter was discovered recently in a Boston bookstore in a journal published in 1814, which was sent to the Ross County Historical Society as a gift. Emphasizing the antiquity of the ruins, Foster says in his letter in part:

It [the fort] contains about one hundred acres and is enclosed by a stone wall, which, if we may judge from the quantity of stones (for it is in ruins) must have been twelve or fifteen feet high and four or five feet thick. . . .

There are trees now growing on this fortification which are four or five feet in diameter and they appear to have been preceded by a race still more gigantic if we may judge from the long traces left by those that have rotted in their native dust. Some of the largest grew out of the foundation of the wall in places where the stone had tumbled down on the side of the hill. . . .

At the bottom of the hill on the southwest side are the ruins of a town, or rather city. The cellars and stone foundations of the houses still remain. The streets are in regular squares. . . . It was from all appearances the residence of a warlike race. . . .

Of that long-destroyed race of people we know nothing except what we learn from their works; even their traditions have sunk with

2

them into a common grave. But we have enough left in these vestiges of their labors and their wars to convince us that they were
much more civilized than the present Indian inhabitants of any portion of our continent.[1]

Three or four hundred feet above the valley, at the summit of
Spruce Hill, one can see the collapsed walls today. Obviously of ancient vintage, these fallen walls have long been among the most puzzling relics of America's past. During my brief residence in Ohio in
the 1930s, I first heard about the mysteries buried at the top of the hill
a few miles to the south. Later, my research on prehistoric America
included examination of many prehistoric masonry structures of unknown origin scattered throughout the northern and the northeastern
areas of our country. As an experienced mason, I determined that
these structures were the work of expert masons, technicians of an advanced civilization. Spruce Hill and the crumbled walls then came to
my mind repeatedly.

Such a heretical idea was, of course, nonsense. For more than a
century, archaeologists and historians have been in agreement[2] that
only Stone Age Indians lived in America before Columbus, savages of
the Mongolian race who came to this continent originally from Asia by
way of the Bering Straits. Their date of arrival, some authorities believe, was probably during the Wisconsin glaciation around 20,000
B.C., when the ice fields covering our northern lands held so much
water that the sea level was reduced and the Bering Straits was a land
bridge.[3] Arriving probably as bands of hunters, so the theory goes,
they settled from the Arctic shores in the north to the southern tip of
South America, developing through the ages a great variety of cultures, depending upon the ecology of the area of settlement.

Archaeologists and historians have been unyielding in their assumption that the people of pre-Columbian America did not smelt and
cast metals. They grant that some of the earliest settlers cold-hammered into usable shape some raw metals and minerals, including copper and silver, which they thought were stones, and iron from fallen
meteors, which they thought were gifts from the gods, "never dream-
ing that they could be melted, refined, and cast into implements and
ornaments."[4] Accordingly, authorities have explained that the rare
pieces of prehistoric iron and iron tools are meteoric iron, and that the
more than 100,000 copper tools stored in our museums are raw copper
hammered into shape by Stone Age Indians.

The startling fact, however, is that these copper tools were cast by expert metallurgists of an advanced civilization and not hammered into shape by Stone Age Indians. In the 1940s, I assembled, with the guidance and assistance of scientists and museums, metallurgical evidence that these tools were cast, proof that there were skilled metallurgical craftsmen in prehistoric America. (See Appendix A for an account of this discovery, including the report of the New York Testing Laboratories and comments of metallurgical experts.)

If they had wanted to, these early craftsmen could have produced iron from the bog ore which was close at hand in the swamps, moors, and other lowlands of many ancient settlements. The earliest method of extracting iron from this common ore was so simple that, like firing of pottery, extraction of iron may have been one of the first crafts practiced by primitive man when he emerged from the Stone Age.[5] Besides bog ore and charcoal for fuel, the earliest ironworker needed only a clay-lined pit dug in the ground close to a hillside or on the bank of a hill to catch the prevailing wind or the updraft from the valley below. An ancient potter may have discovered the process of smelting iron when, by mistake, he attempted to use bog ore instead of pottery clay and hours later found a mass of malleable iron in his kiln. Or he may have discovered that he could extract iron from bog ore by baking the ore in intense heat, when he found chunks of iron in the ashes of his fires, iron which the heat had extracted from bits of bog ore on rocks or in soil in the fires.

In September 1948, I returned to Ohio to examine the masonry of the decomposed walls on Spruce Hill that researchers believe circled a fortress rising high above the mountain in prehistoric times. In the design and the structure of the walls, I expected to find evidence that these walls had been laid by skilled masons, technicians comparable in sophistication to the builders of the masonry structures I was then examining in the northern and northeastern sections of the country and also to the expert metallurgists who had cast the pre-Columbian copper tools piled up in our museums.

Picking my way up the mountain by jeep, I came upon an astonishing phenomenon at the top. Extending for more than 2 miles around the summit lay more than 200,000 tons of quarried stones, obviously the ruins of a very old wall, a tremendous structure. Huge trees covered the line of the wall, which, in the words of E. G. Squier, were "twisting their roots among the stones, which at many points had become embedded in their trunks."

The longer I pondered the piles of crumbled stones, the more probable it seemed to me, as an experienced mason and builder, that the wall had been part of a stockade. The builders had piled up large quarried stones, mostly red sandstone from the side of the hill, as though for a garden wall. At regular intervals behind the wall, they had erected four long posts. To hold the posts in place, they had used cross bars of saplings, anchoring them on one side in the wall and on the other side in a wall of smaller stones back of the posts. Standing on this platform, they could pelt attackers with rocks and spears. The stone wall acted also as a firebreak to protect the wooden parts of the stockade from fires set to burn them down. Samuel de Champlain describes a stockade like this in use by the Iroquois.

It was no surprise to me to find assurance that sophisticated builders had laid these walls. At several locations, they had provided entrances to the fort by curving the walls to form openings so ingeniously that from both sides of the openings, with a barrage of rocks and spears, they could have forced back any enemies trying to sneak through.

While examining the construction of the ancient wall, I noticed tons of cinder scattered about, around and inside the piles of fallen stones. It was a peculiar substance which had obviously been subjected to intense heat for a long time, and so I assumed that it was refuse of very extensive operations involving fire. I was puzzled, for although it resembled most slag from iron smelting, it was too dark and too heavy to be slag.

Soon I was asking myself if this strange cinder could be refuse of prehistoric iron smelting, and then I realized that I was looking at ancient slag for the first time in my life. Recalling my metallurgical studies, I identified the cinder as ancient slag by its distinguishable features: color and weight. Unlike modern slag, lighter in color and in weight, ancient slag retained much of the iron in the ore, which gave it color and weight. The earliest crude hearthpit furnaces were wasteful smelters, for they did not extract all of the iron from the ore. Under normal conditions, these primitive furnaces operated below the melting point of iron. Consequently, the iron did not melt in them as it does in modern high-temperature blast furnaces. Instead, most of the nonmetallic elements in the iron ore melted, and the iron was left mixed with impurities as a solid in an accumulated mass.

The general belief that in the extraction of iron from iron ore it is necessary to melt the iron is a misconception based on the modern process of melting the iron in high-temperature furnaces that operate at a heat above the melting point of iron. The remaining slag is almost devoid of iron, having usually as little as 1 percent or less, whereas ancient slag had an iron content often of 50 percent or more.

After a moment's review of what I had read about the ancient process of producing iron, there was no doubt in my mind. The cinder was the refuse of prehistoric iron smelting.

As I contemplated with wonder the presence of ancient slag in the ruins of an ancient stone wall, I realized that somewhere nearby there would be an ancient smelter for heating bog ore, a primitive hearthpit—in fact, many primitive hearthpits, considering the tons of slag lying around. If they had not been obliterated by man or the natural elements through the ages, it should be possible to find them or at least their remains. Eagerness to find the old furnace, or furnaces, grew as I reasoned that there would be clues to determining who these prehistoric ironworkers were in the kind of furnaces we would find. We would be able to track down their identity with the help of the records of the step-by-step advancement in the development of the craft of iron extraction through centuries. (See Appendix B for description of ancient methods of iron production.) The message of the slag was that it was produced in the earliest hearthpits. My interest now was to find to what stage of development the primitive smelters belonged: the very crude, very old type, which I had classified as *Celtic,* or a later, improved type distinguished by the addition of a flue to increase the draft and to carry the slag and the mass of separated iron down to a receptacle. This later type of hearthpit I had named *Nordic.* The possibility that the hearthpits which we were certain to find would be a more advanced type seemed unlikely, for the slag was too rich in iron.

With the assistance of several aides and a bulldozer, I set about to try to find some hearthpits or their remains, curious about the stage of development to which they would belong. After several hours of digging in promising areas, with the slag as a guide to its location, we finally uncovered a hearthpit on a ledge below the stone wall. Only since recent excavations by Swedish and German scientists have the exact appearance and the method of operation of such a furnace been known to the modern world. This hearthpit is large, about 12 feet long and 8 feet wide. The bottom and the sides are covered by a layer of clay a foot thick.

But this furnace is not the earliest type which I call Celtic. It belongs to a later stage of development because it has an opening at the bottom about a foot square to a stone-covered flue the same size and 8 feet long. At the end of this flue is a small clay receptacle, whose purpose is to bring in air and to carry out the porous mass of iron to the receptacle where the bloom—the accumulated iron—is formed. This flue identifies the furnace as the Nordic type, as does the rough sandstone wall, 2 feet high, surrounding it.

In 1919, George Shoemaker, a resident of Bourneville, came upon this furnace on a visit to Spruce Hill in search of gold. He found the pit filled with cinder, rotten wood, bits of charcoal, and glazed pieces of Berea sandstone and clinker. Certain that there was some gold in the hodgepodge, he cleaned out the pit. What he discovered was not gold but an oval bowl with bottom and sides lined with potter's clay. Shoemaker had worked in a pottery, and so he recognized the lining as clay from a pit or vein on the bank of Paint Creek directly below. We found the pit from which the bog ore had apparently been dug about 60 feet from the furnace. In 1919, Shoemaker had cleaned out this pit and found that it was about 16 feet deep.

At the moment we uncovered the oval pit with the clay lining, elation sent my thoughts soaring into the world of Heinrich Schlie-

Fig. 1-2. Nordic-type iron-smelting furnace on Spruce Hill. Arlington Mallery is pointing. (Photograph by Marcus T. Orr.)

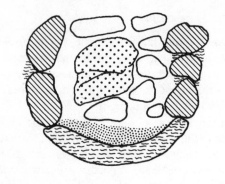

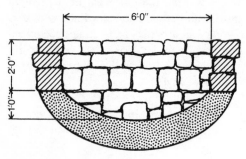

Fig. 1-3. Section of pre-historic Celtic-type furnace found at N. Tralebo, Sweden, above and section of prehistoric Celtic-type furnace found on Spruce Hill, in Ross County, Ohio.

mann and his Troy and the realm of forbidden fancy: here, on the crest of Spruce Hill, in the center of our great continent, lie the remains of a prehistoric Iron Age civilization. We, my associates and I, have discovered—or stumbled upon—proof that America was the home of an advanced civilization centuries ago!

Uncovering this Nordic-type hearthpit was only the beginning of a successful search for more remains of the ancient Iron Age civilization on this continent. Encouraged by metallurgical tests[6] showing that the iron content of the slag in the furnace was around 30 percent and that approximately only 40 percent of the iron in the ore had been recovered in this Nordic-type furnace, we returned to Spruce Hill many times. Each time we uncovered more furnaces, including several of the Celtic type, more primitive. Metallurgical tests showed that the slag in these furnaces had twice the content of the slag in the the Nordic furnace, showing that the Celtic furnaces on Spruce Hill were half as efficient as the Nordic furnace we had found there.

In the fall of 1951 we uncovered a Celtic furnace in a mound of quarry stones on Spruce Hill. Tom Porter, a member of our group, cut into the mound of stones and uncovered a reddish area that turned out

Fig. 1-4. Rune stone at entrance to Viking grave on Spruce Hill.

Fig. 1-5. Viking grave on Spruce Hill.

to be the top of a furnace. Digging down farther, we uncovered a hearthpit almost 9 feet in diameter. It had a lining of red clay, 4 inches deep. It did not have the additional equipment that the Nordic furnace had, a flue and receptacle. So, by my classification it was a Celtic furnace, a more primitive type.

To extract iron in a very primitive furnace such as this one, the ironworker had to work much harder than the ironworker with a Nordic furnace. In the Celtic furnace, the accumulated iron—the bloom—remained at the bottom of the pit. Before lifting it out, the worker had to quench the fire with water and remove the unconsumed fuel. To get the bloom into a suitable condition to be forged, it was often necessary for him to reheat it several times, and each time he had to make a new fire and then quench it after the reheating. This very crude type of hearthpit was used by Celtic [7] people in Europe and Ireland before the Christian Era and later, and undoubtedly by other early people. It became obsolete, however, in the developed areas of the Western Hemisphere and in other areas also during the fourteenth century.

Later I cut into the mound of quarry stones and uncovered four more hearthpit furnaces—two underneath the stone wall. One of them is an oval basin with walls of Berea grit, the parent rock of bog ore. Several large stones, which have been obviously subjected to intense heat, show that the wall had been about 16 feet high at this point.

While excavating around the walls with a bulldozer, we discovered that the wood ties of the stockade posts had rotted and the water seeping through the wall had so undermined the stone facing that it had collapsed. When we reached the ground under the wall, we cut into what appeared to be the charred butt ends of stockade posts which had been either cut down or burned down.

Near the Nordic furnace there is a circular stone-covered mound on a high promontory. Set deep in the top of this mound is a stone engraved in runes, letters of the Norse alphabet. The stone marks the entrance to a grave like those found in many locations in Scandinavia, stone-vaulted burial chambers, known as ancient Scandinavian "passage graves." The ruins of nine more of these stone-lined graves lie on another promontory near the furnace. (See Figs. 1-4 and 1-5.)

At one time there were thousands of such stone-lined graves in the Middle West, identical with those in ancient northern Europe. Few of them have survived. Archaeologists have made little effort to preserve the great stone monuments of the ancient civilization which they have not been able to explain.

2

The
Pre-Columbian
Iron Industry
in
Ohio

Ohio newsmen who followed our excavations on Spruce Hill performed their job with gusto. To them we owe the cooperation of their readers, who led us to our next discoveries. Often weighed down by cameras, heavy windbreakers, and boots, they trudged along beside us through mud, over rock piles and refuse heaps, always in high spirits. They clung to our diggers, awaiting the unearthing of the next relic of the vanished civilization. To pick up all they could about methods of ancient iron smelting, the structure of the crude hearthpits, the peculiar slag produced in these primitive smelters, and the probable people whose relics we were finding, they lingered around the sites after the digging was over, unmindful of passing mealtimes, pelting rain, and other discomforts. Occasionally, they took up shovels and picks and joined the digging, and later became members of our group, contributing both labor and ideas.

News accounts of our findings and of the "Mallery claims" sometimes carried the disparaging remarks of some so-called authorities, but on the whole were objective and accurate reports, even of the most technical factors of ancient iron smelting, presented with an air of excitement and wonder. Illustrated by many photographs of sites

Fig. 2-1. Elza Shoemaker, Bourneville, Ohio, looks on as Mallery points to upper rim of fortification from bastion at Blackamore Knob, Ross County, Ohio. January 10, 1953. (Photograph by Leland Puttcamp.)

and digging crews and hand-drawn diagrams of the ancient furnaces, these news stories kindled the interest of many readers in the glazed cinders and sandstone scattered about their land. From farmers in the Deer Creek Valley, about 10 miles from Spruce Hill, came lumps of cinder to be examined by me. It was obvious at first glance that all of the cinder sent to me was identical to the ancient slag on Spruce Hill.

So I closed down the excavation work on the hill and went to the Deer Creek Valley, certain that we would find some ancient hearthpits there. Luckily, our discoveries in the valley during the following two years far exceeded my expectations. Within several days of excavating on sites there, we unearthed fourteen furnaces representing the development of the iron-extraction industry over a period of several centuries.

Most of these furnaces were buried at the bottom of prehistoric mounds that had not been disturbed since the earliest modern settlements except for surface plowing. Some of the furnaces covered three-fourths of the base of a mound. Modern settlers could not have built them there without tearing down the mounds that cover them, and they could not have been intrusive in any other way. And so the antiquity of the furnaces is established by their position in the mounds.

These Deer Creek Valley furnaces are all the Old World type of ancient hearthpit. In the ways in which they differ among themselves in structural details, they present as a whole a record of the advancing steps in the development of the iron-extraction craft over countless years.

As the first site for excavation in the valley, I chose a mound on the farm of George Arledge, about 8 miles north of Bourneville. It is one of the well-known prehistoric man-made earthworks of unknown origin. My attention had been drawn to this particular mound by Professor Edward Keeler of Ohio State University and an archaeologist with the Ohio State Archaeological Museum, who had picked up glazed slag and sandstone plowed out of the mound. When we first met, Arledge told me that his plow was turning up quantities of cinder and sandstone when he cultivated the top of the mound, an increasing amount as time passed.

The mound was then, in December 1948, about 50 feet in diameter and only about 6 feet high. The farmer and his lifelong neighbors said that in 1910 it was 16 feet high and covered with locust trees, and that during the intervening half-century, the trees and the upper 10 feet of the mound had been removed by cultivation. They explained how they had plowed out many tons of refuse—cinders, charcoal, bog ore, and stones in layers. Their description of this waste assured me that an ancient hearthpit was buried in this mound and that the plow of Farmer Arledge was getting so close to it that we would be able to reach it in a few hours of digging. According to descriptions of the prehistoric iron-smelting industry, the prehistoric mounds in Europe covering ancient furnaces had been built of the same waste: that is, by heaping over the furnaces and the graves of the ironmasters the accumulated ashes, iron slag, surplus iron, and refuse and then covering the pile of waste with a blanket of loam.

To uncover the furnace that I felt certain was now close to the ground surface of the mound, I dug a trench through the slag-marked mound with the assistance of several residents of nearby towns. Near the center of the mound, we found the first of the fourteen Deer Creek

Valley furnaces. This one is an oval pit almost 8 feet long and 5 feet wide. The vertical walls are 6 inches of soft, red-burned iron ore, and the inner facing is glazed.

The next day we cleaned out the furnace chamber and found that it was so complex in structure that only highly skilled metallurgists could have designed it. To reach the furnace floor, we shoveled out more than 4 feet of materials in layers. On top was a 2-foot layer of loam with pieces of glazed cinder and sandstone, then a foot of partially burned bog ore, some black ashes, a 6-inch layer of hard-burned bog ore, and finally, resting on the floor, a bed of white ashes and charcoal.

The floor below was a layer of hard-burned bog ore over an inch thick. When we broke up this hard, smooth floor, I saw that this furnace was more technically advanced in structural detail than the furnaces on Spruce Hill. It is probably a type that was in general use as late as two hundred years before the blast furnace came into wide use around the middle of the fourteenth century. The striking structural difference of this furnace was that underneath the floor was a bed of loosely laid cobblestones, about 18 inches deep, and buried in this cobblestone base was a large flue.

These unusual features of the furnace—an underground flue passing through a cobblestone base under the furnace floor—point to the Greenland Norse as the designers, maybe even the builders, of this furnace. Danish archaeologists found a furnace with a flue in a cobblestone base in the ruins of the settlement of Austmannadal, Greenland.[1] The Austmannadal settlement was abandoned by the Norse about 1350.

Our digging in the Deer Creek Valley was interrupted several times by excitement over discoveries of other relics of the prehistoric iron industry. As our picks and shovels tore into the waste-laden mounds, they unearthed iron bars, iron shovels, and an iron ax with a mineralized wooden handle. The first of these relics was found by Elza Shoemaker, a local schoolteacher, in the mound on the Arledge farm. It was a bar of cast iron, 3 feet long and 62 pounds in weight. Seeing the bar stuck in the flue of the furnace, Shoemaker thought it was a stone and asked his son Herbert to dig it out. Herbert, seeing that it was a bar of iron, cleared away the surrounding debris, and his brother Paul photographed the bar as it lay in the flue of the furnace in which it had been made. (See Fig. 2-2.)

This billet of iron is the first iron object produced in prehistoric

Fig. 2-2. The iron bar in the furnace in the Arledge mound, where it was found.

America to be found in the furnace in which it was produced. It was submitted to the National Bureau of Standards for examination. Dr. George Ellinger, who analyzed the bar there, reported that the iron-workers who made it apparently did not know how to eliminate phosphorus in the production of iron. At the time of the earliest settlements in modern times in the area where the bar was found, iron was produced there in abundance in modern blast furnaces. Like other modern iron, it did not have a high phosphorus content.

Ancient furnaces did not produce cast iron; so how can the presence of this bar of cast iron in the flue of an ancient furnace be explained? It can be assumed that cast iron was produced in prehistoric furnaces in small amounts on those rare occasions when the temperature in the furnace was abnormally increased by an accidentally increased blast or unusually high wind at a time when there was an excess of charcoal in the chamber.

In the case of this bar of cast iron, the furnace temperature had probably risen so high that it had completely melted the iron in the ore. The molten metal had filled the flue and then cooled off when the flue became clogged. Finding his furnace blocked by the long bar of iron, the ironworker had evidently broken into the front of the furnace, quenched the fire with water, and tried to pry out the bar. In his unsuccessful effort, he broke it off 37 inches from the end, leaving the flue clogged with the remaining 3 feet of the bar. Instead of repairing the furnace, he evidently abandoned it with the bar still in the flue.

Micrographs of the bar showed that the structure of the iron had been altered by exposure to intense heat for months after the bar had formed. Since the floor of the furnace was still intact, it seemed probable that there was another flue that had admitted air to the furnace after the first flue had been clogged. Ancient German furnaces of this type (Nordic), called *Schmelzövens,* sometimes were equipped with more than one flue.[2]

The following spring we returned to the site in search of a second flue. In the loose, plowed-up loam at the site, we noticed glazed dark-green and purple stones and, about 2 feet from the opened furnace, a ring of red-burned bog ore. Excavating at this point, we uncovered a second furnace, smaller than the first and a later type. Standing on a loosely laid cobblestone base, it was equipped with a cobblestone back wall which would permit the entrance of air, and also a flue constructed of cobblestones and lined with lime to draw off the iron and slag. (See Fig. 2-3.)

The mound had been built over the two furnaces some time after the second one was shut down.

A complete record of our excavations at the Arledge mound was filed at the Smithsonian Institution Bureau of American Ethnology. The report includes the known history of the mound and its previous owners, affidavits, photographs, and drawings that describe in full the position of the furnaces in the mound, their structure and contents, and complete metallurgical analysis of the bar.

Finding cast iron in his furnace meant trouble for the ancient ironworker, for it was useless to him and often a nuisance, especially if it was lodged in such a position that it blocked furnace operation. He no doubt found that he could not hammer it into usable shape because it was too brittle and could not remelt it because his crude smelter operated below the temperature required for melting iron. Annoyed, he would probably discard this abnormal product of his labors.

In these Arledge mound furnaces, I found the first evidence of the use of lime in the craft of iron extraction. The practice of using limestone as a flux may have begun in the Deer Creek Valley. Apparently in order to distribute the draft evenly throughout the furnace, ancient ironworkers frequently spread a layer of small broken stones over the iron ore. Heat formed white and colored glazes on the stones, and so when glazed stones are found in and around a mound, it is likely that there is, or has been, an ancient hearthpit inside the mound. The Deer Creek Valley ironmasters must have used limestone pebbles from Deer Creek to produce a slow, even draft. When they found that the limestone pebbles increased the efficiency of their iron-extraction operations, they may have started to use limestone regularly in place of other stones.

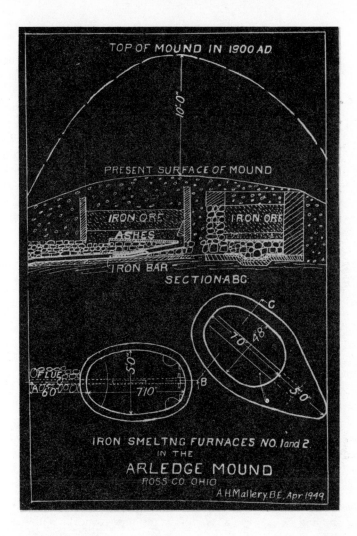

Fig. 2-3. Drawing of the prehistoric iron-smelting furnaces in the Arledge mound. The furnaces were built 50 yards south of a low hill, on the original ground surface of a level 200-acre field. Earth embankments around the furnaces had a dual function. They braced the furnace walls and provided space for the platforms from which fuel and ore were fed into the furnaces. An inclined runway was used for carrying material to the upper platforms, while others at the furnace-floor level were used for removing slag and billets of iron. The drawings above show the relative proportions of the furnaces, their platforms, and the mound. Obviously, the furnaces could not have been intrusive, for with their platforms they occupied almost three-fourths of the base of the mound.

While we were digging out the furnace in the Arledge mound, Fred Keeler, the Ross County agricultural agent, joined us, bringing encouraging news. He said that he had seen the ruins of a structure that might be an ancient iron furnace on the bank of Deer Creek about 100 yards away. Following Keeler to the creek, we saw there in the side of the bank the end of a furnace. Lying in a heap in the gravel of the creek bed 12 feet or more below the top of the bank were the ruins of the remainder of the demolished furnace, where they had fallen.

This furnace was built many centuries ago several feet below the ground surface of a level field. The creek was then a distance away, flowing in its ancient bed. During the ages, it washed away the land and moved nearer the buried hearthpit. By 1900 it was within 150 yards, and there was a road between the creek and the hearthpit. By 1948, the creek had wiped out the road, reached the furnace, and undermined it. All that was left of the ancient structure was an end of the furnace set precariously in the side of the bank of the creek.

As we poked around in the debris of the furnace remains, our picks hit a large, solid object. Pushing aside the loam and other fill covering it, we laid bare a very old shovel. Believing that it might have been used by early settlers to dig in the furnace debris, we hid the shovel in the field above, hoping that nobody would use it to dig further in the furnace and destroy what was left of it. We were overlooking two facts: the furnace had been exposed only a year or so and the shovel was too old to have been used by early settlers. The enigma of the origin of this shovel would become one of the most tantalizing challenges to confront me in my work on the ancient iron industry.

When this furnace collapsed, it contained at least three tons of iron ore. When the ancient ironworkers abandoned it, they filled the chamber with stones, gravel, bits of lime, and other refuse. Then, after roofing the top with a layer of plaster, they covered it with loam.

While watching us uncover the furnace in the Arledge mound, Charles Haskins, a nearby farmer, told us that his plow turned up glazed slag and stones and even some iron when he cultivated a low mound on his land. So Paul Shoemaker and I went to the neighboring Haskins farm to examine the slag and the iron. While escorting us to the low ridge overlooking Deer Creek, Haskins explained that the mound had been reduced 5 feet in height by surface plowing during the fifty years since his father had bought the land.

Deciding at first glance that the slag here was identical to the slag scattered about the sites on Spruce Hill and the Arledge mound where we had unearthed furnaces, young Shoemaker and I dug into the ridge. A few inches below the surface, not more than 10 inches, we struck the walls of a furnace. Haskins's plow would have cut into this furnace the next year.

Piled nearby was a heap of refuse—glazed and unglazed slag, pieces of burned clay, ashes, lime, and charcoal—which Haskins said he had carted away from the mound in many wagon loads during several decades. And yet nobody had even suspected that inside this mound there was an iron-extraction furnace! There were, as we were to learn when we unearthed three more the next year, four furnaces in this mound.

After Paul and I removed the topsoil and uncovered the top of the furnace wall, we found that the chamber was filled with dark loam to within about 10 inches from the bottom. Down to this point the walls were red and there was no evidence that there had been any lime in this furnace. Below the loam was a 10-inch layer of what we thought was lime which covered completely the furnace floor and filled a flue hole in the wall. Not until 1962, over ten years later, did we know that what we thought was lime was white clay. In that year tests by the U.S. Bureau of Standards proved that the longtime assumed-to-be lime was clay.[3]

We removed the layer of clay and found under it a hard concrete floor in which were embedded some boards obviously split from a tree trunk. Paul and I thought the boards were the top of a coffin, and so we decided to suspend the work until the next day so that we could have witnesses to the opening of the coffin. However, when we took the boards up the next day, we found that they were laid on the concrete bottom, not on a coffin.

Paul returned to college, and so several local residents, including Haskins, continued the excavation he and I had started. Under my supervision, they dug a trench about 6 feet wide to explore the area just outside the flue hole. They uncovered there a concrete working platform extending 4 feet beyond the furnace wall. At the end of the platform in a pile of trash, William Miller, who was helping in the work on this furnace, found another bar of iron much like the bar that Elza Shoemaker had uncovered in the Arledge mound. This second bar was smaller, almost 3 feet long and 55 pounds in weight. It was cast iron like the first bar, but it was softer iron. The ironworker had apparently abandoned it because of its uselessness to him, for it was found in the trash.

After cleaning off the platform, Miller started to dig the clay out of the flue end. He found, at the outer end, an old iron shovel completely encased in the white clay. It looked much like the shovel we had found in the remains of the furnace on the bank of Deer Creek, which we had assumed was a very old, but modern, shovel. This shovel was found at the bottom of the mound under the wall of a prehistoric iron furnace, and so it could not be a modern shovel. Its location under a prehistoric mound was proof of its prehistoric origin. I was not present when Miller found this shovel. As he was handing it to me on my return, we remarked simultaneously that it had to be an ancient shovel and the shovel found earlier which was almost identical to this one also had to be an ancient shovel.

This furnace was in perfect condition. It is an improved form of the second furnace found in the Arledge mound. It is over 8 feet long and 6 feet wide. The floor slopes from the back toward an air and draw-off flue. With the flue wide open, slag could be drawn out while ore and fuel were being inserted at the top. It was planned for continuous operation like furnaces described by Ludwig Beck,[4] an authority on ancient German furnaces.

On June 1, 1949, I sent both old iron shovels to the Battelle Memorial Institute for metallurgical examination. Scientists there made elaborate spectroscopic, chemical, and metallurgical analyses of the shovels.[5] They reported that their analyses showed that the shovels were not made by modern processes or of modern iron, although they may have been made in colonial times or earlier. It would be impossible to assign a date to them, they explained, because there are no articles of comparable antiquity of known date available for comparison. (See Figs. 2-4 and 2-5.)

This scientific analysis of the old shovels led to a fascinating revelation concerning the ingenuity of ancient ironworkers (at least some of them): they used an ingenious method for fabricating from their soft iron hard blades for such special objects as axes, shovels, and swords—the famous Damascus sword blades, for example—a technique that became a lost art for centuries after the spread of the use of the modern furnace and the production of steel. Revived in recent times in jet plane construction, this process is now known as *cladding*. Cladding is the welding at less than normal temperature of two thin sheets of steel or carburized iron to produce iron of utmost strength.

Norse iron was so soft that Norse warriors were forced to step out of the battle line to straighten out their swords by stepping on them

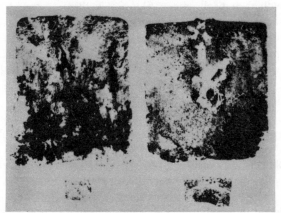

Fig. 2-4. Prehistoric iron shovels found in furnaces in the Haskins and Deer Creek mounds.

Fig. 2-5. Arlington Mallery points to collection of iron bars and implements found in remains of prehistoric furnaces in Ohio.

with their heels after striking only three or four blows. To prepare such soft iron for cladding, ancient craftsmen first hardened it by heating it in crucibles with charcoal at very high heat for days until the thin sheets were transformed into steel by carbon absorbed from the coal. Called carburization, this process is both costly and time-consuming, and so it was used very selectively, only for the manufacture of special objects.

When the Battelle scientists explained the cladding process to me and at the same time said that the blades of both shovels were two sheets of carburized iron cladded, I asked them if they thought the shovels were ancient. If they were of ancient origin, they replied, they would have to have been preserved for centuries in an environment protective to iron, and chemical analysis showed that "they were found in an environment quite protective to iron." A mineral coating formed on the surface of the blades as a result of the soil in which they lay, according to Dr. J. C. De Haven of Battelle, could have preserved the iron for a very long time.

The possibility remained, however, that the shovels were made in our colonial settlements. But it seemed unlikely to me that colonial ironworkers would have used the slow and costly carburizing process to get iron hard enough for tools, nails, and other objects, since modern ironworking methods were in general use in their time and they could produce steel without such an expenditure of time and money. So I decided to have some samples of colonial iron tested to determine if any of them had been cladded. For this purpose, I borrowed some iron nails, hoe blades, and other tools found in the abandoned Jamestown, Virginia, settlement of the early 1600s for testing at Battelle Memorial Institute. Metallurgists there found no sign of cladding of any of these colonial objects, which were loaned for testing by the National Park Service.[6]

The quantity of refuse typical of refuse from iron extraction present in and around the low Haskins mound suggested that the mound had been the site of very extensive prehistoric iron production. So I returned to the site in the summer of 1950, certain that there were more furnaces in the mound. Digging at the other end of the mound, my associates and I unearthed two more iron bars and an ax with a mineralized wooden handle. (See Fig. 2-5.) Going down deeper, we uncovered three more furnaces.

The four furnaces in this mound represent four stages in the development of the ancient iron industry, probably covering a period of

one thousand years. They show the progressive evolution characteristic of a long-continued civilization that was interrupted before its
final end by a different, but related, culture. (See Figs. 2-6, 2-7, 2-8,
2-9, and 2-10.)

Tests of slag found on the sites of the furnaces in both the Arledge and the Haskins mounds showed that these furnaces extracted
about 80 percent of the iron in the ore. This is an exceptionally high
yield for ancient hearthpit furnaces and is an indication that they
operated at a higher temperature than the usual operating temperature
of ancient furnaces.

Several months later, in December 1950, a hunter looking for
rabbits a mile or so south of Austin, Ohio, came upon a strange "rock
formation" on the bank of a stream. Having read news accounts of the
discovery of the prehistoric iron furnaces on Spruce Hill and in the
Deer Creek Valley, he came to Bourneville to tell us what he had
seen, suggesting that it looked like "what's left of one of those ancient
furnaces." So, accompanied by four members of the staff of the Battelle Memorial Institute and an archaeologist of the Ross County Historical Society, I followed him to the location of his discovery.

There on the Walker Overly farm, a stream had cut into its bank,
leaving exposed the remains of a furnace on the side of the bank.
What we saw was a cross section or profile of the original structure,
and it was this that had intrigued the hunter. (See Fig. 2-11.)

During two days of digging nearby, we uncovered two more
hearthpit furnaces. Excavating about 18 inches below ground level
under a large tree stump, we hit the top of a stone wall. Going down 4
feet farther, we discovered that it was the wall of an ancient furnace,
circular in shape and 4 feet high. The pit was filled with earth, and
rooted in the fill was the trunk of a tree. Sixty-five rings on the tree indicated its age as sixty-five years. All three hearthpits had been damaged by the waters of the creek. It was possible, however, to determine that two of them had flat bottoms, one of cobblestone plastered
with clay and the other of hard concrete. We all agreed that these two
furnaces were Nordic-type furnaces, like the first furnace unearthed in
the Haskins mound.

All of the prehistoric furnaces unearthed in Ohio described so far
are like those unearthed in Europe. In the summer of 1950, however,
we found a different type of ancient smelter. Buried in a prehistoric
mound on the farm of William H. Allyn at the foot of Bray's Hill near
Frankfort, Ohio, this exceptional furnace resembles a beehive in struc-

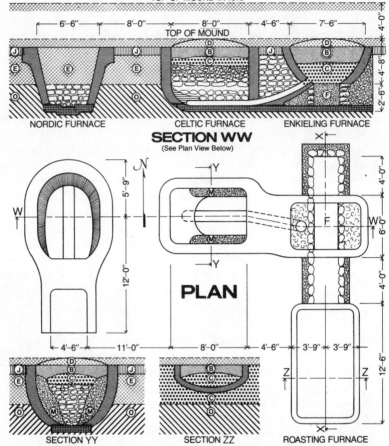

TOP OF MOUND IN 1910

TOP OF MOUND

6'-6" 8'-0" 8'-0" 4'-6" 7'-6"

NORDIC FURNACE   CELTIC FURNACE   ENKIELING FURNACE

SECTION WW
(See Plan View Below)

5'-9"

12'-0"

W

N

PLAN

4'-6"   11'-0"   8'-0"   4'-6"   3'-9"   3'-9"

4'-0"

6'-0"

4'-0"

12'-6"

SECTION YY   SECTION ZZ   ROASTING FURNACE

FOUR HASKINS MOUND FURNACES

Fig. 2-6. Drawings of four prehistoric iron-smelting furnaces in the Haskins mound. The east furnace of the Haskins mound group is an Enkieling furnace similar to those described by Emanuel Swedenborg in 1734. A draw-off flue for the slag produced in this furnace led to a pit on the west. Later this pit was converted to a Celtic furnace by the addition of ruble masonry (M) laid in pure lime mortar. The letters in the drawing of the four furnaces indicate the following: B, burned ore; C, cinders, ashes, refuse, and slag; D, residue of broken stones and slag that had been spread on the ore to ensure even distribution of draft through the furnace; E, earth fill; F, the chamber or basin where the bloom is formed; J, gravel walls topping cobblestone walls and earth bank lined with bog ore; O, ground on which the furnace foundation was placed, about 30 inches below ground level. (All measurements are approximate.)

24

Fig. 2-7. Donald MacBeth standing in the trench between the Enkieling *and the roasting furnaces.*

Fig. 2-8. Celtic furnace lining of rubble masonry laid in clay mortar.

Fig. 2-9. Celtic and Enkieling *furnaces.*

Fig. 2-10. Celtic furnace, showing flue in the bottom. An axe was found in this furnace.

Fig. 2-11. Arlington Mallery working in iron-smelting furnace in Overly mound on bank of stream.

tural outline. Furnaces like it were common in Africa, Asia, and probably in South America. Finding this furnace introduced a tremendously important new dimension to what we were learning about the prehistoric world, for it provided a link between the prehistoric iron industry on this continent and the prehistoric iron industry in Egypt, India, and Peru.

The discovery of this furnace in the Allyn mound is important, too, because it tells us that pre-Columbian Americans were skilled in the use of powder metallurgy. We had assumed that the process of powder metallurgy in America was a modern industrial process! The Allyn furnace is a replica of furnaces used in India for the extraction of iron by the process of powder metallurgy. (See Figs. 2-12 and 2-13.)

What is powder metallurgy? The following comments, which ap-

Fig. 2-12. Exterior of the kiln-type iron-smelting furnace in the Allyn mound near Frankfort, Ohio. Built of clay on the original ground surface, the furnace had a 12-inch opening in the base and a 7-inch flue at the top. It was similar to the primitive Agaria iron-smelting furnaces of India, like the furnace shown in Fig. 2-13.

Fig. 2-13. Open-air furnace at Dumarkachhar, Bilaspur District. In firing this furnace, several bushels of charcoal were poured into it through the flue, followed by a charge of powdered ore mixed with charcoal.

peared on page 26 of the April 1954 issue of the trade journal *Steelways,* describe this metallurgical technique:

> . . . powder metallurgy has been around for 5,000 years.
>
> The Egyptians used it as early as 3,000 B.C. They had no furnace that could melt iron, so they powdered their iron ore, heated it as hot as they could and then hammered and shaped it. The particles of iron bonded together just as they do in today's sintering furnaces.
>
> The Incas used it too, but except for a few instances, powder metallurgy became dormant and almost forgotten until comparatively recent times.

In 1950 the Allyn mound was 60 feet in diameter and 7 feet tall. The furnace that we unearthed rested on the original ground surface at the center of the mound. It was built of clay. At the furnace top was a 7-inch flue, and in the base was a 12-inch opening. In the operation of their furnaces similar to this Allyn mound furnace, the Agaria of India poured several bushels of charcoal into the furnace through the top opening and then a charge of powdered ore mixed with more charcoal.

Paul Shoemaker cleaned out the furnace, digging out ashes and charcoal. Donald Macbeth, archaeologist of the Ross County Museum, worked on the platform, brushing aside the charcoal. Very close to the furnace, he came upon a pile of skeletons. Later, while clearing the area surrounding the furnace, we found three more piles of skeletons in layers three to five deep. They averaged 6 feet in length, but were too decomposed to remove.

These skeletons may have been the remains of the victims of a plague epidemic, probably ironworkers, wiped out in such large numbers that it was necessary to bury them all together without the customary grave goods.

3

The Pre-Columbian Iron Industry *in* Virginia

Neither the magnitude nor the capability of the prehistoric iron industry in America will ever be known, even approximately. When I climbed Spruce Hill to examine the ruins of the ancient stone wall there, I came upon piles of ancient iron slag and immediately began a search for the ancient iron furnaces in which the slag had been produced. The discovery by my associates and myself of twenty or more ancient smelters during the following two years in a very small area of Ohio depended upon a series of such fortuitous incidents. It was, in fact, almost by chance that we uncovered the remains of America's ancient Iron Age civilization. And it was also almost by chance that archaeologists were simultaneously digging up the remains of this prehistoric civilization in Virginia.

Chance is, of course, a most unreliable factor on which to depend for the unfolding of the past, and, moreover, it is becoming less and less likely that chance or accident will lead to future discoveries regarding the past. A Smithsonian archaeologist, Dr. Frank H. H. Roberts, has warned us of "the little short of appalling problem" facing archaeologists of the future: "Because many American aborigines lived along river banks, about 80% of the archaeological remains in the nation will be lost forever as rivers are dammed and reservoirs are filled.''[1]

Archaeologist Roberts was speaking from experience, for he had just completed work on a project with other archaeologists to salvage prehistoric relics on land soon to be flooded by a new dam.[2] On Buggs Island near the Virginia–North Carolina border, the government was then building a large dam for flood control and hydroelectric power. In cooperation with the other archaeologists, Roberts had unearthed in the area iron slag, iron nails, and iron fragments—relics of a prehistoric ironworking people—which would have been lost when the area was inundated several years later (1952).

A few miles from the future Buggs Island dam, an amateur archaeologist was almost simultaneously picking up iron slag and fragments of iron on his estate and nearby land. The archaeologist was James V. Howe, a famous small-arms expert who was spending much of his retirement time prospecting for ancient Folsom points and Indian relics. One day while he was searching for relics, a neighbor's bull broke through a fence and wandered onto his land. After chasing the bull back to the neighbor's pasture, he sat down on a large rock, exhausted. Prodding the earth at his feet with his archaeologist's pick as he sat there, he unearthed a large lump of cinder just below the surface. From then on, he continued to uncover cinder as he dug for relics. Noticing that there was an abundance of bog ore all around, he decided that the cinder was slag—refuse of Indian campfires that had burned so long that they had baked the iron out of the bog ore.

During the following months Howe uncovered iron relics in association with ancient stone tools, spearheads, and arrowheads on six different sites on the north side of the Staunton River near Clarksville, Virginia. Archaeologists at the Smithsonian classified the stone spearheads as pre-Columbian. Howe decided, therefore, that the iron must be of meteoric origin, and not, as he had thought, bog ore baked by Indian campfires.

Howe's land was virgin soil. Examining official records, he found that no iron had been smelted on his property since 1782 when a previous owner had received the estate as a government grant. And, as stated above, the Smithsonian had declared that the stone spearheads were pre-Columbian. Putting all these facts together, Howe came to the conclusion that the iron, iron objects, and an old bronze vase found embedded in slag had to be of prehistoric origin. He therefore decided there could be only one explanation for the presence of the iron and iron objects on his estate and neighboring areas: the iron had been deposited as debris from an exploding comet and had been hammered into shapes by unknown prehistoric people!

Nobody challenged this theory!

Realizing that the so-called Howe iron sites were faced with obliteration as he saw progress in the building of the Buggs Island dam, Howe spoke out in distress over the loss of these sites and the "most important .Folsom sites in the Eastern states," calling all these ancient sites "a physical part of the American heritage that should not be lost to future generations." He sent specimens of his slag and iron discoveries to the Smithsonian Institution for examination. George Ellinger, metallurgist of the National Bureau of Standards, was asked by Smithsonian officers to examine the specimens, and in March, 1949, Dr. Ellinger invited me to join him at the Smithsonian to assist in the examination.

Among the Howe specimens there, we found fabricated items including carburized dies that appeared to be ancient. To me the slag in the collection was of special interest. Magnetic tests and color comparison of this Virginia slag with the Ohio slag showed that they were similar, but that the Ohio slag seemed to contain more iron. So I went to Virginia, feeling certain that I would find there, on the Howe estate, and also on the other "Howe sites" relics of an ancient ironworking civilization.

At the Howe home were hundreds of iron artifacts which Howe called cometary iron. Easily identified among the items were many Viking-type tools: spikes and rivets, scribers for marking wood, caulking tools used in building Viking ships, chisels and axes, boat spikes and boat rivets. The chisels and axes were formed by welding together thin sheets of iron by cladding. The rivets were duplicates of rivets found in a Viking ship, the *Oseberg,* which was discovered in 1903 under a mound on the shores of Oslofiord, Norway. It has been believed that the ship had been buried under the mound eleven hundred years ago. (See Figs. 3-1 and 3-2.)

An iron boat rivet which was dug up on a Howe site at the junction of the Dan and Staunton rivers is a duplicate of the rivets used in Viking ships. Also unearthed on the Virginia sites were several round nails like those the Vikings had so painstakingly made. These nails are very important, for they are uniquely different from nails made by modern ironworkers.

Scattered over the Howe sites were pieces of slag that indicated

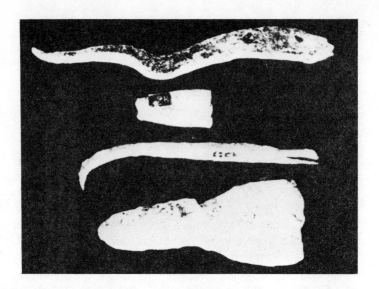

Fig. 3-1. Iron relics from the Howe Collection. At the top is a sickle handle like those used in northern Europe in ancient times. The second object is a nail die such as ancient iron-workers used to produce nails from hearthpit iron. The third item is a scriber used to mark boards for sawing, and the item at the bottom is a caulking tool similar to those used by the ancient Norse. (Photograph by Charles E. Sapp, Richmond, Virginia, *Times Dispatch*.)

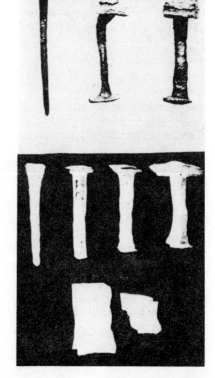

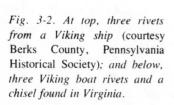

Fig. 3-2. At top, three rivets from a Viking ship (courtesy Berks County, Pennsylvania Historical Society); and below, three Viking boat rivets and a chisel found in Virginia.

there was a primitive smelter nearby. Using the slag as a guide, I located an ancient hearthpit of the Celtic type under a pile of slag on Oak Hill, a low eminence overlooking the five iron sites in the valley below. This furnace is an oval pit, 7 feet long and 5 feet wide. It was originally enclosed by a stone wall that has been torn down for the stones used for grave markers in a nearby cemetery. Fig. 3-3 shows similar Celtic-type furnaces found in Sweden and Virginia.

The press related the story of the finding of this furnace accurately as follows:

> He [Mallery] asked to go immediately to the site of the discovery [of one of Howe's relics]. He, Howe, Will Hundley, and one of Hundley's sharecroppers named Johnnie Hester went into the woods. At the site, Captain Mallery studied the area.
>
> "Dig here," he directed Hester.
>
> After digging a bit, Hester was told to move to another spot. Captain Mallery then explained what he was looking for.
>
> "If my beliefs are true," he said, "we are going to find a fire pit which has been used to melt down ore."
>
> Mallery described the shape of the oven and how it would be built. He said that he thought that they would find nails that resembled Colonial nails and that if they did, they were close to a great discovery.
>
> Hester kept digging. Soon he hit the furnace that Mallery had described.
>
> And there were the nails, along with other bits of metal and a great amount of slag.[3]

I had felt certain that we would find the ancient nails because in the Howe collection of artifacts I had seen several dies of the Viking type for making nails. Nails formed by hand in such dies have off-center heads. These nails had off-center heads. Colonial nails, on the other hand, were machine-cut and machine-headed, and so the heads were all concentric with the shaft. The difference between ancient iron and modern iron shows up in the respective nails. Ancient iron was too soft to make nails that could be driven into wood without special treatment. To harden them, the ancient ironworker baked the soft iron sheets from which they were to be cut or the nails themselves at a high heat in a charcoal fire for days. During the baking, the outer shell of the iron was carburized or turned into steel by carbon absorbed from the charcoal.

To confirm my identification of the ancient nails, I took some of them to Jamestown, Virginia, for comparison with colonial nails

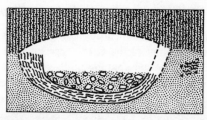

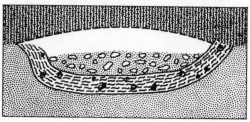

Fig. 3-3. Sketches of Celtic-type furnaces in Sweden and Virginia. The sketch at top shows a cross section of the base of a Celtic-type furnace found in Essuaga Parish, Västergötland, Sweden. The sketch at the bottom shows a similar section of the pre-Columbian furnace found on Oak Hill near Clarksville, Virginia.

Fig. 3-4. Slag bottom of Celtic-type furnace on Oak Hill, Virginia. (Photograph by Luc Secretan.)

found in the abandoned settlement there. In contrast to the round ancient nails, the hundreds of colonial nails dug up in the excavations at the Jamestown settlement are all rectangular and their heads are concentric with the shafts.[4] For metallurgical comparison of the ancient and the modern nails, the National Park Service loaned iron nails from Jamestown to Battelle Memorial Institute and to Dr. Ellinger of the National Bureau of Standards. Battelle metallurgists reported that the hardening process used in the ancient nails was not used in the iron nails or other iron tools from Jamestown that they had tested.

After we found inside the furnace fragments of slag like the slag found by Howe on the sites in the valley below, Howe abandoned his theory that the iron was of cometary or meteoric origin. Mineralogists of the National Museum later proved that the Virginia iron was neither cometary nor meteoric.

The ground on the Virginia sites was quite thoroughly impregnated with slag during the operation of the very old Celtic furnaces. (See Fig. 3-4.) All of the iron and iron tools found there were covered with a thick coating of slag. As soon as we removed the slag for laboratory examination, the iron began to disintegrate, rusting very rapidly. Evidently only furnace slag and a few slag-protected tools have survived through the centuries. Those tools, from which the protective coating of slag was removed in the process of production, apparently did not survive for long.

The iron and iron tools unearthed by Howe were found in close association with ancient stone tools, arrowheads, and spearheads on all of the sites of discovery. In the same way, similar iron and stone artifacts that I had found on the beaches of Newfoundland in 1946 were lying together. It is a generally accepted rule that all artifacts found in such close association are the products of a single civilization. If this is a sound rule, the Iron Age on this continent apparently began at a time when Folsom points were still being used. It is, of course, possible that the Folsom points found in association with the iron were copied from earlier models by arrowmakers of more recent times.

Archaeologists believe that the Folsom people lived in America ten or fifteen thousand years ago. They base this theory on the discovery of Folsom points embedded in the bones of animals assumed to have become extinct about that long ago. Both the Folsom-type points and the samples of the iron and slag from the Howe sites have been accepted as authentic by the Smithsonian Institution, where they were left for storage.

It is not possible to determine the age of the iron sites in Virginia by their height above sea level, for the land there is practically stationary. By contrast the land in Newfoundland is rising at the rate of about 4 feet per hundred years. By measuring the height of the raised beaches in Newfoundland, I was able to determine the approximate age of the sites and to show that the settlements there were contemporaneous with the historic Scandinavian settlements in Greenland and Ireland. (See p. 135 for measurement of height of Newfoundland beaches.)

In the summer of 1950, R. W. Breckenridge, a professor of metallurgy at Iowa State College in Ames, visited the Virginia iron sites uncovered by Howe. In a letter Dr. Breckenridge says:

> . . . I examined specimens from that region. I found no meteoric iron. I did find old-style wrought iron and what would be classed at present as dirty steel—containing slag inclusions, iron oxide and steels of varying carbon contents, all in the same piece. We found furnace slag under the roots of an oak tree estimated to be 300 or more years old. We found no furnaces, but we did find what appeared to have been a bowl-shaped pit with a little burnt clay at the bottom. . . . The ground in many scattered areas contained at shallow depths irregular masses of iron (not gray cast iron) and many nails and partially formed tools.[5]

Howe excavated in all sixteen sites within 60 miles of his estate in Mecklenburg County, Virginia. He found more than 400 pounds of iron, much of it worked for industrial use. The iron remains a "mystery" that baffles professional archaeologists. Unfortunately, as Howe feared, the sites of discovery for the most part have been lost in the flood waters of the Buggs Island dam.

Although there are, in this collection of old Virginia iron, Viking-type round boat rivets, caulking tools, scribers, and cladded chisels, the most solid evidence of a pre-Columbian iron industry near Clarksville is in the thousands of pieces of iron slag, many of them in undisturbed hard pan. This slag is a type found only around the ancient furnaces such as those in Scandinavia, Germany, Belgium, and Greenland.

4

The
Clash
of
Theories

It was 1848—the year of the *Manifesto*. In Europe, two young socio-
logists, Karl Marx and Friedrich Engels, were biding their time, following publication of their monograph enshrining the doctrine of
Communism. In America, two young amateur archaeologists, Ephraim
George Squier and Edwin Hamilton Davis, were bickering over credit
for their joint research on antiquities of the Mississippi Valley following
publication of their monograph on these antiquities. This remarkable
first publication of the new Smithsonian Institution also enshrined a
doctrine: that iron was not produced on this continent before the coming of Columbus.

Marx and Engels did not live to see their disciples demolish the
ruling forces of a nation, set up a new order, and draw down an Iron
Curtain to shut it off from the outside world. Squier and Davis lived
almost long enough to see their doctrine demolish the credibility of
veteran researchers and eventually become an essential prop for the
axiom that only Stone Age Indians lived in pre-Columbian America—
an axiom that drew down an Iron Curtain on America's past by restricting research on prehistoric America to the investigation of Stone
Age Indians. Squier, the versatile opportunist, and Davis, his complai-

sant collaborator, accomplished all this in their leisure time—in less than three years!

No effective challenge would arise to their rejection of evidence that antiquarians, including at least one professional archaeologist, had found relics of an ancient Iron Age civilization in America. That is, not until 1948, when I came upon slag on Spruce Hill, identified it as refuse of ancient iron smelting, and found prehistoric furnaces nearby.

My misconception that I was the original discoverer of an ancient iron civilization on this continent was short-lived, however, for very soon after my "discovery," I learned that many ancient iron furnaces had been discovered on Spruce Hill and had even been identified as such by investigators nearly a century and a half before. The earliest discovery and identification of the furnaces must have been prior to 1811, for in that year James Foster wrote a letter referring to them as he had seen them. In this letter, from which a passage describing Spruce Hill has already been quoted, Foster says:

> . . . Within the area [Spruce Hill] there are about thirty furnaces from which I took cinders that resemble in every way those forged in blacksmiths' forges. From some of them I got pieces of burnt wrought clay that looked somewhat like pumice stone, but are of a pale blue color. Those lying on the surface of the earth are covered with coats of rusty mail, which probably had lain there since the days of Lycurgus. . . .[1]

In this letter, Foster expounds his theory that an ancient people had built these "furnaces" in his description of a city nearby, "the residence of a warlike race," and in his statement that these "long-destroyed" people were "much more civilized than the present Indian inhabitants of any portion of our continent."

Nine years later, Caleb Atwater, who was recognized as Ohio's first professional archaeologist, also described furnaces and cinder on Spruce Hill as such. In Atwater's report, which was published in *Archaeologia Americana,* he gives an account of his exploration of various ancient forts, including Spruce Hill. The account is illustrated by maps which Atwater says are "actual surveys." These maps and the naming, in some cases, of the professional surveyors who worked with him give an air of authority to the report, in which he says about the furnaces and the cinders on Spruce Hill:

> . . . inside the wall, at line D (the 700 Gate line) there appears to have been a row of furnaces or smiths' shops where the cinders now lie many feet deep.

I am not able to say with certainty what manufactures were carried on here, nor can I say whether brick or iron tools were made here or both. It was clay that was exposed to the action of fire. The remains are 4' to 5' in depth now at some places. Iron ore, in this country, is sometimes found in such clay; brick and potters' wares were manufactured out of it in some instances.[2]

Greatly impressed by the geometrical expertise of the prehistoric builders of the mounds, Atwater described the exact manner in which these early people "laid down their square and circle," saying that "the works described . . . were erected by a race of men widely different from any tribe of North American Indians known in modern times."

Atwater, one of the most notable contemporaries of James Foster, lived in Ohio at this time. A graduate of Williams College, he was first a Presbyterian minister and later a lawyer and state legislator. Prominent for his advocacy of canals, improved highways, and forest conservation, he eventually became distinguished as the founder of the Ohio public school system and the first historian of the state.

After settling in the town of Chillicothe, the first capital of the state and the capital of the ancient builders of mounds, in 1815, Atwater spent his spare time during the next six years studying and writing about the nearby earthworks and other antiquities. It was believed by many that he was the most knowledgeable person in the state on the antiquities of Ohio. His knowledge extended beyond the state boundaries, for he investigated also the remains of past civilizations from New York to the Tennessee Valley. He became counselor for Ohio of the American Antiquarian Society.

For decades, Atwater's theories were generally respected. They were in accord with findings and claims of other investigators of antiquities. Professional engineers, professional archaeologists, several physicians, a famous scientist, and the editor James Foster, in their explorations of the mounds and other sites in the Middle West and the South, were finding iron and copper tools, smelting furnaces, metal money, brick, lime mortar, and masonry, showing techniques they recognized as European.

In recognition of this evidence of technological skills, the prevailing archaeological theory during most of the nineteenth century maintained that the mounds had been built by a long-vanished, highly civilized people, the ancient Mound Builders, who were distinct from and superior to the American Indians. To the white settlers, this idea was an appealing explanation of the mystery in their midst, for they saw the seminomadic Indian hunters as a subhuman species who lacked the skills, the ingenuity, and the industry to construct the great symmetrical earthworks. But who were these ancient Mound Builders? To what race did they belong? And when were they here? Such questions spawned countless romantic theories concerning the identity of the vanished people, including the myth of the Lost Tribes of Israel and the myth of the survivors of sunken Atlantis, each defended with passion and at times with quackery.

It is difficult to imagine today the bitterness of the contest waged for decades among both professional and amateur archaeologists for acceptance of their fanciful, often fantastic, theories and to understand the force with which the feuding caught the fancy of the public. It was a double-edged conflict, however, for a few scholars of antiquity rejected the concept of a distinct ancient race of Mound Builders and insisted that the builders of the mounds were ancestors of the present Indians. For decades, the protest of this minority was lost among the more appealing claims of the divided majority. That is, until the 1880s, when the minority, with their down-to-earth theory of a prehistoric America populated only by Stone Age Indians, won out over the majority, with their theory of a prehistoric America populated in antiquity by a superior people with an advanced technological society.

It was in such a milieu of speculation and contention in the mid-nineteenth century that the attack on the "romantic" notion that prehistoric Americans had smelted iron began. In an article published in *Transactions of the American Ethnological Society,* in 1848, Ephraim George Squier stated:

> All accounts of the discovery of iron in the mounds . . . are vague and unsatisfactory. . . . The only authority for the discovery of iron in the mounds is the author of a paper on American antiquities in the first volume of the *Archaeologia Americana.*[3]

A more telling attack on Atwater's suggestion that there were iron-smelting furnaces in the remains of the ancient fort on Spruce Hill came in the Squier-Davis report, *Ancient Monuments of the Mississippi Valley,* published by the Smithsonian Institution the same year. Describing the remains, the authors say:

> . . . Nothing is more certain than that powerful fires have been maintained for considerable periods at numerous points on the hill; for what purpose, unless as alarm signals, it is impossible to conjec-

ture. . . . *The suggestion that these are traces of "ancient" furnaces is not to be entertained for an instant.* [Italics added for emphasis] [4]

In the same monograph, the authors continue their attack:

> The traces of these fires are only observed upon the brows of the hills; they appear to have been built generally upon heaps of stones, which are broken up and sometimes partially vitrified. In all cases, they exhibit marks of intense and protracted heat. *They are vulgarly supposed to be the remains of "furnaces"* from the amount of scoriaceous material accompanying them, which often covers a large area and is several feet in thickness. This popular error has led to some very extravagant conjectures as to the former mineral wealth of the vicinity in which they occur; an error which has perpetuated in various works on American antiquities. [Italics added for emphasis] [5]

Squier (for he was the "idea man" in the Squier-Davis partnership) seems to have been determined to wipe out all thought about the smelting of iron in ancient America, for he brings up the subject several more times in the same report, saying at one point:

> No iron or traces of iron, except with the recent deposits, have been discovered; nor is it believed that the race of the mounds had any knowledge of that metal. The copper and silver found in the mounds were doubtless obtained in their native state, and afterwards worked without the intervention of fire. [6]

And shortly thereafter he extends his remark to include the art of metallurgy in general:

> . . . the knowledge of welding and of working metals through the assistance of fire . . . does not seem to have been possessed by them. Their acquaintance with metallurgy appears to have been confined to working the native metals in a cold state. [7]

But the audacious Squier was fighting reality. Since 1794, settlers and archaeologists had been uncovering in the mounds artifacts revealing that the builders of the mounds, whoever they were, were sophisticated in the craft of metallurgy. And Caleb Atwater, obviously knowledgeable in the craft, as early as 1820 had described in his less dramatic style several of these finds as follows: ". . . a sheet of copper, copper articles, all seem to be pure copper covered with green carbonate of that metal''; ''. . . ornaments of copper overlaid with a thick plate of silver . . . pieces of a copper tube filled with iron rust''; ''. . . a plate of iron which had become an oxide, but before it was disturbed by the spade, resembled a plate of cast iron''; and six inscribed brass plates fastened together by two iron wires, uncovered 12 feet below the surface of a mound in Illinois.[8]

The Illinois find was dismissed by Squier as a ''harmless imposition got up for local effect,'' fabricated by the village blacksmith who had taken the letters for the inscription from the lid of a Chinese tea chest.[9] Faced with the challenge of a find obviously betraying the metallurgical sophistication of an ancient worker, like many of his contemporaries, he dismissed the find as native metal cold-hammered or as intrusive after the arrival of the white settlers, or more often as meteoric iron.

Throughout his handling of the enigma of ancient metallurgy, Atwater showed more knowledge of the ancient craft of iron smelting than Squier did. When he was confronted with the fact that no tools that the builders of the mounds might have used had been found, he pointed out that wooden shovels would have been adequate for constructing the mounds, but if the builders had used tools ''manufactured from iron, by lying either on or under the earth, during all that long period which has intervened between their authors and us, they would have long since oxydized [sic] by rusting and left but faint traces of their existence behind them.''[10]

Even before Squier spoke out against Atwater, several scholars were calling for a more up-to-date and comprehensive report on the mounds than Atwater's 1820 report, which for twenty-five years had been the major work on antiquities of this country. In disagreement with the prevailing theory of an ancient superior race of Mound Builders, this minority believed that the builders of the mounds and the Indians were the same race. Foremost among them was Albert Gallatin, founder of the American Ethnological Society. An emigrant from his native Switzerland, Gallatin became a noted financier and promoter of interest in ethnology. Eventually as president of the Society, he was called ''the father of American ethnology.'' Gallatin based his theories on the aborigines of America on his finding in his linguistic research that the Indians of North America, South America, and Mexico spoke languages ''of substantially the same structure and grammatical form.'' This fact, he declared, ''connected with the similarity of physical type . . . prove a . . . common origin.''

Another scholar among the minority of scholars who rejected the theory of an ancient distinct and superior race of Mound Builders was the eminent craniologist Dr. S. G. Morton, who based his theory on his examination of skulls. Morton concluded that skulls from the Peruvian crematories, the tombs of Mexico, and the mounds of this country were of the same type, and that this physical conformation "excludes every branch of the Caucasian race from any obvious participation in the populating of this continent."

By 1846 the theories of Gallatin and Morton, despite the high regard for their competence in their professions, had not achieved the popularity enjoyed by the more appealing concept of a special race of Mound Builders. As president of the American Ethnological Society, Gallatin knew this. He began then to "search for a man who would compile all that was known about the mounds, conduct extensive new research, and produce a definitive study. They [the Ethnological Society] found their man in Ephraim George Squier. . . ."[11]

At that time (1846), young Squier had been in Ohio a little more than one year and was working as an editor on the Scioto (now the Chillicothe) *Gazette*. Only about twenty-five years old, he had already been an editor on a newspaper in Hartford, Connecticut, a contributor to papers in Albany, New York, and elsewhere, and founder of the short-lived *Poet's Magazine*. The son of a Methodist minister serving in Bethlehem, New York, Squier had had little opportunity for schooling, and in his early youth he had worked on a farm and taught school to support himself. The diversity of his remarkable talents and of his interests was to continue throughout his life to drive him into a variety of occupations, ranging from research and writing on the antiquities of North America to diplomatic assignments in Central and South America.

An Ohio acquaintance of Squier has left us an impression of him as he appeared to him during his earliest days in Ohio:

> Mr. Atwater did good service by his work on Western Antiquities and this leads me to speak of two other archaeologists, Ephraim George Squier and Dr. Edwin Hamilton Davis. They were then engaged in making their explorations and surveys. Dr. Davis was a native of Chillicothe and was then about thirty-five years old. He was a very reserved and somewhat diffident gentleman, and one of the highest character. The latter part of his life was passed in New York pursuing his archaeological studies. Mr. Squier was an entirely different man. He had come to Ohio to assist Mr. Seneca Ely, now the agricultural editor of the Cincinnati *Commercial Gazette* [Scioto

Gazette]. He was then about twenty-six years of age, blond, small and boyish in figure, but one of the most audacious spirits I have ever known. In coming to Columbus with a friend of mine just prior to the opening of the legislature, Squier said to him that he was going to get the clerkship of the House. Surprised, the other replied, "Why, Squier, you can't do that. You have just come to the state. You are not even a citizen." "I don't care, I shall do it." And he did.[12]

Squier's introduction to the antiquities of Ohio is described as follows by the same acquaintance:

> One day he [Squier] was riding out with the same friend when they came in sight of ancient works. He thereupon inquired about them. The latter told him, on which he became greatly interested and said that would be his field of work, he didn't care for politics.
>
> In the course of conversation, Squier asked if there was anyone interested in archaeology. "Yes, there is Dr. Davis who ten years ago assisted Charles Whittlesey in his explorations and surveys of the Newark antiquities and is still gathering relics." The result was that he united with Davis who furnished the funds and they worked together.[13]

For over two years, the young editor and the young doctor enjoyed a friendly and fruitful association, which culminated in 1848 with the publication of *Ancient Monuments of the Mississippi Valley*. During their leisure hours, together they examined Ohio earthworks, drew plans of sites, and prepared their manuscript for publication. Records are in agreement regarding the division of labor and reponsibility for their joint project. Dr. Davis paid all expenses incurred in their work, and he also contributed most of the scientific expertise required in the analysis of relics, while Squier did most of the writing of the report and took over the job of finding financial assistance and professional sponsorhip for its publication.

Squier was a neophyte in antiquarian research and analysis, and so in Davis he acquired an expert well qualified to lead him by shortcuts through the unfamiliar world of antiquaries. With this guidance, the financial and scientific support of Davis, and his own brilliance in discourse, he emerged after less than three years at the pinnacle of that world—the final authority on the antiquity of this country!

To the anatomy of his phenomenal rise, Squier also contributed ambition, imagination, and zeal. Ardently bent on achieving eminence, he pursued every available angle to achieve it in his newly found hobby. Adroit in winning others to his purpose, he obtained from various competent surveyors many previously drawn plans of sites. To these borrowed plans—for which he often failed to give full credit—he added four plans of sites drawn by Davis and himself in 1845, thirteen drawn in 1846, and three drawn later to constitute the body of the joint report. To the account of his research on antiquities, he added also a quality hitherto unknown in descriptions of long-defunct civilizations—a sparkling, animated style. So it was in a setting of élan, if not of scientific accuracy, that the basic doctrine of the history of prehistoric America was launched.

Within scarcely a year after Squier first entertained the notion of investigating the earthworks of Ohio, a year during which he had spent his spare time with Davis digging in the mounds, he was traveling around in search of funds and of a publisher of his prospective report. He apparently did not find financial help, but he did find a publisher: the American Ethnological Society. On July 27, 1846, he received a letter [14] from an officer of the Society saying that Mr. Gallatin, president of the Society, was much pleased with his plates and "wished you to extend the paper and add as many plates as you think advisable." The letter refers to another officer of the Society who "thinks that no steps can be taken at present toward promoting the larger work. . . . get out your account of recent explorations as soon as possible . . . accompanied with a prospectus of the large work we propose to do." The officer ends his letter with the suggestion that "in the meantime, you and Dr. Davis will be prosecuting your labors and preparing materials for the large work."

In a letter to Dr. S. G. Morton, dated January 16, 1847, Squier states that he is preparing "a volume for the New York [State] Ethnological Society" and that he is "pretty well advanced . . . in addition to duties as Clerk of the House of our General Assembly." In this letter he refers to his associate, saying that he is devoting "all leisure time to investigation in connection with Davis" and he admits his indebtedness to Gallatin "for his generous aid."

The Ethnological Society would not be the publisher of "the large work." To the Smithsonian would go this honor in an agreement to be reached very soon. On April 3, 1847, Secretary Joseph Henry of the Smithsonian tells Squier in a letter that he has been authorized by the Board of Regents to publish his manuscript "in quarto form . . . in the first number of the Smithsonian Contribution to Knowledge."

And so, on May 15, Squier submitted the manuscript of the joint

Squier-Davis report to Secretary Henry. On June 2, Henry referred the manuscript to Gallatin for an examination by a committee of the Ethnological Society, explaining that the memoir would be published by the Smithsonian if the committee report was favorable. Two days later Gallatin held a meeting of the committee, and five days later, he received from the committee a resolution recommending publication. A week later, he forwarded the resolution to Henry, and without investigation or further consideration, the Squier-Davis manuscript was published by the Smithsonian.

In a letter to Alexander Bache, dated June 25, 1847, Henry voiced his gratitude for the opportunity to publish such a remarkable report as the first number of Smithsonian's Contribution to Knowledge, saying in part, "This paper was recommended to me by Mr. Gallatin. . . . A committee of the Ethnological Society of New York has pronounced it the most interesting article on the subject which has ever been produced and eminently worthy a place in the Smithsonian Transactions." [15]

In the Smithsonian pamphlet, the "cinders" that James Foster, Caleb Atwater, and I saw on Spruce Hill and identified as slag from ancient iron smelting are "light, porous scoriae" or "scoriaceous material." And, declared Squier, not for an instant was the suggestion to be entertained that these scoriae were traces of ancient furnaces! Squier, undoubtedly, was acquainted only with modern furnace slag such as that produced at the nearby Rapids Forge furnace owned by John Woodbridge, whose Seip site he had examined. There he would have seen light-colored lightweight slag, very different from the dark slag of the ancient reduction furnaces at point D on Spruce Hill and the blue, corallike slag from the roasting furnaces at point A. Atwater correctly described both of these types.

The wonder is that apparently the Ethnological Society committee did not question the feasibility of the claim of the two amateur archaeologists regarding the great amount of work they had done in their leisure time. Persons acquainted with the time-consuming procedures of research, especially in the case of amateurs, should have been tempted to ask many questions. How could Squier and Davis, as they claimed, in two years of leisure time (1845–1847) have "personally examined or surveyed upwards of 100 enclosure works, excavated 200 mounds," and more specifically have personally surveyed and mapped thirteen more sites between January, 1847 and May, 1847? Some of these sites are very extensive, particularly Spruce Hill, which covers nearly 14 square miles. During this three and one-half months, they also revised their manuscript, adding three more maps and about twelve pages of text. To have done all this surveying, mapping, and manuscript preparation while pursuing their respective duties as clerk of the state legislature and practicing physician would have been impossible even with the assistance of squads of surveyors and draftsmen.

Squier-Davis maps of sites they surveyed agree in general with aerial photographs of the same sites as closely as could be expected in the work of inexperienced surveyors, especially inexperienced surveyors working only in leisure hours. Examination of several of their maps and comparison of these maps with aerial photographs of the same sites, however, raises skepticism regarding the authenticity of at least two of them: the drawings of Spruce Hill Fort and Jones Fort.

Reproductions of the aerial photograph of Spruce Hill and of the Atwater and the Squier-Davis maps of the same enclosure expose some important points of agreement and of disagreement among the three illustrations. First, it is evident that the Atwater map resembles the aerial photograph more than the Squier-Davis map does. The general contours of the two are quite similar. The pond and the serpent mound surrounding it are in the same position on the photograph and the Atwater map.

Also evident is the fact that the Squier-Davis map differs from the aerial photograph more in general outline than the Atwater map does. The pond on the Squier-Davis map is not in the same location as on the aerial photograph. It is quite obvious that the Squier-Davis map resembles the Atwater map more than it resembles the aerial photograph and that certain features of the Atwater map which differ from the aerial photograph appear also on the Squier-Davis map.

The fact that a professional surveyor, Perrin Kent, drew the Atwater map and Squier and Davis drew their map, according to their claim, should be taken into consideration. It is possible that their map is merely a freehand sketch of the site drawn as they walked over it, and that it is based on the professionally drawn Atwater map?

Success brought trouble for the Squier-Davis partnership. Immediately after the Smithsonian accepted the manuscript for publication, Squier increased his claim for credit, at the same time reducing credit for Davis. A letter written by Squier on January 8, 1848, to George Marsh, explaining the role of Davis in their collaboration, throws light on Squier's capricious thinking. In this letter,[16] which is too long to quote in full, Squier reviews the report of the investigations, claiming that he did all of the work, and paid half of the expenses, "or nearly half." On the last page, however, he claims "nine-tenths of the time and five-sixths of the expense of these investigations have fallen on me." Declaring that he is the sole author of the manuscript, he says, "I now assert my rights and shall insist upon them. . . . Now my position is fixed."

Shortly after writing the letter from which excerpts appear above, Squier wanted to change some of the conclusions he had previously come to and which he presented in the manuscript then being considered for publication by Secretary Henry of the Smithsonian. Henry objected to changes in the manuscript. In the early days of 1848, while completing his manuscript for publication, Squier, who was then in New York City, had an opportunity to study reports of British archaeologists. Information in these reports which was new to him convinced him that the hilltop forts and mounds of the Mississippi Valley were identical to those in the British Isles and in Scandinavia. In an effort to include this information in his report, he revised his manuscript. But his revision was rejected by Secretary Henry.

In a letter to Squier, dated February 16, 1848, Henry demands that Squier adhere to the manuscript as it was submitted and remove everything he had added later. From then on, Squier must have harbored doubts about the validity of his theory that pre-Columbian Americans did not know how to extract metals from their ores. Almost immediately after the Squier-Davis report was published in 1848, denouncing even a suggestion that these early Americans might have extracted iron or copper, Squier reversed himself on one of his denunciations. Having declared in the first report that they did not "understand the art of plating," he now declares that the copper ornaments under examination "are absolutely plated, not simply overlaid with silver," adding, "and if it is admitted that these are genuine remains of the Mound Builders, it must at the same time be admitted that they possessed the difficult art of plating one metal upon another." [17] (Was the plating referred to in the case of these ornaments and of several other relics an example of the ancient lost art which has recently been revived as *cladding*? See page 20 for a description of this process for strengthening metal objects.)

Years later, during his diplomatic service in Peru, Squier directed an extensive survey of local antiquities. In an article personally addressed to the Library of Congress, he touchingly mentions "my already *matured* opinion'' and further on describes a chamber 10 feet square and open at the top, which he thinks may be a furnace: "Its walls are burned and blistered like those of a furnace to a depth of 20' and show every sign of having been exposed to severe and protracted heat. . . . I am more disposed to regard this mass as a furnace in some way connected with ancient metallurgical operations." [18]

A decade later, Squier broke down. After partially recovering, he broke down again and became permanently insane. He died in Brooklyn in 1888, forty years after he exploded the idea that there was an ancient Iron Age civilization in America.

5

An
Iron Curtain
on
America's Past

Although speculation on America's past during the forty years following the publication of the Squier-Davis report was dominated by the belief in a superior ancient race of Mound Builders, fresh and formidable opposition to this popular theory irrupted during these years. By the time of Squier's death, such opposition was in command and very soon thereafter laid to rest permanently the theory that prehistoric America was the home of people with an advanced civilization distinct from the Indians.

This fresh opposition resided in the Bureau of Ethnology of the Smithsonian Institution, which was established by Congress in 1879. Under Director John Wesley Powell, who was determined to obliterate the theory of a vanished distinct race, the Bureau, strengthened by appropriations for excavation of archaeological sites, demolished the credibility of all claims in support of that theory. Even Squier did not escape exposure of countless errors in his calculations and conclusions which supported the belief in the ancient race of Mound Builders. His comments, however, on the lack of metallurgical sophistication in the vanished civilization remained unsullied, for these comments served the purpose of the opposition. They were, in fact, essential to the new dominant theory that only Stone Age Indians had lived in prehistoric America.

During the 1880s and increasingly after 1890, the Peabody Museum of American Archaeology and Ethnology also funded archaeological explorations. Founded in 1865 as a depository for relics of ancient cultures, the Museum followed the shift from interest in ethnology to an emphasis on excavation that became general in archaeological activities.

In the 1890s, archaeologists from the Peabody Museum excavated Ohio mounds and uncovered ancient furnaces like those that my associates and I found in those mounds nearly sixty years later. They failed to identify their finds as furnaces. From the Museum field notes, I have identified one of their finds as a Celtic furnace similar to the first furnace that we found in the Arledge mound.

In 1890, Peabody archaeologists cut trenches through a mound at Foster's Crossing in Ohio. In this mound, they found a furnace like one we uncovered at Deer Creek[1] and like a furnace found in Smaland, Sweden, soon after 1890 by John Nihlen.[2] The walls of the furnace had evidently been constructed of hard-burned bog ore backed up with loose stones and earth. The bottom was paved with flat stones laid on loosely piled stones. A flue, built of stones, conducted air into this pile, which filtered through the loose stones into the furnace. This flue served also as an outlet for the molten slag and iron, which dripped down and flowed into an outside collecting basin.

The builders of this mound had apparently used the method used in northern Europe:[3] First, the walls of the furnace were demolished. Then the accumulated furnace refuse—cinders, ashes, and unused bog ore—were heaped together to form the base of the mound. Often layers of loam were spread over the conglomerate heap, but sometimes, as in this case, the entire mound was built of refuse.

The Peabody archaeologists also uncovered a variety of flues and pits which seem to have been furnaces of different types evolved from the use of a second pit and flue. These furnaces were in Turner group mound number 3.[4] Two-pit furnaces have been found in Sweden, on the hilltops and on the plains, and two-pit furnaces similar to the one found by the Peabody archaeologists in mound 3 of the Turner group have been found in Germany.[5]

It is unfortunate, indeed, that the Peabody archaeologists were not aware that they had uncovered the remains of an ancient iron industry on this continent. By 1890, the triumph of Squier over Atwater and other early investigators in the argument regarding the smelting of iron in pre-Columbian America was complete. No archaeologist of repute would even contemplate the possibility that prehistoric Americans had smelted ores to produce malleable metals.

Over thirty years earlier, the Smithsonian Institution published an article by an officer of the American Antiquarian Society evaluating the work of American archaeologists in uncovering the past. The author of the article published in 1856, Samuel F. Haven, referring to American Mound Builders, declared: ". . . There is no proof of the practice of reducing metals from their ores and cutting them for use and ornament—none of the knowledge of chemistry and astronomy."[6]

An Iron Curtain had been drawn on America's past!

6

Pre-Columbian Viking
and
Celtic Migrations
to
America

On a sunny June day several decades ago, I stood on the bank of a river near Sherbrooke, Quebec, watching a gang of ironworkers climb about the skeletal framework of a steel arch bridge rising far above the waters. I was proud of that bridge. It was the first steel arch that I had designed, the first one that our company had built in Canada. But it was not the bridge that was holding my attention; it was the iron-workers.

The sight of bridgemen at work was not new to me. Born into a family of bridge builders, as a boy I had worked in my father's quarries in northern New York. I had forged and tempered tools, stone drills, cold chisels, axes, and adzes. I had laid many a stone in bridge foundations and had often helped erect the steel structures built by our company. As an experienced bridgeman, I could appreciate the skill of these master craftsmen at their trade—their able handling of tools, their alertness, and the ease with which they moved about on the slender, slippery beams at a dizzying height above the ground.

But it was not their skill which had caught my attention; it was their physical appearance. They looked much like the usual gang of ironworkers. They had the same weather-beaten skin and essentially the same build, except that they were a little taller. The arresting thing about the group as a whole was that they all seemed to be Swedes or Norwegians. It prompted me to ask Jim Foote, the foreman, where he had picked up "all these Squareheads." Grinning, he replied that they were full-blooded Indians, not Squareheads.

"Every one of these men," Jim said, "carries a card from Uncle Sam showing that he's a full-blooded Indian, a Mohawk from the St. Regis Reservation in northern New York. They all belong to a bridge-men's union that takes in only registered Iroquois Indians."

I recall thinking idly at the time that these Iroquois of striking Nordic appearance could easily pass as descendants of the legendary Vikings—those ancient tall, blond warrior-sailors who were supposed to have settled somewhere in North America. I had no inkling then of the fact that both Norsemen and Celts were sailing across the Atlantic for more than a thousand years before Columbus, and, furthermore, that they had settled in communities stretching from Newfoundland and Labrador as far south as Virginia and westward throughout the Great Lakes region.

Even today the Viking settlements in North America scarcely receive mention in histories of the New World. Despite the massive accumulation of evidence attesting to their impact on America, the Vikings remain virtually ignored as a formative influence. Unfortunately, centuries of cultivation by farmers and excavation by archaeologists have destroyed the earthworks and masonry remains of Viking occupancy. And historians have consistently misinterpreted the origin and function of these evidences of a long-forgotten civilization.

The questions which I asked myself then concerning the possibility of the infusion of Viking blood in the veins of the Sherbrooke bridgemen—in fact, of the Iroquois Indians as a whole—were the beginning of an extensive probe into the enigma of pre-Columbian America, a probe not yet concluded.

The New World trail of the Vikings started in Iceland. It is in Iceland that the *Sagas of the Vinland Voyages,* the records which they themselves began, have been preserved by their descendants for almost a millennium. To these accounts of Viking expeditions I turned first. I studied them as a navigator studies his pilot books, looking for changes in the course of the ocean currents and clues to the location of the landmarks described in the sagas which can not be found anywhere on modern maps. It seemed plausible to me that these guides for the ancient voyagers often mentioned in the sagas had in fact existed at the time of the Vikings and that they had disappeared from sight as the earth's crust became warped during the centuries since the voyages.

Among other Icelandic documents, copies of ancient sailing charts turned up, showing the routes followed by the Vikings in their voyages to America. At first these charts appeared to be what they in general have been thought to be: merely meaningless scrawls, inventions of the imagination, or at most early man's notions regarding the geography of the sea and the land over which he traveled. But I found that, on the contrary, they were actually practical sailing charts platted on a projection system unknown in modern times. I deciphered this projection system, and then I saw that these charts totally disregarded by modern scholars are accurate plats of the Arctic coastline of America, obviously drawn by skilled cartographers. They reveal detailed knowledge of the coastline and indicate far more extensive navigation of American waters before Columbus than scholars have ever suspected.

The sagas describe the route from Greenland to Leif Ericsson's camp in Vinland. Using these ancient sailing charts preserved in Iceland and the sailing directions recorded in Icelandic history, the experienced navigator can follow this route. He can check the detailed descriptions of the landmarks given in the sagas with the actual characteristics of the North Atlantic coast along the way to Newfoundland.

All of this I did, beginning with the first-known Viking voyage to America—that of Gunnbiorn Kragesson in 876—and continuing through all seven voyages from Iceland and Greenland to Leif's camp in Vinland. One by one I picked up the landmarks described and traced the course from Iceland past the recently found Gunnbiorn's Skerries to Greenland, from there to Baffin Land, and down the coast of Labrador to Belle Isle about 20 miles or so above the tip of the Newfoundland peninsula, and finally into Pistolet Bay at the tip of the peninsula.

To my great surprise, the navigation charts substantiate the revelations in the sagas that another maritime people, the Celts, were crossing the Atlantic centuries before the Vikings and had even established a settlement in the New World. Appearing on the charts as Albania, this Irish country, according to my interpretation of the charts, was in the area now known as the St. Lawrence Valley. (See Chapter 9 for details concerning this settlement.)

In following the leads provided by the sagas and the charts, the first step was to determine if there was any tangible evidence in these locations sufficient to justify a claim that they had actually been occupied by the Celts and the Vikings. A later step would be to extend the search for evidence of ancient occupation to other areas of the American continent where there are still pre-Columbian relics which have baffled scholars since the earliest days of modern settlement.

For proof of a Vinland in Newfoundland, I went to that island. There, on the raised beaches, I found hitherto unidentified ruins of long central hearths like the hearths in the longhouses of the Norse in Norway and Greenland after A.D. 1300. In and around these ruins, I found scattered iron chisels, boat spikes, clinch nails, and a battle ax side by side with stone tools, arrowpoints, and spearheads exactly like those found in all the areas of northern Europe once occupied by Scandinavians. Later metallurgical analysis of the iron tools showed that they had been fabricated not of modern steel but of plain or carburized wrought iron like the Viking iron which archaeologists have found in Norse ruins of Scandinavia and Greenland.

Then I turned my attention to one of the most puzzling vestiges of lost civilization on this continent: the expertly laid stone structures scattered along the coasts from Victoria Island in the Arctic to Newport, Rhode Island, and inland as far as the Ohio River Valley. At one time hundreds of such structures were strung along the St. Lawrence River, across New York and into Ohio, but for the most part they have vanished as wreckers have pulled them down to salvage the stones for new buildings. Still standing, however, is the mysterious stone tower near Newport. The subject of dispute for more than a century, the origin of the tower became a matter of international controversy when a Danish antiquarian declared that it had been built in the eleventh or twelfth century by Christian Scandinavians.

Intrigued by the enigma of the tower, as an experienced mason, I decided that the resolution of the mystery of its origin might lie in an analysis of the masonry, particularly in the manner in which the stones were joined. So after completing extensive research in libraries on the comparative characteristics of ancient Norse and Celtic masonry practices, with the assistance of local citizens, I excavated deeply in and around the supporting columns of the tower. My associates, including professional engineers who had followed previous investigations of the tower, and I examined the construction of the tower in detail. Our finding was that the technique of construction provided evidence that the tower was built by the Celts, not by the Norse.

The earliest crossing of the Atlantic on record was made in 330

B.C. or thereabouts by a daring Greek, Pytheas, who was then an astronomer and navigator residing in Marseilles. According to some scholars and the explorer Vilhjalmur Stefansson, Pytheas landed in Iceland. The permanent settlement of Europeans in America, however, was probably not accomplished until the Celts (Irish) came. That the Celtic Irish settled in America before the Norse seems certain, for reports of traders from Iceland who entered Vitramannaland were recorded by both contemporary and later historians. Using these reports, saga references to Vitramannaland (Albania) on the sailing charts, and the conventional history of Ireland, one can piece together an account of the Irish in pre-Columbian America.

During the golden age of Irish civilization, contemporary with the disintegration of the Western Roman Empire, Celtic navigators and settlers were voyaging to Iceland and Greenland. Twenty years after Leif Ericsson discovered Vinland, so the *Eyrbyggia* saga relates, a party of Norsemen landed in Vitramannaland and found there a thriving Irish settlement. It seem obvious that these settlers must have explored the area and established their settlement long before the Norse found them there in A.D. 1020.

A central enigma of Viking civilization in the New World confronts all researchers in pre-Columbian history of America. That enigma is the seemingly total disappearance of that civilization. When Cartier explored the St. Lawrence region in the sixteenth century, he met no Vikings or Celts. He saw no traces of their culture. He found only Indians in a Stone Age culture, naked and illiterate.

But continuous infiltration into America by Celts and Vikings over a period of three centuries would necessarily have left many marks, and it did. Yet the stories of Vinland the Good and Great Ireland have been thought of as fables just as King Midas and the Labyrinth and historic Troy were long considered to be products of a poet's imagination.

There are, of course, several factors which at least partly explain this phenomenon. For one, although it is not customary to think of Vikings as prehistoric people, during a considerable period of their existence they were just that.

Latin and Greek were the written languages of the European world in the days of the Vikings—a world that, except for the Vikings, was Christian. The Viking rural communities did not accept Christianity in everyday life for almost two hundred years after the first colonization of Greenland. The scanty records that they finally made were for the most part documents of the Church and the state. Extant today are only fragmentary copies of priceless Church documents which were lost when Greenland finally disappeared behind the great Arctic ice barriers or were burned when the cathedral at Skalholt, Iceland, and the Royal Library in Copenhagen were destroyed by fire. Consequently the only surviving documents which mention the settlement of Norse in America are the *Sagas of the Vinland Voyages,* a few brief, widely scattered historical memoranda, and recently deciphered sea charts.

Another explanatory factor is that no iron artifacts of the Viking type were found in America until very recently. Pertinent to this circumstance is the statement of Donald B. Macmillan, summing up the generally accepted belief about the settlement of the Norse in America:

> The belief is widespread that the Vikings explored the coast of North America long before the voyage of Columbus. But while there are some sixty ancient sagas in which such explorations are mentioned, and on our own northeastern coasts archaeologists have discovered the remains of stone houses similar to those found in Iceland, no genuine artifacts—instruments, tools, or utensils—used by the Vikings have ever been discovered.[1]

To historians and archaeologists, "genuine . . . artifacts used by the Vikings" means iron instruments, tools, and utensils, for they have incorrectly assumed that the Vikings used only iron implements after 500 B.C. But, on the contrary, the Vikings continued to use stone tools for centuries after they began making and using iron tools. They made some of the finest stone tools ever produced, and were still making and using them long after most European peoples had substituted iron for stone.[2]

Shortly after I recovered the Viking-type iron tools on the Newfoundland sites and in the mounds of Ohio, it became apparent why "no genuine artifacts . . . used by the Vikings" have ever been found in America. The recovered ancient tools, when exposed to the air for several months, disintegrated! Impurities left in the bog iron in the low-temperature, natural-draft furnace caused such iron to vanish in decay within a few years of exposure to the air. With no iron artifacts as evidence, the archaeologists and historians have declared that the presence of the Norse in America cannot be established. And, furthermore, posterity has never even suspected that there was an Iron Age in pre-Columbian America.

What eventually stopped the movement of trade and settlement in the New World before A.D. 1400? Unquestionably it was the gradually changing climate. In the centuries of Viking ascendancy, the Arctic was far warmer than it is today. The northern waters were navigable, and in the cold lands of Labrador, Greenland, and Newfoundland, grain could then be grown and forage for large herds of cattle was at hand. Through the later centuries, however, the Arctic regions became more and more frigid until by the time of Columbus, Greenland and the nearby Gunnbiorn's Skerries were blanketed by an ominous barrier of ice floes. The tiny ships of that time could not fight their way through the barrier, and so the links between the Scandinavians in Europe and their outposts in the New World were severed.

But these explanations, while they contribute to an understanding of the total picture, are not sufficient. Settlements of Europeans in America, we now have reason to believe, stretched from Newfoundland and Labrador through the St. Lawrence–Great Lakes area and southwest as far as Virginia. The Vikings were outstanding seamen, intrepid, formidable warriors. They were able to record basic facts on rune stones and on vellum. Their culture was far in advance of the cultures of the surrounding Eskimos and Indians. Their own records tell us how they successfully maintained and extended their settlements in the New World against opposition by the natives for at least four hundred years.

7

The Adventurous Vikings

The people of the viks, or small bays and inlets of the southern portion of the Scandinavian peninsula, were the preeminent voyagers, pirates, and maritime adventurers of Europe in the Middle Ages. To their westward surge belongs the story of American discovery.

Like the Hellenic and Teutonic peoples, the Vikings pushed south from their Arctic homeland, overrunning the countries in their path. Bred on the cold shores and islands of the Arctic seas, they landed on the northern coasts of Europe a thousand years or more before they settled in their viks. A fully developed maritime people, they were then in the Copper Age and just entering the Bronze Age. Like the ancient maritime Minoan Cretans, they were skillful, adventurous sailors, shrewd traders, and courageous fighters. And, too, like the Cretans, they frequently turned to piracy. When they became predominantly pirates, they called themselves Vikings, and it is by this name that they have been known in history.

In their purely acquisitive invasions, the Vikings captured and enslaved whole populations. The era of the Pax Romana had hardly come to an end when Europe experienced the first raids of these pirates from the north. Overnight they seemed to be swarming over all the European coasts. Magnificent in physique, highly skilled in military tactics, possessing a battle formation superior to any other of the time and enormous fleets, they were able to seize command of the sea rapidly and to conquer and rule throughout almost all of civilized Europe. The terror-stricken natives called them the Northmen, but they were in reality three different peoples: Danes, Swedes, and Norwegians (Norse).

The Danes raided Germany, France, and southern England, established temporary sway over all of Britain, and occupied Normandy. They overthrew the Saxon kings of England and the Norse kings of Scotland and Ireland. They secured dominion over Italy and Sicily. Except in Ireland, they were subsequently amalgamated with the peoples of their subject nations.

The Swedish migrations were to the east and south. Sweeping down the Volga, the Swedes established great kingdoms in Russia and were finally merged with the Russian people.

Sailing from the Norwegian fiords, the Norse quickly turned the Irish Sea into a Viking lake. They set up trading and manufacturing centers in harbors along its shores, and carved out kingdoms in England, Scotland, and Ireland. After crossing the Atlantic Ocean, they began to settle in Iceland in 875 and in Greenland 110 years later. In the year 986, Norse voyagers sighted the mainland coasts of North America.

About the time that Columbus started on his first voyage, Greenland disappeared behind great barriers of ice. When explorers found the island a hundred years later, the Norse settlements which had been there were gone. Only scanty signs of the former Norse occupation remained. Modern Danish archaeologists have unearthed a few relics: two axes (one of iron and one of bone), a handful of iron nails, a few planks, some trinkets, and the skeletal remains of long-forgotten men and women. No written records have been found in Greenland; all have vanished.

Icelandic historians, however, recorded the discovery of Greenland by their countryman Eric Thorvaldsson. And contemporary official documents, both secular and ecclesiastical, preserved the record of life in the Greenland settlements from the time of their founding by Eric in 985 until their disappearance.

Sagas preserved by farmers in Iceland recount activities of the Norse settlers in both Iceland and Greenland. The two sagas which have not been lost give conflicting reports of the voyages to Vinland.

One of these sagas was composed in Iceland, and the other was put together in Greenland. The Icelandic report is titled the *Hauksbók Saga of Thorfinn Karlsefni*. It describes the heroic exploits of Icelanders on voyages to Vinland. The other, which is called the *Flatey Sagas,* commemorates similar deeds on the voyages, but credits them to Greenlanders. The contradictions between these accounts of the Vinland voyages gave rise to the belief that there never was a Vinland, in fact that Vinland was merely a creation of skalds (poets) picturing a mythical paradise in mysterious lands west of Greenland. Granting that the Norse who lived in Greenland may have sailed along the North Atlantic coast of America, historians concluded that they had never settled on the American continent. Recent discoveries, however, have established the fact that they did settle here.

These sagas relate the story of the discovery of a country—now known to be America—by Leif, the son of Eric the Red, of later voyages to this country, and of Norse settlement there. Called Vinland, this country is described in the sagas as a wondrous land where trees and vines poured out luscious wines, where cattle browsed on far-flung pasturelands and tall grass in wild meadows invited the harvester's scythe, where self-sown grains grew thickly at the edge of great forests of finest woods, where for a tiny bit of red ribbon the natives offered a whole gray fox skin.

The story of this land, discovered in A.D. 1000 by Leif Ericsson on the shores of the North Atlantic Ocean, spread all through the northern world. From Greenland to Vinland later went Leif's brother, Thorvald, to explore its wonders, and he, too, made a startling discovery. Far to the west of Vinland he found a grain shed—proof that somewhere back in the interior was an agricultural country populated by civilized people. An Icelandic voyager, Are Marsson, went on into the interior west of the grain shed and found there a land which traders called Vitramannaland (Land of the White Men).

After Thorvald, other Greenlanders and Icelanders sailed to Vinland—among them Karlsefni and Bjarne Grimolfsson, with three ships, 160 men, their women, household goods, and cattle. Somewhere south of Leif's Vinland camp, they found a beautiful landlocked harbor in a mountainous country which they called the Land of Hop. There, too, they found self-sown grain, wine trees and wineberries, great forests, and a rare mauser wood, a small piece of which could be traded for yellow gold. They found game swarming in the forests and every river teeming with salmon. They saw the "sacred fish" * come up with the tide and fill the Norsemen's pits.

Karlsefni, like Leif, returned to Iceland a wealthy man with a ship loaded with products of Vinland. Lured by hopes of quick riches, Leif's sister, Freydis, also voyaged to Vinland and picked up a valuable cargo.

From the broken Danish Viking kingdoms of Ireland came the pagan Danes, and in A.D. 1054 an Irish Christian bishop went to Vinland and there lost his life.[1] Sixty-seven years later the Church was still attempting to spread the gospel in that pagan land; a missionary bishop left Denmark for Vinland in A.D. 1121 but was never heard from again. That was the last mention of Vinland in contemporary records now extant.

---

* Young flatfish, probably a small variety of flounder, locally known as "flatfish," which come in with the tide in northern Newfoundland. When the tide goes out, they are left in the pools on the shore. They are trapped in pits by the natives and used for hog feed.

8

Stepping Stones
to
America

Because of Iceland's traditional contacts with Europe, the island is generally thought of as a part of the Old World, but geographically it is really in the Western Hemisphere. The voyage from Europe to Iceland was, therefore, a major stepping stone in the westward tide of navigation and settlement.

The Vikings were not the first European emigrants to reach Iceland and to settle there. Evidence to be presented shortly places the Celts (Irish) in settlements in Iceland and also in Greenland and in the St. Lawrence Valley long before the Vikings arrived in the New World, probably as long as thirteen hundred years ago.

If there ever was a record of the date and the circumstances of the first arrival of Celts in Iceland, it has gone the way of most records during the Dark Ages in the history of man. However, revealed in records still extant is the fact that as far back as 330 B.C., the Celts in the British Isles were in contact with the Celts in Iceland. The English documents which are reported to have told about regular voyages between the British Isles and Iceland may have disappeared, but the statements of Roman and Irish historians remain to attest the fact.

Mention has already been made of the first recorded voyage between the Old World and the New World, the voyage undertaken about 330 B.C. by Pytheas. This famous astronomer of Marseilles, one of the first Europeans to determine latitude, sailed up the Irish Sea, stopping at various ports. Somewhere along his route he learned about a country far north of Britain called Thule where during the summertime the sun never set. Intrigued by these reports about this land of the midnight sun, he set out for Thule.

Only excerpts from Pytheas' account of his travels in and near Thule survive;[1] but they give the latitude of the places he visited, recorded, according to the customs of the day, in terms of the longest day of the year at these places. This record of latitudes along the way traces out his route to Thule.

Just where Thule was has been a controversial subject for centuries. The renowned Arctic explorer Stefansson and some scholars maintain that Thule was present-day Iceland. It may have been, for Pytheas seems to have followed the customary route between the British Isles and Iceland, which sailors used for thousands of years: up the Irish Sea, through the Hebrides, due north to the Faroes, and then slightly west of north to Iceland. Stopping first in a land where the longest day in midsummer was eighteen hours and then at a place where the longest day was nineteen hours, he finally reached his destination. The journey took five or six days' sailing north from Britain. In Thule Pytheas found that the longest day in one place was twenty-one hours and in another place was twenty-two hours. In the north beyond the Arctic Circle, the sun was above the horizon at midnight. One day's sailing beyond Thule, he found the frozen sea covered by a peculiar material which could not be traversed on foot or by boat.

Using Pytheas' record of his voyage based on the length of the longest day at places along his route, it is possible to reconstruct his voyage in modern geographical terms. And so the following account of his voyage is based on that rational assumption. After landing in England at some point on the coast of the Irish Sea, he stopped first in the north end of Scotland, where the length of the midsummer day is eighteen hours. His second stop was in the Faroes, where, in the southern islands, the midsummer day is nineteen hours long. That his final stop—Thule—was Iceland is likely, for southern Iceland has the twenty-one-hour day; the region farther north, the twenty-two-hour day; and the extreme northern part of the island, the midnight sun. The frozen sea, such as he found one day's sailing beyond Thule, is for most of the year approximately 100 miles north of Iceland—one day's sailing for the ancient ships. Irish priests who went to Iceland centuries later also ran into a frozen sea one day's sailing north of Iceland.[2] The "peculiar material" covering the sea which blocked Pytheas' passage was evidently the ice sludge which forms along the edge of drift ice when it is ground to pulp by the action of the waves.

It has been contended by some scholars that Pytheas went to Norway, not to Iceland, on the grounds that he could not have reached Iceland in a six-day voyage from Britain. But all ancient records of voyages between the British Isles and Iceland give the required sailing time as six days or less. Then, too, at the Arctic Circle the frozen sea was several days' sailing north of Norway, and Pytheas could not have reached it in one day from any point in Norway where he could have seen the midnight sun. Furthermore, it is maintained that during the navigation season ice sludge does not form in the sea around Norway.

Fortunately we have very definite records of the average distance per day traveled by ships in Pytheas' time. Herodotus, writing about 450 B.C., gives the time required for a voyage in the Black Sea. The *Scylax Codex,* probably compiled about 330 B.C., gives the distances and sailing time for ships between most of the ports of the Mediterranean and the Black Sea. According to the data supplied by these two authorities, the usual day's sailing for a ship was between 75 and 80 miles, and the average speed per hour was about 3¼ miles.

Since the distance from the north end of Great Britain to Iceland is about 480 miles, Pytheas' statement that Thule was six days' sailing north of Britain agrees almost exactly with the sailing time for the distance as figured from the known speed of the vessels of his time. The later Viking ships apparently were nearly 20 percent faster than the Mediterranean ships of the third century B.C. This is indicated by Icelandic records which give the sailing time between Iceland and Ireland as from three to five days.[3]

At the time of Pytheas' voyage, the Celts were the leading maritime people of northern Europe. Long before the Christian Era, they had oceangoing vessels with which they ruled the northern seas. Their rule finally came to an end, however, in 56 B.C. when the Celtic Veneti navy was shattered by Roman sea power under the command of Julius Caesar.

In his *Commentaries on the Gallic Wars,* Caesar has left us an excellent description of the Celtic ships in his account of his naval victory over the Celtic Veneti. It is apparent from this description that the Celtic ships were capable of long voyages over the storm-ridden Atlantic.

The Veneti state is by far the most powerful and considerable of all the nations inhabiting the sea coast. And that not only on account of their vast shipping, wherewith they drive a great traffic to Britain, and their skill and experience in naval affairs, in which they greatly surpass the other maritime states, but because, lying upon a large and open coast, against which the sea rages with great violence and where the harbors, being few in number, are all subject to their jurisdiction, they have most of the nations that trade in those seas tributary to their state.

. . . the Venetian ships were built and fitted out in the following manner: Their bottoms were somewhat flatter than ours, the better to adapt themselves to the shallows and sustain without danger the regress of the tides. Their prows were very high and erect, as likewise their sterns, to bear the hugeness of the billows and the violence of the tempests. The body of the vessel was entirely of oak to stand the shocks and assaults of that tempestuous ocean. The benches of the rowers were made of strong planks about a foot in breadth and fastened with iron nails an inch thick. Instead of cables, they secured their anchors with chains of iron and made use of skins and a sort of pliant leather by way of sails. . . . Between our fleet and vessels of such a make, the nature of the encounter was this: that in agility and a ready command of oars, we had the advantage; but in other respects, regarding the situation of the coast and the assaults of storms, all things ran very much in their favor. For neither could our ships injure them with our beaks, so great was their strength and firmness; nor could we easily throw in our darts, because of their height above us, which was also the reason that we found it difficult to grapple the enemy and bring them to a close fight.[4]

The Veneti assembled their entire fleet of 220 ships for the battle which was to result in Roman control of the northern seas for more than four hundred years. Even though the Romans raised turrets upon the decks of their ships, the lofty sterns of the Veneti ships still towered above them. The Romans could not hurl spears over the thick open bulwarks of the Gallic ships to any effect. The battle hung in the balance until Caesar ordered the Romans to mount scythes on long poles, to hook the scythes into the Venetian tackles and slash the ropes holding the sailyards to the masts. When this was done, the Veneti could not maneuver their vessels quickly, for they had very few oars. At once several of the well-oared, fast Roman galleys closed in on each disabled Venetian ship, and the Romans boarded the crippled giant from all sides. With the battle lost, the Veneti attempted to flee, but the Romans captured most of their ships. Only a few managed to escape in the night.

Caesar's account of the battle continues:

> This battle put an end to the war with the Venetians and all the nations. For as the entire body of their youth and all those of more advanced age who were capable of serving their country by their knowledge and counsels were present in the action, and as they had likewise drawn together their whole naval strength, such as survived this defeat, having neither any place of refuge nor means left of defending their towns, surrendered themselves and their all to Caesar's mercy. But he thought it necessary to proceed against them with the greater severity that he might impress upon the minds of the Gauls for the future a more inviolable regard for the sacred character of envoys. Having, therefore, caused all their senators to be put to death, he ordered the rest to be sold as slaves.[5]

And so, at a single stroke, Caesar destroyed the most advanced maritime nation in the ancient world—the Celtic Veneti. The Irish sagas indicate that those Veneti who managed to escape fled to their home ports, picked up the families of their crews, and fled to Ireland. There as the Gall-Gaels, or the Galians, they carried on the maritime traditions of their ancestors. It is likely that they were soon joined in their new home by other Celts who had been engaged in coastal traffic around the British Isles and in transoceanic traffic. Certain Gallic (Celtic) words in Icelandic records indicate that some of the surviving Veneti settled in Iceland as well as in Ireland; in both places they would have found hospitable and familiar cultures and probably personal relatives.

The cultural exchange between the British Isles—particularly Ireland—and Celtic Iceland continued through the following centuries. Some seven hundred years after the defeat of the Veneti, inhabitants of the British Isles were still going to Iceland. Bede the Venerable, who lived from A.D. 672 to 735, tells about frequent voyages between the Isles and Iceland, where Christianity had probably been established through Irish contacts two centuries before (finally to be extirpated by the pagan Norse). Bede remarked that ". . . the island which the books designate as Thule is situated so far toward the world's north pole that a day dwindles to nothing there, while the night is extremely long and the reverse takes place in summer."[6]

That the Irish priests and missionaries did reach Iceland is not a matter of conjecture or folklore, though there is an old Irish saga telling the story of St. Brandon who, in A.D. 500 or thereabouts, was the first Christian missionary to carry the faith to Iceland. Irish history also has an account by a contemporary historian, Dicuil, of three Irish priests going to Iceland in February, 795 (more than seventy-five years before the Vikings began their invasion of that island). The three priests stayed until April of the following year, presumably to serve the local Christians and to try to further the expansion of the Church. Dicuil tells what they subsequently related to him:

> . . . not only at the time of the summer solstice, but also during the days before and after, the setting sun at evening conceals itself as it were behind a little mound, so that it does not grow dark even for the shortest space of time. But whatsoever work a man will do, even picking lice out of his shirt, he may do it just as though the sun were there; and if they had been on a mountain, perhaps the sun would never be concealed from them . . . those who sailed thither reached it in the natural time for great cold, and, while they were there, always had day and night alternately except at the time of the summer solstice. But a day's sail further northward from it, they found the frozen sea.[7]

The sailing route of the priests from Ireland to Iceland was evidently via the Faroes. For, according to Dicuil, they reported visiting or seeing on their voyage small islands "filled with countless sheep." The Faroes derived their name, Faer-eyjar, the Sheep Islands, from their many sheep. The priests said that the small islands were separated from each other by narrow sounds, that for a century they had been inhabited by hermits from Scotia (the ancient name for Ireland), who had left them because of the northern robbers.

It is not surprising that Irish priests undertook a mission to Iceland around A.D. 800. There must have been a substantial Christian population in both Iceland and Greenland by that time, for during the next century, both countries, still Celtic, were often mentioned in papal bulls.

Records of early Christianity show that in 834—150 years before the Norse settlement of Greenland—Iceland and Greenland were made a part of the Arch-Episcopal see of Hamburg under the jurisdiction of Archbishop Ansgar. In the following year Pope Gregory IV appointed Ansgar as his delegate to "northern peoples, including the Icelanders and Greenlanders." The authorizing bulls were confirmed by Nicholas I with specific reference to Iceland; by Pope Adrian II in November, 872; by Pope Anastasius III in January, 912; and by Pope John X in October, 920.[8]

All mention of Iceland and Greenland in documents preserved in the Church archives, however, stops after the last notation by Pope John X in 920. By this time the pagan Vikings had almost completely occupied Iceland, which they had begun to invade forty-five years before. As they moved in, they enslaved those Celtic-Irish Christians who had not fled before them. The subjected Irish then adopted the pagan religion, and few, if any, Christians were left on the island. Through an account of the famous eleventh-century historian Ari Thorgillsson, in the *Landnamabok,* we learn that the Celts were in Iceland and that they fled from the Vikings:

> Before Iceland was settled from Norway, there were there men whom the Northmen call *Papar*. They were Christian people, and men think they landed from the west across the sea; for that were found after them Irish books, bells, and staffs, and some other goods. So it was readily known that they were West men that were found in East Papey and Papyli; and it is told in English books that in that time there was faring between the lands [British Isles and Iceland].[9]

In the *Islendinga-bok,* Thorgillsson also refers to the presence of the Celts in Iceland prior to the establishment of the Norse there. Calling them Irishmen, the historian states that "they went afterward abroad for they would not be here with heathen men."[10]

The fleeing Irish abandoned their belongings at Patricksfiord on the eastern coast of Iceland, where assorted remains of them were found by the incoming Vikings. Unable to defend themselves and their settlements from the battle-seasoned invaders, they knew that they would have to submit to enslavement if they did not escape the Vikings by fleeing west across the island. Vikings apparently seized control of the islands off the east coast and gained command of the eastern approaches to Iceland.

Mention has been made of how certain Irish and Gallic words are retained in the Icelandic records, or, indeed, still cling to the original sites which they designated. These words prove that the Celtic culture existed at some time in Iceland, and that it was a Christian Gallic culture. Names like Patricksfiord[11] utilize a distinctly Christian proper name. Many others are variations of the word *papa,* the Gallic-Celtic for "priest" or "Father," such as Papey (Priests' Island), Papafiordr (Priests' Fiord), and Papyli.

Greenland, too, has records made later by invading Vikings or their descendants of a previous occupation by another civilization. Historian Ari Thorgillsson relates that Eric the Red and his countrymen found traces of previous settlements—building sites, remains of boats, and stone implements—when they first landed in Greenland in 982. Thorgillsson suggests "that such people had lived there which now live in Vinland and which the Greenlanders called Skraelings."[12]

The assumption that Eskimos had been in Greenland before Eric the Red landed there and that it was they whom the Greenlanders called Skraelings no longer suffices as an explanation for this evidence of previous occupancy. Explorations by Danish archaeologists have established the date of the arrival of the Eskimos in southern Greenland as after A.D. 1400. The word *Skraeling* in Denmark meant a wretched or miserable person,[13] and during the twelfth century may have been the name used by the Norse for the despised Celts. Later writers applied the name to the Eskimos.

Papey and Papafiordr, respectively an island and a fiord off the east coast of Iceland, were evidently the center of Christian activities in Iceland during the era of Celtic occupation—activities stimulated by contacts with Ireland. The New World Celts were obviously much in debt to the European Irish for sharing with them the learning and the progress fostered by the Christian priests of Ireland, then a world center of learning and ecclesiastical training.

Ireland's Golden Age occurred in the very early Middle Ages, during and after the decline of the Roman Empire of the West and the ending of the Pax Romana. When St. Patrick and his followers preached Christianity in Ireland during the fifth century, they taught the Irish the art of writing. Never a Roman province as other Western countries were, Ireland preserved her native speech, developed a native script, and produced literature which has been called "the earliest voice from the dawn of western European civilization." The Christian monasteries of the country became centers of the arts and crafts as well as of religious training. Scholars and artisans from devastated Britain and starving Europe brought to these centers the accumulated culture of the Romans, while Irish craftsmen produced indigenous masterpieces in bronze, silver, and gold.

To Irish universities of the era flocked students from Britain and Gaul for instruction in the essentials of the higher education of the period: Latin, Greek, astronomy, grammar, writing, and decorative arts. Almost a thousand years before the time of Columbus, the Celts in Ireland were teaching that the world is round. An Irish abbot, Dungal, explained solar eclipses to Charlemagne. Missionaries from

Irish monasteries carried Western civilization, along with Christianity, to the German hordes then ravaging the entire European continent. Christianity and Western civilization flourished in Ireland alone.

Then came disaster, complete and overwhelming, and the culture of Ireland was snuffed out. Its first harbinger was the slow disorganization of the political state and the decay of military power. During the peaceful four centuries of the Pax Romana and the three succeeding centuries of the barbarian invasions of Britain and the Continent, Ireland was broken up into petty states. Gone was her national unity and organization for war. Forgotten was the science of military tactics. Except for the Gall-Gael,[14] the Irish had let their ships rot. Norse traders not only took over the seaborne commerce with the British Isles and Europe, but also established trading posts in many of the harbors and intermarried among the Gall-Gael and other Irish.

Realizing that the Irish monasteries with their vast endowments of gold, silver, and rare treasures were defenseless, Norse Viking raiders landed on the island in 797. Swarming down the Irish coasts and up the rivers into the lakes of the interior, for half a century they looted and burned, unchecked until Danish Vikings in turn drove them from the principal seaports. It was then that the Norse, themselves refugees, went to Iceland and brought to an end the Celtic occupation of that remote, peaceful island. The harried Christians had been residents of Iceland for more than a thousand years. After the Viking conquest of Ireland, they were the last outpost of the Golden Age of Irish civilization. The subsequent Norse victory in Iceland destroyed all relics of the earlier occupation except those names which the Celts had given to the hills, rivers, fiords, and the outlying islands.

9

Vitramannaland:
Refuge
of
the Celts

The first settlement on record of Europeans on the American mainland was a haven for harried Celtic peoples. Located immediately south of the St. Lawrence River, this overseas home of Celts was known in the beginning by contemporaries as Vitramannaland (White Man's Land). Some time later it became known as Irland Mikla (Great Ireland), and eventually as Albania (also White Man's Land). Bit by bit, references in the sagas, in Icelandic records, and on ancient charts and maps to Vitramannaland, to Irland Mikla, and to Albania tell the story of this civilized society in pre-Columbian America. And yet the onetime existence of this community has not hitherto even been suspected in modern times.

Documentary evidence that there was a Vitramannaland or Albania has been ignored because modern scholars have been unable to determine its location. Apparently, they lacked the know-how necessary for translating geographical terms of saga-time into modern geographical terms, and so were unable to interpret the old charts (or maps) that gave the location of Vitramannaland or Albania.

Just before World War II, during the course of my research, I stumbled upon a statement made about 1605 by a noted Icelandic his-

Fig. 9-1. Thordsen map of Albania, or Vitramannaland. This chart was apparently made by a group of navigators who were making regular voyages to central Canada, then known as Einhyrningialand, "Land of the People of the One-Horned Ax."

Grids showing latitude and longitude have been added to the original map by the author.

torian, Bjorn Jonsson, that sent me on a search for the ancient chart giving the location of Vitramannaland. The statement follows:

> Sir Erlend Thordsen, a priest in the parish of Staden, Iceland, in the year 1568 obtained from abroad the geographical chart of that Albania or Vitramannaland which is situated opposite Vinland the Good and which the merchants formerly called Hibernia Major or Irland Mikla (Greater Ireland).

Realizing that such a chart would be important documentary evidence of the exact location of Vitramannaland and, in fact, even of its onetime existence, I searched for the chart for years in every conceivable place. Not until 1946 was I fortunate enough to find it. Meaning nothing to historians and archaeologists, this chart (or map) had lain for centuries in musty archives, undeciphered (see Fig. 9-1).

According to my interpretation of this ancient map, which has been checked at the Hydrographic Office of the U.S. Navy, Vitramannaland (Albania) included all the territory west of the Gulf of St. Lawrence and south of the St. Lawrence River as far as the area which is now upper New York State and the northern ends of Maine,

New Hampshire, and Vermont. On other recently deciphered maps of ancient vintage, the northern end of Newfoundland is labeled "Vinland." The reference on the chart to Albania or Vitramannaland as being situated "opposite Vinland the Good" is, therefore, in agreement with the maps showing Vinland. For the St. Lawrence Valley is "opposite" Newfoundland—on the opposite side of the Gulf of the St. Lawrence.

It is possible to reconstruct a partial history of Vitramannaland by correlating references to it in Icelandic history, in the sagas, and on the ancient maps with the pertinent history of the Celtic and the Scandinavian peoples. These sources indicate that successive tides of Celts, Norse, Norse from Ireland, and, finally, Scots made the dangerous trans-Atlantic voyage to seek new homes in this thriving area. Frequently, the spur was defeat in the numerous conflicts between Norse and Irish, Norse and Danes, and Irish and Danes which raged within Ireland from the eighth to the thirteenth centuries. Facing death or enslavement, the vanquished would flee their homes in Ireland, disperse, and seek new lands. This process created waves of settlement of Vitramannaland with accompanying changes in the name of the area from the original Vitramannaland to Irland Mikla, and finally to Albania.

During the second Viking expedition westward from the Greenland settlement in A.D. 1002, Thorvald, the son of Eric the Red, came upon a grain shed on an island which my research places in the northwestern corner of the Gulf of St. Lawrence. Turning about, he headed back at once to Leif's Vinland camp on the northern end of Newfoundland. He probably realized that the shed marked the eastern outskirts of a country that he dared not enter—Vitramannaland; in fact, that Vikings caught in that neighborhood would be enslaved or slain. He was surely aware of the historical strife between his people and the Celts, in particular of the resulting hostility of Celts toward Vikings. For centuries the Celts had been robbed, forced into bondage, and slaughtered in their European settlements by Viking pirates, and more recently the Celts of the New World had been slain or driven out of Iceland and Greenland by his Viking forebears.

Peaceful traders from Iceland, however, did succeed in entering Celtic Vitramannaland. Contemporary records tell us that they knew it as a place where they could do a profitable business, and so they made frequent voyages there with their wares. Traders rarely risk their vessels and their cargoes on voyages to unknown places. Before setting out for prospective markets, they know the route to their destination, what wares are needed there, and what they will receive in exchange. Reports of these traders, recorded by both contemporary and later historians, give us a description of the location of Vitramannaland and an account of its customs and overseas commerce.

The *Eyrbyggia Saga* relates the experience of an Icelandic trader, Gudleif, the son of Gudlaug the Wealthy of Straumfiord, who returned to Iceland from a voyage in or around 1020 to Vitramannaland. According to his account, he found there a country well populated by people of the white race. Their language, he observed, was so much like the Norse that he could grasp the meaning of their discussions. He concluded that they were speaking Irish. They were organized into a society with well-articulated laws and regulations, providing, among other things, that Vikings attempting to enter the country would be enslaved or put to death. According to Gudleif, some traders were allowed to enter, and at least two well-known former Icelanders resided there, one of them an aged man who was spending his final years as a respected chief.

Gudleif's experience is retold in the saga as follows:

> Gudleif was a great merchant trader and had a big ship. It was late in the days of King Olaf the Saint that Gudleif went on a trading voyage to Dublin; and when he sailed, he was bound to Iceland. He sailed west about Ireland and met northeasterly winds and was driven far west into the sea and into the southwest.
>
> A strong northeast wind apparently drove Gudleif's ship into the great fog bank south of Greenland. Here the ship drifted with the currents. On emerging from the fog, Gudleif and his men were tired and discouraged:
>
> . . . they did not know where the land lay and how much of the summer was past, and they made many vows to get out of the deep, and now it came about that they got sight of land. It was a big land, but they did not know what land it was. Gudleif and his men took this plan to sail to the land because they were tired of striving longer against the might of the deep. They found a good harbor there, and when they had been on land for a short time, men came to see them. They knew none of them, but rather thought they were speaking Irish. Soon there came to them such a great gathering that it came to many hundreds.
>
> They laid hands on them all and bound them and drove them up into the country. Then they were brought to a council and judgment given over them. They understood that some men were for killing them, but others would have them distributed among the inhabitants and made slaves. And while this was going on, they saw a great

body of men approaching, and a large banner was borne in the midst. They thought there must be a chief in the troop; but when it came nearer, they saw that [in a litter] under the banner rode a large and dignified man, well along in years and his hair was white. All bowed to him and received him as well as they could. Soon they saw that all opinions and decisions referring to them were submitted to him.

Then this man ordered Gudleif and his companions to be brought before him; and when they had come before him, he spoke to them in Scandinavian and asked them from what country they came. They answered that most of them were Icelanders. The man asked which of them were Icelanders. Gudleif said that he was an Icelander. He then saluted the old man, who received it well, and asked him from what part of Iceland he came. Gudleif said that he was from that district called Borgafiord. Then inquired he from what part of Borgafiord he came, and Gudleif told him. Then the man asked about almost every one of the principal men in Borgafiord and Breidafiord; and after they told him this, he asked after Snorregude and Thurid of Froda, his sister; and he asked minutely after all things at Froda and especially after the boy, Kjartan, who was chief at Froda.

In the meantime the people of the country were demanding that the chief give some decision about the ship's crew. Then the big man left them and called out by name twelve of his men along with himself, and they sat a long time talking. After that he walked back to the crew. Then the chief spoke to Gudleif and those that were with him: "We men of this country have talked over your case, and the natives have left your fate to my decision. Now I will give you leave to go where you wish to go; and, though you may think that the great part of the summer is gone, yet I advise you to get away. For the people here are mistrustful and hard to deal with, and they think the law has already been broken in your case."

Gudleif said, "What shall we say if we are fated to return to the land of our fathers as to him who set us free?" The leader answered, "I will not tell you because I would not have my kinsmen and foster brethren make such a journey to come here as you would have had if you had not been helped by me. And now I have reached an age when at any hour age will step over my head or overcome me. But though I were to live yet awhile, there are here in this country those who are more powerful than I, that would give small quarter to strangers, though they do not live where you have come." Then this man had their ship made ready for them and stayed with them until the wind came fair which was ready for them to put to sea. And before Gudleif and he parted, this man took a gold ring off his arm and gave it into Gudleif's hands and with it a good sword. And then he said, "If you be fated to come to your fosterland, thou shalt take this sword to Kjartan, the chief at Froda, and the ring to Froda, his mother."

As they were ready to sail away, the man said, "I forbid any man to come to see me; for it is the worst kind of a voyage, unless you take the way by good luck and land where you have landed. And this land is also bad in harbors, and war certain to all strangers." After that they parted. Gudleif and his men put out to sea and made Ireland late at harvest time and were in Dublin through the winter. But in the summer they sailed to Iceland, and Gudleif handed on the treasures to whom they were sent. And all men took it as truth that this man must have been Beorn, the champion of the Broadwick men.[1]

This land where Gudleif found the old Icelandic chief living as a ruler is not named in the saga, but traders who later followed Gudleif to this new country identified it as Vitramannaland. Other stories which traders told about this land are preserved in an old Icelandic manuscript and also in the authentic *Landnamabok*. Retold more than once is the story of the finding in Vitramannaland of another old Icelandic chief, Are Marsson, who had disappeared from his homeland long before. Traders reported seeing him in Vitramannaland. Although he was a chief there, it was explained that he was also a captive of the country's rulers and could not return to Iceland.

The account of the discovery of Are Marsson in his new home is thus recounted in an Icelandic manuscript now preserved in the library of the University of Copenhagen.

Now there are, it is said, south from Greenland which is inhabited, deserts, uninhabited places, and icebergs, then the Skraelings, then Vinland the Good. Next and farther behind lies Albania, which is Vitramannaland. Thither was sailing formerly from Ireland. There Icelanders and Irishmen recognized Are, the son of Mars and Katla of Reykjanes, of whom nothing had been heard for a long time and who had been made a chief there by the inhabitants.[2]

Marsson, an important Icelander, was listed in the *Book of the Chiefs of Iceland*.[3] A cousin of the wife of Eric the Red, he was probably a generation older than his nephews, the sons of Eric: Leif and Thorvald. Both Marsson and Beorn of Broadwick may have been on some of the ships which attempted to follow Eric to Greenland but never arrived there. Blown past Greenland, they probably drifted in the fog along the Labrador coast and through Belle Isle Strait, finally landing somewhere on the shore of the Gulf of St. Lawrence, where they were captured by the Celtic inhabitants of the region.

At any rate, that there was an Are Marsson, that there was a Vitramannaland west of a sea near Vinland, and that Are was living in Vitramannaland are facts recorded by contemporary historians and based on the evidence of well-known persons in personal contact with the merchants who went to Vitramannaland. The most reliable Icelandic historian, Ari Thorgillsson, also related the story of his countryman, Are Marsson, in his *Landnamabok:*

> He was drifted by sea to Vitramannaland, which some call Irland Mikla. It lies west of a sea [the Gulf of St. Lawrence] near Vinland the Good. . . . Are could not get away from there, and he was baptized there. The first who told the story was Rafn the Limerick-Farer, who had been in Limerick, Ireland, a long time. Thorkell Gelleson also said that an Icelander told him that he had learned from Thorfin, Earl of the Orkneys, that Are had been recognized in Vitramannaland but could not get away from there, although he was held in great esteem.[4]

Evidently, at the time (ca. 1076) when Thorgillsson was writing his history, Vitramannaland was also known as Irland Mikla. Thorkell Gelleson was an uncle of Ari Thorgillsson, the historian who recorded this data. Thorfin, the Earl of the Orkneys, an outstanding man of his generation, was the ruler of the Hebrides and almost two-thirds of Scotland. He was well informed on the current news of his day, especially the affairs of the Vikings.

About fifteen years after Thorvald Ericsson found the grain shed, so the sagas relate, another Norse sailor, Karlsefni, came back from the western lands with a significant report. After an unsuccessful attempt to establish a settlement in Vinland, he had captured two Eskimo children in Labrador on his return voyage. After the children had learned to speak the Scandinavian language, "they said that there was a land on the other side over against their country, which was inhabited by people who wore white garments and yelled loudly and carried poles before them to which white flags were attached. People believed this must have been *Vitramannaland* or *Irland Mikla.*"[5]

Since the early Irish Celts and their priests wore white garments, probably made of the linen for which Ireland has always been famous,[6] the Eskimo children may have been describing a festival procession of the Irish Celts in Vitramannaland. It was not long after A.D. 1020 that Vitramannaland became known as Irland Mikla. It seems reasonable to assume that only an impressive change in the nationality of the inhabitants could have brought about this change in name. Since the new name is Scandinavian for "Great Ireland," the assumption is that the country was now occupied by Scandinavians—Norse or Danes—who had been living in Ireland. The available records show merely that various voyages from Ireland to Irland Mikla occurred, but give no clue to the racial stock of the voyagers. The situation in Ireland at that time was such that only Norse or Danes living there would have been under a compelling desire to emigrate. Neither then nor in the immediately preceding decades would the Celtic Irish have abandoned Ireland, for they had just regained control of their homeland and had compelled both Danes and Norse who were living in kingdoms which they had established on Irish soil to acknowledge the sovereignty of Irish kings.

The so-called Norse Era in Irish history (795–1014) had come to an end at the battle of Clontarf in 1014, when the Irish finally defeated the Norse decisively and broke forever the power of the Northmen in Ireland. Those Norse and Danes residing there who chose not to accept Christianity and become subjects of Irish kings would now be looking for new lands in which to settle. That the Norse among them migrated to Vitramannaland and the Danes to Vinland (Newfoundland) and later to Virginia seems probable from the evidence of artifacts and historical circumstances. The newcomers to Vitramannaland, it can be assumed, renamed the country Irland Mikla in memory of the land that their forefathers had ruled for nearly two hundred years.

Another change in the name of the country first known as Vitramannaland and then as Irland Mikla points to a new occupation, this time by immigrants from Britain. For Irland Mikla eventually became known as Albania. (Alban was the ancient name for Scotland.) After the Norman conquest of Scotland, many of the more energetic Scots, particularly those with Norse connections or with money to pay for their passage, took advantage of the ships crossing the Atlantic to escape to the New World. Eventually so many of them settled in Irland Mikla that the country's name was changed to Albania, land of the people from Scotland.

The name apparently became so well established and the country so well known that the Norse navigator who made the last copy of the Thordsen map of eastern Canada designated the entire area as Albania.

In the sixteenth century—five hundred years after Gudlief found the old Icelander in Vitramannaland—French explorers reached the St. Lawrence Valley area that had been Vitramannaland. They found two different peoples residing there: the Iroquoians and the Algonquians. The Iroquoians were sedentary, living in well-built wooden houses in strongly fortified villages and cities. The remarkable resemblances of their culture to the culture of the Vikings (described in Chapter 20) as well as the Scandinavian loan words in their language confirm the historical and geographical evidence of an earlier Viking occupation of Vitramannaland.

The Algonquians, on the other hand, derived their living mainly from hunting and fishing, resided in lightly constructed houses or tents, and had no strongly fortified villages. Their culture had some Celtic characteristics. Analysis of their language reveals a number of words that could conceivably have been loan words from the several Celtic languages. The original Celtic settlement may have been prior to Pytheas' voyage of 330 B.C., and the Algonquian language was not recorded until two thousand years thereafter. During twenty centuries, the pronunciation of both vowels and consonants would have changed. *G* might have shifted to *j, k,* or *t; l* to *r* or *n; dh* or *th* to *d* or *t; e* to *a, ei,* or *i.* Consequently, only an expert linguist could make a valid selection of loan words.

Archaeological excavations have disclosed that the original occupants of northeast America were tribes similar to the Algonquian. Since the sixteenth-century occupation of that area by Iroquoian and Algonquian tribes is known, the conclusion may be drawn with reason that Viking invasions through the St. Lawrence and Virginia valleys pushed some of the Algonquian tribes north and east and pocketed others against the Atlantic seaboard between Maine and Virginia.

10

New Horizons *for* the Norse

The legends of Eric the Red and of Leif the Lucky have come down through almost a millennium as the principal reminders that Vikings at some time saw the New World that was to become America and may even have planted a settlement there. The names of this father and son have persisted through the centuries as mythlike symbols evocative of this hazy "Viking episode." Who were these two most illustrious Vikings, and to what do they owe their enduring place in history?

Their adventure in the New World began with the arrival in Iceland of Thorvald, an outlaw from Norway. When Thorvald came to Iceland with his redheaded son, Eric, all of the choice farm sites there had been taken. Having no better choice of a homesite, he built a home for his family in one of the most desolate areas of the island. When Thorvald died, Eric, being more resourceful than his father, abandoned this home and cleared land for a homesite in the more desirable area of the famous valley of Haukdale.

In time, however, Eric, like his father, was looking for a new location, for, like his father, he was finally outlawed and banished from his homeland. Happy-go-lucky, courageous, and friendly, Eric had many friends, but his quick violent temper had made him many enemies, and he had killed three men. His first victim was a man who had slain several of Eric's slaves in the belief that they had caused a landslide which had damaged his farm. Instead of bringing the neighbor before the governing council and taking *wergild* (legal recompense for injuries), Eric slew him. Since his victim was *odal*-born (a noble), his murder was a serious crime for which the council, or *Thing*, outlawed Eric from the district.

It was for the slaying of two other man later, however, that he was finally banished from all Iceland. After being outlawed from the district for the first murder, he found it difficult to find a permanent home in a good location on the crowded island. Like other Viking chiefs, Eric had valuable seat posts at the end of the platform, the *Ha-Seta*, in the center of his *skala*, on which he sat in his carved armchair at feasts and celebrations. Cut from the rarest of hardwood and elaborately carved, his seat posts were among his most valued possessions. While looking for a new homesite, Eric left them with a neighbor named Thorgest. After he had established what he expected would be his new home, he returned for the posts. Thorgest refused to give them to him, and Eric, in the ensuing fight over them, killed Thorgest's two sons. Those victims of Eric's violence also were *odal*-born, and so for their murder, Eric was outlawed and banished from Iceland.

The order for his banishment placed Eric in a most serious predicament, for there was apparently no place to which he could go. The Scandinavian countries were not to be considered as possibilities for his future home for several reasons. They were all overcrowded, particularly Norway, where the population had expanded far beyond normal during the Viking period of the accumulation of vast wealth. And, too, Eric's father had been banished from Norway.

To put an end to the piratical practices of the Viking chiefs, the king of Norway had ordered them to operate as units of the royal forces. In this, he had met strenuous opposition. During the ninth century many Vikings had fled from Norway to places overseas such as Iceland, the Shetlands, Orkneys, Caithness, or Ireland. Here they could continue their raids on the British Isles without interference by the Norwegian kings. These fugitive Vikings saw no sense whatever in risking their lives and their valuable ships in campaigns profitless to them. But the natives of the British Isles were now uniting; and, wherever the Vikings landed, they met stiff resistance from Scot, Saxon, and Gael. The day of the small Viking chief was over, even in Iceland. With the ending of the Viking days, many Norsemen were left without revenue. Scandinavian countries, including Iceland, as a result of this, had surplus populations, too heavy to be supported by agriculture alone.

The desperate Eric decided that he would go farther west into the unknown seas in the hope of finding there a land in which to settle. Like most Icelanders, he had heard about Gunnbiorn's Skerries, a group of islands between Iceland and Greenland—their discovery one century before and their probable location west of Iceland. (See Chapter 17 for an account of the disappearance of the Skerries.) And so Eric Thorvaldsen set out from Iceland in 982 to "search out the land which Gunnbiorn, Ulf Kragesson, saw when he was driven westward across the ocean" a century before. He told his friends that he would come back for them if he found a place for a settlement. In this promise he revealed his hope of finding land suitable for settlement either on Gunnbiorn's Skerries or in some unoccupied country to the west or south.

It was, however, his discovery of the route through the fogs then blanketing the Western world for most of the year that made this voyage of Eric's so outstanding. (At that time the cold East Greenland Current, then flowing through the strait between the Skerries and old Greenland, met the warm Atlantic Current in Denmark Strait at the south end of the Skerries. The contact of the cold Greenland waters with the warm Atlantic Current created a bank of fog so thick that it blanketed Denmark Strait the greater part of the year and hid the Skerries from Iceland.)

Sailing west from Iceland, Eric first reached the southern end of the largest skerry. Rounding this island, he sailed into the strait then lying between Greenland and Gunnbiorn's Skerries, which today are hidden under a sheet of ice. In the cold, fog-free East Greenland Current there, he could see on his right, to the east, the part of the skerry which is now submerged. (Soundings reveal this submerged southern end, now clearly marked by a shelf which stands about half a mile above the bottom of the main channel of the strait.) [1]

To the north, high peaks and many islands were visible. Surrounded today by a sea of ice and partially covered by the glaciers, these peaks and islands of the Skerries form the southern shore of Greenland as it is outlined on modern maps. To the northwest, almost in the middle of the great strait which then separated Gunnbiorn's Skerries from Greenland, one of the highest peaks of the Skerries towered more than 2 miles above sea level.

To the northeast lay the high mountain now named Mount Gunn-biorn. These peaks are all still visible today. Owing to their height, the parts of the island of which they were the high points would even then have been covered by the glacial formations to which Eric gave the name Midjokul.

As he approached these peaks, Eric came in sight of the coasts of Greenland. Aware that the habitable land would be to the south, he undoubtedly turned immediately in that direction. (During his three years of exile, he explored the coasts and fiords of Greenland, proba-bly selecting the best of the abandoned Celtic sites for homesteads.)

In order to keep out of the fog, Eric had to sail close to the east coast of Greenland. Although he had learned the course to be followed to avoid the fog banks, the voyage was still hazardous. Almost any wind from the north could drive a ship off its course and into the fog. At least twenty-five ships set out for Greenland during the year after Eric returned to Iceland, but only fourteen reached their destination.

Greenland well deserved the name by which it had been known for at least 150 years before Eric's arrival. With its clear channels for sailing, harbors everywhere, and long, deep fiords with islands out-side, this new land was much like Norway. There was good seal-hunt-ing in the fiords in the winter and on the drift ice in early summer. There were whaling and fishing in the sea and fiords, as well as hunt-ing for walrus, reindeer, and a variety of edible birds. Grain* could be grown in the fields, and there was plenty of pasture for cattle and sheep.[2]

At the time of Eric's discovery, spring came earlier and summer was much longer than it is now. The climate was then probably much the same as it is in southern Norway today. Part of the circulating warm water from the Atlantic Current passed up the narrow channel between Iceland and the Skerries, and another part greatly enlarged the Irminger Current. The warm water melted the pack ice which was brought down by the East Greenland Current, thus causing a perpetual fog in Denmark Strait. Flowing around southern Greenland, the warm water which merged with the Irminger Current then turned north, giv-ing west Greenland a warm climate and melting part of the ice brought down by the Labrador Current. The entire southwestern part of Green-

---

* Grain-grinding mills were found on the Greenland farms by modern Danish archaeologists. The climate in southern Greenland in the eleventh century appears to have been the same as in Iceland, and grain was grown even in northern Iceland in the eleventh century.

land bordered on a warm sea and consequently had climatic conditions closely approximating those usual in the central portions of the North Temperate Zone.

Eric returned to Iceland and in the spring sailed back to Greenland, taking with him his family and his possessions. So appealing to the overcrowded and land-hungry Icelanders was his account of Greenland that many of them followed him to this outpost in a new world. To them it was an island at the western end of Europe, probably connected to the mainland of Asia. It was farther from Norway than Iceland, but that was not very disadvantageous. Traders would come to Greenland as readily as to Iceland, undoubtedly, if they could make a profit there.

The basic policies for the settling of Greenland were established by Eric. He made the final decisions, and everybody obeyed him. In time he became the *landstjornamadr* (ruling chief) of the area, with a number of lesser chiefs under him. They divided among themselves all the available land, giving to the uninfluential immigrants the right to settle in the domains only under certain conditions. Each chief defended the interests of the settlers (thingmen) in his domain at the moot, or local court, and, when it was necessary, even took the law into his own hands.[3]

Each chief or land-taker was restricted in the amount of land he could acquire to a space which he could "pass over with fire" in the course of a day. After selecting the area that he wanted, he was required to light a fire at the mouth of every river within his chosen land. After lighting the first fire when the sun was in the east, he would walk until the sun was in the west, lighting the last fire then. Thus were the boundaries of the land he could take set by fires burning at nightfall.[4]

Upon their arrival, Eric and his followers found throughout Greenland the building sites and stone implements left behind by previous settlers. The Norse built their homes, barns, and outbuildings on these abandoned sites, using sod and driftwood and thatching their roofs with reeds, hay and sod, and driftwood. The work of establishing their homesteads was in itself a tremendous task. Only a very limited quantity of provisions could be brought from Iceland in the boats, loaded as they were with household goods, cattle, sheep, goats, and their fodder. For food the early settlers had to rely mostly on fish, seals, and the few wild animals they could kill. They conserved their herds, allowing them to multiply as rapidly as possible. Providing winter forage for the herds was a necessity, and, in the early days especially, a tiring task, which would have been much harder if some of the land had not been cleared and cultivated by previous settlers, the Celts. To meet the need for fuel, peat had to be cut, dried, and stacked. To all this indispensable labor was added the work of building houses, barns, and outbuildings. Eric personally performed these many tasks for his own homestead and, in addition, carried all the responsibilities imposed upon him as the discoverer, founder, and leader of the new colony. His skill in accomplishing all this won him a secure place among the great Norwegians of history.

Though at the time of the founding of the settlement, the shores were lined with timber and driftwood, probably from Labrador,[5] wood soon became scarce. During the last years of the colony, all that they could find was the little brought down from Siberia by the Arctic currents. The annual deposit of driftwood was not sufficient for the settlers' needs even if none of it was used for firewood. The growing lack of wood taxed their ingenuity, but, for domestic purposes at least, they were able to find substitutes.

They used soapstone for cooking vessels, oil and peat for fuel and light, stone and sod for buildings, and whalebones to support their roofs. But nowhere in Greenland could they find anything to replace wood in the construction of their ships.

Their prosperity, in fact their very existence, depended upon an adequate supply of ships. Since travel by land was rendered almost impossible by the many fiords, separated by high, steep ridges, communication between the villages was by water. Their food was, in large part, derived from the sea. The scanty surplus of hides, tallow, and wool from their herds was insufficient to pay for needed supplies of manufactured goods such as fine cloth, pottery, and silverware from Norway. From the whale, seal, and walrus out in the open sea, they procured ivory, hides, and oil for trading purposes, as well as meat to supplement their food supply.

The few trading vessels that came to Greenland could not afford to carry timber for the price the islanders could pay. Shipbuilding required several special kinds of trees. Tall, straight, sizable trees which could easily be hewn into long, flat timber were needed for keels. Trees without large knots and with a straight grain for splitting into ship plank were required, the wood soft for easy cutting by hand and long-lived, even though it became alternately wet and dry. Inside and above the water line, spruce could be used, but under water the best planking was juniper. If juniper was not available, birch or oak would do, but easily splintered fir was not desirable. The joints between the planks had to be thoroughly caulked, and the caulking could not be driven home in fir planking. Even with thick planks, the seams had to be tightened with iron clinch nails and rivets.

Another kind of tree was also needed in shipbuilding: a tree with a large bent taproot whose main root was nearly the size of the tree trunk. From such naturally bent timbers the curved ribs necessary in a Norse ship could be easily hewn. With the exception of the keel and cross frames, every stick in the frame of a Norse boat was a naturally curved piece of wood which had been hand-hewn to fit exactly the place in which it was used. In the spruce forests of northern Newfoundland and Labrador, growing on rocks overlaid with a thin topsoil and constantly exposed to the high gales, there is an abundance of these bent taproots and trunks—moors, as they are called by Newfoundland shipbuilders. Today these builders still use the moors and hand-hew their frames from the natural bent wood, although they no longer use the clinker-type planking fastened with thongs or rivets (see Fig. 10-1).

Within a decade after they had started their settlement, the Greenlanders faced a shortage of wood for many purposes. The ships in which they had come from Iceland were wearing out and would soon have to be replaced. So short of ships were they by A.D. 1000, when

Fig. 10-1. The Newfoundland "moors."

Leif Ericsson set out on his voyage to Vinland, that he had to buy and refit a vessel that was at least twenty years old.

But shortage of wood was not the only perplexing problem that the Greenlanders faced at this time. In the first place, the available homesites were by then nearly all occupied. Immigrants were arriving in a steady stream from Norway and probably from Iceland, too, where volcanic eruptions were devastating large sections of the country.

Moreover, the recent demand by King Olaf of Norway that the Greenlanders officially adopt the Christian religion was fully as disturbing a blow to them as the growing shortage of wood and desirable land. Eric's oldest son, Leif, had returned from Norway during the summer of 999 with bad news. King Olaf, he said, had embargoed Iceland as a means of enforcing his demand that the Icelanders adopt Christianity. Norwegian ships would no longer be allowed to trade there unless the Icelanders acceded to his demand. The Greenlanders probably feared that an embargo would be placed against them, too, unless they accepted Christianity, and the majority of them objected to a change in religion.

They wanted, instead, to retain their worship of the pagan gods and their old customs. Most of them had come from the district of the Thorsnes Thing, where the cult of Thor had been followed more devoutly than in any other place in Iceland. These Thor worshipers objected to the Christian ban on plural marriages, then customary among the Norsemen. Their wives, however, were enthusiastic about the new religion. Some of them, including Eric's wife, Thorhilde, even adopted Christianity. In Olaf's demand that they make Christianity their official religion, the men saw merely a pretense to hide the king's intention to win absolute control of their island. The presence of the priest sent by the king to preach the mild and gentle doctrine of Christianity only inspired them to build more temples for the worship of Thor.

But King Olaf was a most persuasive Christian. One of his odd habits was to immerse worshipers of Thor in boiling oil. Another was to put a snake in a warhorn, place the horn's end into the unfortunate heathen's mouth, and then place a red-hot iron against the horn. The snake would crawl out of the horn and down the victim's throat, eating his way out through his vitals.

Leif had himself been a quick convert to the Christian religion during his winter with the king. Perhaps, being in the power of Olaf, he had no alternative but to embrace the new religion. As the saga states, "The king expounded the faith to him as to other heathen men who came to visit. The king was easy with Leif. He was Christianized and all his shipmates with him. Leif was with the king all winter and well treated."

According to the saga, Olaf asked him to "proclaim Christianity there [in Greenland]." Leif replied that that decision was for the king to make, but gave it as his opinion that it would be difficult to carry such a mission to a successful issue in Greenland. The king answered that he knew of no man who would be better fitted for the undertaking—"And in thy hands the cause will surely prosper." "This can only be," said Leif, "if I enjoy the grace of your protection."

Leif had good reasons for his misgivings. The king's order to "proclaim Christianity" in Greenland was an assumption of the king's right to rule there. If carried out, it would reduce free Greenland to the status of a fief of the crown, subject in all respects to the will of the absolute monarch of Norway. Even Leif's position as son of Eric, the ruling chief of Greenland, might not have been sufficient to save him from severe punishment by his fellow countrymen, or even exile. As the king's ambassador and consequently under royal protection, however, he could act resolutely.

In the year 1000 Olaf sent Gissur the White and Hialte Skeggiason to Iceland to proclaim Christianity there. So hazardous did he consider the expedition that he retained four Iceland nobles in Norway as hostages. The government of Iceland nominally accepted Christianity that year in order to lift the embargo which Olaf had placed on Icelandic trade with Norway.

It may have been due to the stubborn resistance of the Icelanders that Olaf decided to try a more subtle approach to the Greenlanders. He had the son and probable successor of the chief of that island in his power. If Leif issued the king's proclamation, Eric and the *Althing* (national council) might let it pass without open opposition. Thus the king would have accomplished his purpose, and Leif, when he became chief, would be bound to acknowledge himself the vassal.

The dwelling of Eric was often the meeting place for an assembly of the settlers. Sometimes these gatherings were formal, attended by all the chiefs and leading men of the locality, called together to discuss a coming session of the *Althing,* at a time when the *Althing* was about to alter the laws or act on a national policy on a question such as the king's demand that Christianity be officially accepted.

It is not difficult to picture these frequent meetings at Eric's home. His hall stood high up, with a slope down to the fiord and a mountain behind. A doorway on the south side afforded a splendid view out over the fiord. Nothing approaching over the open waters could escape the watchful eye of the thralls (slaves) who stood on guard. There the men stood and chatted, leaning against the great door pillars, looking down the fiord for seal or an approaching ship, while inside the women attended to their household duties.

The *skala* was long and narrow, like all the great Norse halls of saga time. Eric's hall was about 50 feet long and 17 feet wide. According to the *Grettis Saga*, "it was customary to have large fire houses on the farms, and there the people would sit of an evening by the long fire; there the eating tables were also set out at meal times for the people of the house, and there, too, they slept. By day the women sat there with their wool work." [6] These halls were large enough for a gathering of local leaders and one or more traders from Norway. The traders usually made their winter quarters with the chief of the settlement. (The striking similarities of the longhouses used by the Norse and the Iroquoian Indians are described in Chapter 20.)

Extending over half the length of Eric's hall was a row of hearths. The stone flags of the hearths covered a stone-lined trench, through which trickled a stream of water fed by a spring bubbling up in a small basinlike well. A little distance from the door, just below the gable end, there was a handsome well in which the water was trapped in two small basins, one above the other. [7] The fires in the hearths formed a single line of flame in the center of the hall. In Norway the hearths would have been filled with huge brightly burning logs from which pillars of smoke rose straight up to the openings in the roof above. But as already noted, in Greenland, within a few years after the settlement, logs had become too scarce to burn as fuel. Dried turf or peat was the usual fuel, supplemented on festive occasions by branches of birch and alder. Illumination in the *skalas* was provided by soapstone lamps and blazing torches.

On each side of the hearth stood portable tables with benches for seats. It was customary for the male members of the family, the guests, and the chief officers to be seated at the center tables. Highly honored guests would usually be seated at the table of the head of the household. Tapestries, shields, swords, axes, and spears usually adorned the center of the right-hand wall of the main hall. Beneath this adornment Eric probably sat in an elaborately carved armchair, oc-

cupying the center of the *Ha-Seta*. Women and children of the household ate at tables at the end of the hall. Thralls and thrall maidens
served the food, which was prepared in kettles on the hearth or roasted
over the open fire.

After the evening meal was over, the portable tables were removed. The dogs, having feasted on bones and scraps thrown to them
on the packed earth floor covered with boughs or straw, were put out.
The men found seats on the benches. If Eric's *skala* had a sleeping arrangement called a *set,* the visitors would take their seats on these
platforms along the sides of the hall. The *sets* were used as beds at
night and seats during the day.

At the nightly gatherings at Eric's *skala,* traders would be called
upon for stories of important events in Norway, particularly the latest
accounts of King Olaf's torture and murder of Norwegians who dared
to defy his order to become Christians. The king's motives were self-
evident to the rough, free-speaking Greenlanders, who were always
alert to any attempt to bring them under his rule. Their comments may
have been embarrassing to Leif, a recent convert to Christianity. Also
embarrassing to both Leif and his neighbors was the realization that as
the son of the ruling chief, he was the probable successor to the chieftainship of this pagan society.

But the ruling chieftainship was not hereditary in the case of Eric
and Leif, as it was for many Norwegian chiefs. Eric was one of the
few who had won their positions by virtue of superb leadership alone,
both in war and in peace. This factor had been greatly strengthened by
the obvious fact that it had been he who had discovered for his people
this new land and had, in the trying days of the new settlement,
organized them into a well-disciplined self-governed colony.

When his son Leif returned, bearing his—to the Greenlanders—
ominous news, Eric must have realized that now, for the first time in
the fifteen years of its peaceful existence, the colony faced a serious
crisis. Some solution would have to be found for a fourfold problem:
the threat of Christianity must be staved off; the colony must be saved
from rule by the king; some way must be found to replenish the timber
supply; and more land must be acquired.

First, he would in some way make it impossible for Leif to carry
out the order of the king to proclaim Christianity in Greenland. Then
at the annual meeting of the *Althing* in the summer, he himself would
recommend to the parliament that Christianity be officially adopted as
the state religion. The worshipers of Thor, of Odin, and of Njord, the

sea god, would, of course, object. But he could satisfy their objections by explaining that the passage of such a law would not affect their freedom to worship as they chose; it would merely authorize the worship of Christ by those who wished to do so. With Christianity adopted, Olaf would have to figure out some other pretext for asserting control over Greenland, and he might be killed or die before he could do it. This solution to the problems of Christianity and domination by the king would be especially satisfactory to Eric for a personal reason. It would save the imperiled status of his son Leif. In view of the Norse tradition relative to family heritage, Eric doubtless considered it highly important to preserve his son's position in the colony.

But the increasingly serious problems relating to the shortage of wood and timber for shipbuilding and land for the new settlers pouring in from Iceland and Norway, where Olaf's persecutions were driving out heathen worshipers, could be met in only one way: by the discovery of new land—forested land. The time had come to seek out and explore the woodlands which Bjarne Herjulfsson, a fellow Greenlander, had reported seeing years before after being blown off course on his way to Greenland.

11

The Norse Discover *a* Continent

The distinction of being first on the record to sight the mainland of North America belongs to young Bjarne Herjulfsson. Bjarne was a Norwegian seaman and trader who regularly plied the ocean routes between the Scandinavian peninsula and Iceland. On his first voyage west of Iceland, he was driven off his course to Greenland by a combination of foul winds and accident. Blown into the foggy areas south and west of Greenland, he drifted for several days and was finally carried by the current within sight of wooded lands. From Bjarne's description of these lands and of his voyage, it is apparent that he had sighted the wooded shores of Labrador. The failure of modern scholars to identify Bjarne's course as it is described in the sagas [1] has obscured his major role in the history of American exploration. (In this and the following chapters, quoted materials are translated from the *Sagas of the Vinland Voyages,* unless other citations are given.)

Among the men who had relinquished their homes in Iceland to accompany Eric the Red to Greenland was Herjulf Bardsson. While the other settlers selected sheltered homesites inland along the fiords, Herjulf picked out a homestead on a high headland in south Greenland near a fiord which is even now one of the most picturesque in Greenland. This headland, upon which Herjulf's home stood out boldly during the days of the Norse settlement, was thenceforth known as Herjulfsness. A famous landmark both before and after the Norse occupation, Herjulfsness retained that name for more than four hundred years. Through a nearby port, the last Greenlanders made contact with England and Norway, and it was there that the last living Greenlanders were seen 450 years after Herjulf landed in Greenland. And it is from the excavations in the graveyard at Herjulfsness that much of our information about the last Greenlanders has been derived.

Herjulfsness has another claim to historical importance: it was the destination of Bjarne, the son of Herjulf, on the voyage that was to take him by accident within sight of the American continent.

Bjarne was an enterprising young man. Like many Norwegians, he went to sea when he was quite young and soon owned a trading vessel of his own. In saga time, trading was just that: simply trading. Bjarne, like other traders, would spend a fall and winter in Iceland exchanging his Norwegian goods for Iceland's walrus ivory, furs, wool, hides, dried fish, tallow, and other local products. In the spring he would sail to Norway to trade his Iceland produce for Norwegian goods. This method of barter was time-consuming, and so he customarily spent one winter in Norway and the following one in Iceland.

Norse merchant ships like Bjarne's had marked drawbacks despite their general seaworthiness. Rising easily over the waves with favoring winds or currents, these vessels normally shipped very little water but were not able to face a strong head sea. Having to turn and run before a heavy gale, they were built with high sterns and were steered by oars instead of rudders. With their flat bottoms, they were absolutely at the mercy of the wind when it reached the proportions of a gale. They might be blown as far as 50 to 80 miles off their course within twenty-four hours. If the mast and sail were carried away, the crew had to drift with the currents and wind until carried within sight of land, when they could get out the oars and row in. Nor could these Norse merchantmen bear up well against unfavorable winds. They could sail, however, with the wind slightly forward of the beam.

Bjarne probably had a clinker-built ship about 80 feet long and 16 feet wide, with one mast and a square sail. His crew, if normal, was about twelve men. The ship was equipped with oars, which were generally used only in approaching land against an unfavorable wind or for maneuvering about in a harbor. With fair winds a ship like this would average between 70 and 100 miles per day, depending upon the wind and currents.

Because of the relatively slow speed of the Viking boats and the shortness of the navigation season, the most important element to be considered in planning a voyage was the time required. Hence, the length of a voyage between two points was reckoned by the number of days' sailing (*daegr*) required. This method of reckoning the length of a voyage was used throughout the Old World prior to the fourteenth century. On a course such as that from Bergen, Norway, to southern Greenland when both prevailing winds and ocean currents were favorable, a day's sailing was 125 miles; around the coast of Iceland, it was 120 miles. The effect of an opposing ocean current was frequently more than counteracted by the favorable prevailing winds on courses such as from Cape Stadt, Norway, to Horn, Iceland (80 miles per day's sailing), and from Snaefjeldnes due west to Greenland (82 miles per day's sailing).

When Bjarne returned from Norway to his home in Iceland in the summer of 985, he learned that his father had moved to Greenland. Deciding immediately not to unload his ship, he made plans to go on to Greenland. His crew was evidently made up of freemen whose cooperation he had to win, for he discussed the voyage with them, saying, "I will go to Greenland with the ship if you will bear me company." He did not minimize the dangers of the voyage when he added, "Our voyage may well be thought reckless since none of us has been in the Greenland sea."

Bjarne, of course, would have obtained all the information that he could about Greenland and the location of his father's home and, being an experienced navigator, would have procured all the sailing directions available. Undoubtedly he received the usual instructions to sail directly west across Denmark Strait for two days and two nights, when he would sight Gunnbiorn's Skerries halfway on the route to Greenland.

As soon as his ship was ready, Bjarne put out to sea. He "sailed for three [sea] days until the land was out of sight under the water, but the fair wind failed and changed into north winds and fogs." Sailing before an east wind, Bjarne had passed the Skerries—the one and only landmark on the route—and gone west of them. The east wind died down, and a north wind followed, driving them south into the area of perpetual fog. After a time the north wind also died down, leaving him lost and helpless. The only thing he could do was to furl his sail and wait for the appearance of some heavenly body by which he could determine his location and set a course for Greenland. "These fogs lasted for many days and they did not know where they were or whither they had drifted."

By this time Bjarne was far south of Gunnbiorn's Skerries. His ship had become the captive of currents running close to the continent of North America. South of the Skerries he drifted into the warm Irminger Current. Much larger then than now, this current carried him southwest and then west, around southern Greenland. Part of the current continued north along the west coast of Greenland, but Bjarne was in the stream which turned west across Davis Strait. This warm current then turned and flowed south alongside the cold Labrador Current, giving rise to dense fogs out at sea. Bjarne drifted south in these fogs for "many days. Thereafter they got sight of the sun and could distinguish the quarters of the heavens."

With clear weather and a sight of the sun, Bjarne's only choice was to continue west with the hope of reaching Greenland. A careful navigator, he had lowered the sail as soon as the fog set in, in order to hold his ship as nearly as possible to his then known position.

Within a few hours Bjarne first sighted land—undoubtedly the coast of Labrador.

> Now they hoist sail and sail that day ere they saw land and deliberated with each other what land that might be, and Bjarne said he thought it could not be Greenland. They asked whether he will sail to this land or not. "My intention," said he, "is to sail close to the land." And so they did, and soon saw that the land was *mountainless,* and *woodgrown, with small hills on the land.*

Now that he was out of the fog, Bjarne could readily determine his latitude by sight on Polaris at any time during the night. With his years of navigation in that latitude, he could tell his approximate position during the day by the sun, and his observation of the highest point the sun reached would give him his latitude almost exactly. But after the long drift in the fog, he would not know his longitude, even approximately. He would know, however, that he was south of Herjulfsness, the southern end of Greenland. When he saw the forests, moreover, he knew that the country was not Greenland because Greenland was treeless. Because of the set (direction) of the flow of the ocean currents, the only land he could possibly have sighted was Labrador. As seen from a vessel well out at sea, the Labrador coast between

Cape Harrison and Cape Makkovik, in fact, appears to be moun-
tainless, wooded, and with small hills on the land. Bjarne was thus, as
the remainder of his voyage also reveals, the first man on record to see
the mainland of America. He was to see it again soon.

When they approached near enough to see that this new land was
wooded, Bjarne was certain that it was not Greenland; so they "left
the land on the larboard and let the sheet turn toward the land. After
that they sailed for two days before they saw another land." Sailing
with a favorable wind but against the current, they probably made
around 80 miles per day. When, after sailing two days, they sighted
land again, they had gone north along the Labrador coast about 160
miles. There, in the vicinity of Nain, the Kiglapaik Mountains rearing
above the horizon were their first signs of land in two days. The
mountains along the coast which they had passed receded, and the
shores were deeply indented.

Bjarne's companions asked him if the land they were sighting
was Greenland, and he replied that it was not, because Greenland had
very large glaciers. Sailing closer to the land, they saw that it was *flat*
and *wooded*. By *land,* the saga meant *mainland,* not the islands off the
coast which in this area are now treeless. In 1900, geologist R. G.
Daly described the coast south of Nain as seeming to be *flat* from the
deck of a boat several miles off shore and as being *covered with
woods.* [2]

Bjarne resisted the urging of his crew to land. Soon "the fair
wind failed them" and the crew muttered that it "would be wise to
land there." But Bjarne remained adamant against landing, even when
they declared that they were in need of wood and water. Bjarne later
was criticized by his countrymen for failing to land: his decision cost
him the honor of being acclaimed the first known European to set foot
on the American continent.

Hoisting sail and "setting the prow from the land, they sailed out
upon the high seas with southwesterly gales for three days [about 240
miles]," and then they saw a third land, *"high and mountainous and
with glaciers on it. . . .*They did not lower their sail, but went ahead
along the land until they saw it was an *island."*

The only small island along the Atlantic Coast west of Greenland
with a glacier on it is one of the Resolution Islands group, located at
the entrance to Hudson Strait. From out at sea, the group looks like a
single island, and for three hundred years it was so marked on all
modern maps. It was not until 1948 that a U.S. Navy captain flying

over the area discovered that what had been thought to be one island is actually a group of islands. The Norse, however, for whom the islands became an important landmark, soon found that there were several in the group. In accordance with their custom, they named them Bjarney-jar (Bjarne's Islands) in honor of their discoverer. On a later voyage, Icelandic explorer Karlsefni went directly from Greenland to the islands and landed there.

This third land, then, which Bjarne saw was the group of islands called Resolution Islands. In failing to identify this "island with glaciers on it"—the Norse Bjarneyjar—historians have missed the one clearly identifiable landmark of the *Sagas of the Vinland Voyages,* and, in doing so, have missed the key to the identification of the routes of later Vinland voyages.

Knowing that there was no island with a glacier on it at the south end of Greenland, Bjarne realized he was west of Greenland. In order to reach that island, he had only to sail east until he sighted it and then turn south and continue down along the Greenland coast until he made out the rugged peaks of Hvarf and Hvidserk. There, below the peaks, would be the only headland in Greenland with a house on it—his father's house, and so

> again they set the stern towards the land and held out to sea with a fair wind. But the wind waxed at once, and Bjarne bade them to reef and not to sail faster than the ship and rigging could bear. They sailed now for four days. Then they saw the fourth land.

This was Greenland, about four days' sailing from Resolution Islands. Then they asked Bjarne whether or not this was Greenland, and Bjarne replied, "This is most like that which has been described to me as Greenland, and now we shall steer towards the land." When they were near enough to distinguish objects on the shore, they simply followed the coast south until they saw the house on the headland lying under the two peaks.

> . . . and they came to land below some ness at evetide . . . and there dwelt Herjulf, Bjarne's father, on that ness, and from him the ness has taken name and is afterwards called Herjulfsness. Went now Bjarne to his father and gives up now his sailing and stays with him as long as Herjulf lived, and afterwards he dwelt there after his father.

12

Leif the Lucky
and
Vinland the Good

The first recorded landfall and settlement in North America was that of Leif Ericsson in A.D. 1000. Although his adventure of sound seamanship and brilliant planning and organization is narrated in detail in the sagas, the record has been obscured by generations of scholars who have perversely followed false trails. In the erroneous belief that the newly discovered region was named Vinland because grapes flourished there, rather than wineberries, investigators have searched in vain in New England for evidence that Leif's settlement was there. But Vinland was in fact in Newfoundland!

Tracing the trail of Leif's route of exploration and discovery was for me a fascinating quest. The sagas describe the course. Using them as a guide and comparing the saga accounts with ancient sailing charts only recently deciphered and with sailing directions recorded in Icelandic history, I believe I have pieced together the more important parts of the mosaic. My method was to correlate detailed descriptions of the landmarks seen on the saga voyages with known changes in climate, ocean currents, and fog belts, with the rate at which the land rose throughout the centuries, and with known habitats of the Eskimo. My identification of the glacier-topped Bjarneyjar, a landmark of the Viking voyages, as one of the Resolution Islands was a major clue in solving the mystery of the route of Leif's voyage and of later Viking voyages as well as the earlier voyage of Bjarne Herjulfsson.

In order to meet the crisis facing his colony, it will be recalled, Eric was confronted with the need to send an expedition to search out the wooded lands which Bjarne had reported seeing to the west. To Leif, eldest son of the ruling chief, would go the responsibility for organizing and executing this undertaking sponsored by his father. The saga relates that he prepared for the voyage with the same foresight and thoroughness that later characterized his conduct of the expedition. First, he purchased a boat from Bjarne, presumably the same boat in which Bjarne had made his notable voyage fourteen years before. Leif than proceeded to equip the vessel in the manner of the Vikings. It was their custom to carry enough oarsmen to drive a boat at a good speed independently of the sail. In calm weather, or if they had to go against the wind, they used the oars. With this extra motive power they could run in and out of the fiords and close to the head-lands, confident that they would be able to get out to sea if a sudden storm blew up.

Bjarne's boat had been equipped as a trading vessel with a crew of ten or twelve, but Leif, apparently realizing he might land in enemy country, converted it to his purpose of exploration by increasing the facilities for a crew of thirty at the oars. As a merchant vessel, the boat had been left open at the center, or midships, for storage of cargo. Passage from bow to stern was by narrow gangways along the gun-wales. For Leif's use, these gangways were widened into plat-forms for the rowers' benches. The bow and the stern of the boat, both pointed, were decked over to provide sleeping quarters for the crews and platforms for fighting. The oarsmen's shields were hung on the rails in order to protect the rowers from arrows and spears and also to permit the oarsmen to pick them up easily in case they had to shift suddenly from rowing to fighting. The author of the saga must have been aware of the work involved in the preparation of the ship, for the saga relates that "now they built their ship and went to sea [in the summer of A.D. 1000] when they had finished."

Retracing Bjarne's route, they "found then that land first which Bjarne found last." To reach this place so readily, it was necessary to have accurate sailing directions, which could have been obtained only from Bjarne. Most important were the directions which would enable Leif to avoid the fogbound areas south and west of Greenland. That he did so we are assured by the saga:

> They found then that land first which Bjarne found last. There sailed they to land and cast anchor and put out the boat and went ashore and saw there no grass. Great glaciers were seen far away, but like one stone field was all from the sea to the glaciers, and it seemed to them that this land was good for nothing. Then said Leif, "It has not happened with us as it did to Bjarne that we have not got upon the land. Now I will give name to the land and call it Helluland [Land of Flat Stones]." Afterward they went to the ship and sailed to sea.

The land which Bjarne had found last was the projecting peninsula of Baffin Land on the north side of Frobisher Bay. He had to be close to this peninsula before he could see the strait between the mainland and Resolution Islands. Leif, in retracing Bjarne's course, would go to Baffin Land instead of to the island, for the tidal currents are very swift around the island, and there are no good anchorages there.

The name that Leif gave to Baffin Land—Helluland—was well chosen. The coast at that point is exactly as the saga describes it. As far as the eye can see, the shore is covered with innumerable large, flat black stones; and in the background are the snow-and-ice-covered mountains and the glaciers. It is literally "good for nothing," a bleak, bare, mountainous country where the land in every direction, up to the glaciers, is completely covered with large flat rocks, roughly piled. In a thousand years no one except a few Eskimos has found a use for this land or has settled around Frobisher Bay.

Having determined that these rocky lands were not habitable and knowing from Bjarne's description that the woodlands were much farther south, Leif sailed down along the coast until he saw a definite change in the appearance of the shoreline—probably beyond Cape Mugford, where the high land ends abruptly and sweeps away into the bell-shaped Okkak Bay.

At any point south of the cape, he would have found a wooded area (Labrador) entirely different from the barren waste of Baffin Land. As the saga relates, Leif actually

> found another land and again sailed to the land and cast anchor; then put out the boat and got ashore. That land was level and wood-covered, and there were wide white sands wherever they went, and it was not steep at the shore. "Then," said Leif, "after its quality shall this land have name and be called Markland [Woodland]."

There are several locations between Cape Mugford and Nain to which this description could apply. It is quite probable that Leif landed somewhere on the northern part of the coast where, near the shore, he would have found mostly spruce trees. Had he gone into the deep inlets near Hopedale, he would have seen large spruce and juniper, but only small birch. It is evident that he did not locate the large trees, since he continued on to Newfoundland, where he did find them, loaded up his ship, and returned to Greenland, thus indicating that his purpose was to find ship and building timber as well as settlement sites.

(Markland is the first area of the American continent on which the Norse are definitely known to have landed; they were in contact with Markland for 350 years.)

On later voyages the Norse did find the larger timber around Nain and Hopedale, as well as curved moors of both spruce and juniper. The spruce and fir there grow to a diameter of 18 to 24 inches, and the juniper is almost as large, but the birch is usually less than 8 inches in diameter.

According to the port record of Reykjavik, Iceland, for the year 1347:

> There came thirteen sea ships to Iceland. . . . There came also a ship from Greenland, smaller than the small Iceland craft. It came into the outer Straumfjord. It had lost an anchor. Therein were seventeen men who had been to Markland, but on their return were driven in here.[1]

The name, location, and products of Markland were so well known in the days of early Greenland that, in the above document as well as in others of the time, neither description nor comment was considered necessary in referring to it. Markland (Labrador), it will be recalled, was primarily useful to the Greenlanders as a source for lumber for ship construction.

There could be no doubt in my mind that Markland existed. The truly important question was: Where was it located? As I indicated earlier, the Nain-Hopedale area of northern Labrador seemed to fulfill the necessary requirements—it is south and west of Greenland; it has large forests of trees suitable for shipbuilding, as had the Markland of the sagas; and it is the region nearest to Greenland in which shipbuilding timber could have been obtained. Fortunately, however, the question was not destined to be settled solely by deduction.

When the Greenland Norse began lumber operations in Markland, they would have had to set up lumber camps to house the crews. Since these operations took place over an extended period, it is reasonable to assume that more or less permanent dwellings would have been constructed, probably on an island as a safeguard against a surprise attack by hostile natives. In short, if the Nain-Hopedale area was indeed Markland, definite traces of a Viking occupation would still be there. As indeed they are.

On Sculpin Island, near Nain, are to be found the ruins of prehistoric stone houses—twelve of them with walls still standing—apparently all that is left of what used to be a permanent village on the island. Extending in some places 3 feet above the present surface of the ground, the stone walls are 3 feet thick.[2] The claim that these houses were built by the Eskimos is fallacious: they were constructed with the skill of experienced stonemasons, whereas the Eskimos simply threw stones together in loose piles. The masonry is, in fact, characteristically Norse, identical with the remnants of Greenland farm buildings[3] and the ancient Norse rubble walls in Norway and the Hebrides. The Norse were good masons; even in their poorest masonry, the joints are carefully broken and the stones firmly bedded.

In the Hopedale area, moreover, among groups of Eskimo ruins, Junius Bird of the American Museum of Natural History uncovered a number of fragments of steatite pots which had been ornamented on the top and outside of the rim with parallel grooves.[4] They are almost identical with other steatite fragments found in the Norse ruins of Greenland. He also found a number of typical old Norse iron boat spikes and clinch rivets which were hand-forged from Viking-type iron. One of those tested by him had been cut from a carburized iron plate.

The evidence of these archaeological findings is supplemented and confirmed by the Friseo and Stephansson charts, both of which definitely place Markland in northern Labrador. Therefore, insofar as circumstantial and tangible evidence can produce a true historical conclusion, it seems certain that Markland was in the Nain-Hopedale area of Labrador and was, consequently, the first place on the American mainland where the Norse are definitely known to have landed.

Leif had located an ample supply of good, though small, softwood timber at Markland, but he also needed to find larger timber for ship plank and trees with curved taproots for ship frames. Hardwood for bowls, kitchen utensils, and ornamental carvings was required also. For this ship timber and hardwood, Leif knew he would have to go farther south.

Then, too, winter was approaching. He had to find a place where he could draw his ship up on shore to avoid its being crushed by the ice, preferably at some secluded spot where he would not be exposed to attacks from hostile natives. This retreat should be in the vicinity of game and good fishing. He would be lucky indeed to locate a campsite meeting these requirements in or near a forest containing both hardwood and ship timber.

Lucky he was, for in northern Newfoundland he found a location with all these advantages and one more: complete isolation from Celts, Indians, and Eskimos. Before coming upon this place which the world was to know as Vinland, however, Leif had about six days' sailing ahead. The saga relates in detail the story of his 400-mile journey from Baffin Land past Markland, but passes over the next several hundred miles without giving particulars. Leaving Markland, Leif and his crew passed a succession of steep, rocky cliffs and forbidding, but picturesque, headlands. Then, the saga relates, "They came to an island which lay to the north of the land and went up there and looked about in fine weather. There was dew on the grass."

Leif had reached the northern headlands of Newfoundland, 300 miles south of Markland. Crossing the Strait of Belle Isle, he had arrived at the island "which lay to the north of the land": Kirpon Island, which is separated from the northeastern point of Newfoundland by a channel so narrow that it is scarcely larger than a creek. From the highest hill on Kirpon Island—one of the highest peaks of the region—he had a panoramic view of northern Newfoundland. It was from this same height that Cartier, 500 years later, surveyed the surrounding country before moving on to the St. Lawrence Valley.

The long northern peninsula of Newfoundland is outlined on ancient sea charts, and it is there named Promontorium Vinlandia. While gazing at the peninsula from his point of observation on the 600-foot peak of Kirpon Island, Leif could see Pistolet Bay penetrating the northern tip of the peninsula. Extending back into the slopes of the mountains southwest of the bay was a narrow lake from which a river flowed into the southwest corner of Pistolet Bay. The rays of the morning sun reflected from its waters would have revealed the lake to him across the peninsula. The forests covering the entire country to the south and west were, in this climate and latitude, almost certain to be partly hardwood. The rivers running into the bay would furnish good salmon fishing, while seal and cod could be caught in the bay and sea. The wood surrounding the lake would provide lumber for his camp buildings, conceal the camp, and screen the ship when he had it hauled up on shore.

The land in this area is today 35 feet higher than it was when Leif and his men saw it, because the northern end of Newfoundland is steadily rising, pushing the water line farther out as time goes on. The place where their ship went aground is, therefore, 4 miles or more inland today. With these conditions in mind, the saga account of their landing at the campsite can be retold with the addition of modern geographic names:

> Afterwards they went to their ship [which was anchored in Noddy Bay] and sailed into a sound that lay between an island [Sacred Island] and that cape [Cape Onion] which went to the north from the land . . . steering to the west of the cape, it was very shallow there at ebb tide [a shallow inlet then opened out of the southwest corner of Pistolet Bay], and their ship stood there aground, and their ship was far away from the sea. Yet they were so anxious to go ashore that they would not wait for the high water to rise under the ship but hurried to the land where a river fell into the sea from a lake. But as soon as the tide rose under their ship, they took the boat and rowed to the ship and moved it up the river, after that into the lake and cast anchor there.

With the gradual rising of the land, the inlet, which was known to the French sailors of the seventeenth century as the Baye au Mouc, had disappeared by 1765. Captain James Cook, the famous explorer, mapped Pistolet Bay in that year and noted that there was a river in the southwest corner of the bay. In 1841 Sir Richard Bonnycastle, lieutenant colonel of the Royal Engineers, had the area surveyed, plotted the river on the map, and noted that inland from the river were ponds and marshes. The latest maps do not show either the river or the ponds, but they are still there. A great marsh and numerous ponds occupy the site of the old bay. The marsh, now called the Northwest Marsh, drains into "Leif's River," which flows along its edge.

For about 5 miles from the sea, the bed of the river is graveled, and there is a succession of pools separated by shallow rifts. The banks of the river commence to rise a mile from the bay, becoming gradually steeper. Several miles from the bay, the river has cut a narrow canyon 300 feet wide through solid rock. Here was the entrance to the lake or cove into which Leif took his ship at high tide. (He could not have entered at low tide.) This lake is now a wide marsh about a mile long.

Leif evidently decided to survey the surrounding country carefully before establishing a permanent winter camp. The saga states that his men "brought from the ship their leather bags and put up . . . shelters." They were in a strange and probably hostile country, with return to Greenland impossible except by sea. As long as their ship was free to move and the waterways were open, they were reasonably safe. When winter set in, their boat was hauled up on shore before the lake and river froze over; an attack by natives of the country under such circumstances could prove disastrous. It was most important, therefore, that their permanent camp be away from the traveled paths and as far as possible from inhabited villages.

Leif happened upon an almost inaccessible location where he would not be molested. The shore of the strait extended northeast and southwest about 7 miles away from and parallel to the lake. There was no one living in the area nor any reason why anyone should come there. The nearest landing place was on the strait at Big Brook, 8 miles distant, and the ground between the camp and the strait was a low swamp. Immediately east of the lake the land was low and marshy, and beyond the swamps rose hilly country which could be traversed only with difficulty. The same hills also extended along the northern shore of Hare Bay, running two-thirds of the distance across the peninsula and cutting off access to the campsite by land from the south, except through the ridges of the Long Range Mountains. The highway of the Eskimos, which was on the east coast of Newfoundland, was 20 miles east behind the hills.

During the fifteen years that the Norse used this camp on their later expeditions to Vinland, neither an Eskimo nor an Indian ever visited them, and their permanent buildings were not disturbed. On the other hand, on virtually every voyage to places south of Markland, they encountered Eskimos. Careful examination of most of the coves on the south shore of the strait has confirmed the sagas in this respect. No Eskimo artifacts have been found there. There is, however, ample evidence of Eskimo occupation of the opposite Labrador shore.

Owing to the almost perpetual state of hostility between the Indians and the Eskimos, there was usually a strip of neutral territory between them into which neither ventured except for the purpose of making an attack. The lake near Pistolet Bay happened to be in one of these neutral zones and to be so situated that war parties never crossed near it. Access to this particular spot was too difficult, and there were no villages, either temporary or permanent, in the vicinity. Interestingly enough, in all the wooded sections of the Atlantic coast north of the fortieth parallel of latitude, there was no other location where the Norse could have remained for years without coming in contact with either the Eskimos or Indians. Fisheries were so vital to the existence of the coastal natives and travel along the seashore by land and sea was so continuous that, with this one exception, not a single cove would have been permanently free from visits by them.

Even today, the site is so isolated that the southwestern shore of the bay is uninhabited. Although "Leif's River" is the largest stream flowing into the bay, I was unable to find a single inhabitant in the Pistolet Bay area who knew of its existence. Lifelong residents of northern Newfoundland insisted that there was no such river in that end of the bay. But I noted that the southwest corner of the bay could be seen on a clear morning from the top of Ran Galley Head—the highest peak on Kirpon Island—and that it was the only site which fully complied with the descriptions in the sagas. I knew, too, that the lake bed must now be 35 feet above sea level and at least 5 miles back in the woods.

So day after day, I cut my way back through the dense spruce underbrush behind the grass-covered shore of the bay. Finally, I broke out into a rolling, marshy, moss-covered plain. It was dotted with small ponds and an occasional clump of spruce trees.

This marsh is the partially dried-up bottom of the old Baye au Mouc. When the French mapped it centuries ago, it was an arm of Pistolet Bay. Now it is 10 feet above mean low tide. Driven by the northeast gales, the waves of the bay have formed a bar across the entrance. This bar now forms a rounded ridge covered by an almost impenetrable thicket of spruce scrub which hides the swampy bottom of the former bay.

On the western side of the swamp, I could see a thick woods apparently marking the course of a river flowing into an inlet at the extreme southwest corner of Pistolet Bay. This was "Leif's River." At low tide, leaving my launch at the entrance of the inlet, I had to walk nearly half a mile across the tidal flats of its bottom to reach the river. Numerous small brush-covered islands scattered over the flats had both screened the main stream and split it into rivulets. Five miles from the bay I found the former entrance to "Leif's Lake" about 35 feet above the present sea level. The lake is now a swamp with rocky banks about

10 to 15 feet high. Although in Leif's time it was close to sea level, it must have been as well concealed at that time as it is today.

Northern Newfoundland has not changed much since Leif landed there nearly a thousand years ago, although its climate, like that of Iceland, has grown colder. In Leif's time the people in Iceland were growing wheat,[5] but in neither island can ordinary wheat be raised today. The saga emphasizes the qualities of Newfoundland that were to make it most attractive to the fishermen and cattle raisers from Greenland: an abundance of very large salmon in the lake and in the river, excellent land, and no frost in the winter.

A thorough preliminary reconnaissance probably satisfied Leif that the area was about as good a location for a permanent camp as he could find. It was not large enough for an actual settlement, but the natural meadows on the shore of Pistolet Bay provided ample food for his cattle. So he "took that resolution afterwards to abide there for that winter and made there a large house." His dwelling was a permanent *skala* large enough to house his full crew, and it was used during the entire period of the Norse Vinland voyages described in the sagas. Even if other factors had not been present, the rising of the land would have forced abandonment of the site some twenty-five years after Leif built his camp. By then the Norse boats could no longer enter the lake.

Leif may have seen Eskimos on the islands which he passed after leaving Markland, or he may have feared that either the Celts or the Eskimos might come in from the coast, for the camp routine he established clearly shows that he anticipated attack.

After their housing had been constructed, he divided his men into two groups—one-half to explore the land and the other half to remain at the camp. He stipulated that the explorers were not to go so far away that they could not return in the evening and that they were not to be separated. The routine thus established by Leif was followed for a while, with Leif remaining at home sometimes and accompanying the explorers sometimes.

Those of his crew who remained at the camp would be there to fish and hunt, to obtain a stock of food for the winter, to cut firewood, and to rough-hew timber for building material. Those sent out by Leif to explore the surrounding country apparently did a thorough job, for the next three Norse expeditions seemed to agree that there was nothing to be gained by staying there permanently. They used Leif's camp only as a winter base and a convenient place at which to cut a supply of lumber.

The Greenlanders were much impressed by the number of hours of daylight and darkness. "The length of the day and night was more equal there than in Greenland and Iceland. The sun was there between *Eyktr Stad* and *Dagmala Stad* on the shortest day of the year."

A probable explanation and one that accords with the customs of the sea is that the phrases relate to the change of the watch. It has long been the rule on ships at sea to divide the twenty-four hours into six watches of four hours each, the morning watch starting at eight and the evening watch at four. *Dagmal* in ancient Iceland was eight o'clock in the morning; *eykt* was four o'clock in the afternoon. *Stad* means stand or watch. The saga report, therefore, means that on the shortest day of the year the sun rose at eight o'clock in the morning and set at four o'clock in the afternoon. This could happen only in the latitude of Belle Isle Strait.

Newfoundland has always been known as one of the world's finest fishing grounds, but the most noteworthy feature of the bay is the natural meadows which stretch along its shores for miles at a level a few inches above high tide. Today nearly every family around the bay keeps one or more cows as well as sheep and goats. There is good pasturage for all, and there are many fenced meadows providing the winter fodder for the cattle. The strong winds of northern Newfoundland blow the salt spray inland over unprotected places for a distance of 100 to 200 yards, and in that zone a very fine grass grows which is especially valuable for cattle feed. The spruce underbrush, which in spots sheltered from the wind grows to the water's edge, does not grow in ground which is regularly watered by the salt spray. In the level places, covered with water only for a short time at high tide, grows coarse grass which, when cut and dried, makes an excellent salt hay relished by cattle. The soil is so rich that potatoes of the finest grade are grown there, as well as beets, turnips, peas, carrots, and exceptionally large cabbage. At least eighteen varieties of berries grow in or near the woods, including red raspberries, blueberries, blackberries, currants, and varieties not commonly found farther south, such as squash and partridge berries.

In the forests, through which roamed gread herds of caribou, grew the naturally bent woods required for the frames of the Viking ships, as well as great juniper and spruce trees from which could be split light but strong and durable planking, and big fir trees suitable for making tough and sturdy keels. Here, too, were the great birches—the wine trees whose trunks could be used as house timbers and whose sap made birch wine. In the lowlands near them grew currants, the wine-berries (*vinberja*) from which the Newfoundlanders have traditionally made excellent wine. Scant wonder that Leif named this country Vinland the Good.

It was the wines of Vinland that carried the fame of the Norse of Greenland to the four corners of the earth and made references to Vinland and the Vinland voyages so appealing and so lasting through the ages. Other details of the Viking experience in America were not so enduring. Gunnbiorn's Skerries disappeared. Markland was lost. The story of the advance of the Norsemen into the interior of America remained for many centuries a mysterious tradition of their descendants, always exciting wonder and curiosity, but defying all efforts to prove its authenticity.

Eventually even the one-time existence of the Greenland settlements was questioned. And yet never has the name of Vinland the Good been forgotten. The earliest recorded mention of the Greenland settlement in a foreign history was in connection with the wines of Vinland.[6]

Every attempt to relocate the lost country, except those of Dr. Wilfred T. Grenfell and the Finnish geographer Vaino Tanner,[7] has been based on the assumption that it was a land of wild grapes. The precise descriptions of the voyages in the sagas, the directions of the prevailing winds and ocean currents, the short navigation season, the time required to sail from one point to another, the known habitat of the Eskimos, the short distance to the great forests of Labrador and Newfoundland—all these were ignored. Far-off southern New England was picked by historians as the site of Vinland because grapes were found there and they had mistakenly assumed *vinberja* to be the Greenland name for grapes.

Wineberries and wine trees grew in Vinland, but not grapes. The Norse Greenlanders made their wine from cranberries, which they called *vinberja* (wineberries), and the word has that meaning in the sagas. Wineberries of various kinds and birch wine trees grow abundantly in Newfoundland. It was their discovery that started the myth about the wild grapes of Vinland.

One evening when the exploring party returned to Leif's camp, they learned that a man was missing. Leif reprimanded his men severely, for the man was a lifelong intimate of Leif and his family. He was Tyrker, the German. Accompanied by twelve companions, Leif went in search of Tyrker.

The searchers had gone only a short distance when they ran into Tyrker. Seeing that his friend was very excited, Leif said, "Why wert thou so late, my foster father, and separated from your comrades?" Tyrker, acting strangely, answered Leif in his southern (German) tongue and continued to speak in this language which his companions could not understand. Finally, the unseemly little man with a large forehead and freckles spoke in Norse, saying that not far away he had found wine trees and wineberries (*vinvid ok vinber*).

"May that be true, foster father?" the startled Leif asked. Tyrker assured Leif that it was true, adding that he was born where "there is no scarcity of *vinber* or *vinvid*."

The next morning Leif ordered his men to "either gather wine berries or hew vinvid every day so that they may make a cargo for my ship." And they did as he ordered them to do.

Tyrker, who discovered the wine trees, was so excited that he reverted to his native German. His childhood had been spent in the great wooded lands of Germany, but for more than fifteen years he had been living in treeless Greenland, where the only thing like a tree was the stunted birch or alder bush. All he had seen there were dwarfed imitations of the mighty forest giants of his native land. In the Markland area visited by Leif, there had been only small birch trees. Then, wandering in this new country, probably following Leif's River to its source in the White Hills near the end of Hare Bay, he had found some of the great birch trees like those in his native land. Vivid memories may have come to him of the springtime of his childhood days when he had seen holes bored a few inches below the birch boughs, a little roll of birch bark or a hollow bit of wood pushed in, and a bucket hung on the bough to catch the sap, which soon turned into *birken wein*.

Then returning to join his companions, he had apparently passed through the lowlands at the south end of the Baye au Mouc and found currants which resembled the *vinberja* of Greenland. These Greenland *vinberja* were black cranberries similar to the currants of Germany from which an excellent wine was made.

When he suddenly came upon his Norse companions, Tyrker started to explain in his native German about the birch wine and the wineberries. Finally aware that they did not understand, he started to talk Norse, then recalled that the only birch with which his companions were familiar was the stunted sapless brush of Greenland. He stuttered and stammered for a time. Certain that if he told them that the trees he had seen would give *birken wein,* they would not believe him because wine could not be made from Greenland birch, he then thought of wine wood (*vinvid*) and wineberries (*vinberja* or *vinber*).

Birch wine was also made by the English in Newfoundland in the nineteenth century. Sir Richard Bonneycastle describes the process as follows:

> From the white birch, an antiscorbutic, de obstruent, and diuretic wine is made by the settler by merely cutting to the pith under some large branch, keeping the wound open by a splinter and hanging a bottle under it. A large tree produces two or three gallons of birch wine.[8]

Although the mythical wines of Vinland were to make its name famous, Leif was chiefly interested in the valuable products of Vinland's forests. He had come there looking for various kinds of heavy timber for use in ship and house construction and hardwood for furniture and wooden containers. He found so much lumber that the one cargo which he carried back to Greenland made him a wealthy man:

> So it is said that their aftboat was filled with wine berries. Now was hewn a lading for the ship. And when spring came, they made ready and sailed away and gave Leif name to the land after the land's products and called it Vinland. Sailed now after that to sea and got fair wind until they saw Greenland and the waterfalls under the glaciers. . . . He was afterwards called Leif the Lucky. Leif was now well off both as to riches and honor.

He evidently planned to return for more of this quick wealth, for a few years later he refused to give his dwelling at the camp to other explorers—his sister Freydis and his relative Karlsefni. Having discovered a new continent, according to the evidence of the Norse sagas, Leif did not, in fact, return nor stamp his name on other great adventures.

Even the imaginative Leif would doubtless have been startled to learn that almost a thousand years later, because of the Greenland *vinber,* historians would be still searching for the fabled grapes of Vinland.

The story of Vinland the Good, of its fabulous wine trees and wineberries, the great forests, the freedom and the adventure of life there, was probably told in many foreign lands; but its greatest appeal would have been to the adventurous young Norse of both Scandinavia and the British Isles, who were then chafing under the iron rule of the kings of Norway and Ireland and the rigid enforcement of peaceful Christianity in place of the wild feats and forays of their Viking ancestors.

13

Thorvald
and
Vitramannaland

After Leif returned home, "there was much talk about Vinland and his brother, Thorvald, thought that the land had not been enough explored." Encouraged by the enthusiasm accompanying the retelling again and again of Leif's successful expedition, the Greenlanders soon undertook another voyage to Vinland, hoping to bring home wood and lumber, for which they had pressing need. The lead in organizing this new expedition was taken by Leif and Thorvald, sons of Eric, the ruling chief.

But Leif was unable to go along. So he offered his ship to Thorvald for the voyage. Setting out from Greenland very soon thereafter, Thorvald and his crew must have sailed directly to Leif's campsite at Pistolet Bay, for the sagas do not report details of the voyage, except to say that they arrived there, and that they spent an uneventful winter at the camp. In the spring, ordered by Thorvald to explore "the western part of the land," members of the crew went westward in the aftboat. There they found the land to be densely wooded with the woods coming close to the white sands and the sea, where there were many shallows and islands. They saw no beasts and only one sign of human habitation in this land to the west: a grain shed built of logs "in one of

115

the western islands.'' They then turned back, sailing east to Leif's camp and arriving there at harvest time.

That grain shed—a permanent log building—somewhere west of Newfoundland told the Greenlanders that beyond the shed there was an inhabited country where civilized people cultivated the land and raised grain. They were farmers who had been born and reared in Iceland where grain was then being grown, and so they were familiar with the custom of drying and storing grain crops in buildings constructed for that purpose, a necessity in a cold, damp climate. This shed was the only building reported to have been seen on the American continent by the Norse.

The grain shed was also a warning to Thorvald's men not to go any farther west in their aftboat. In those days when a Viking boat was observed approaching a strange country, the inhabitants of the country rang the bells of the countryside to assemble their armed men to attack the feared Vikings with all the weapons they could muster. Slavery or death was the fate of any Viking captured. The Greenland explorers knew this, and so, as soon as they saw the shed, they turned around and went back to Leif's camp.

After rounding the northern point of Newfoundland, Thorvald's men in this expedition had sailed westward into the Gulf of St. Lawrence along its north shore. If they left Vinland as soon as the ice broke up during the second week in June and returned at harvest time (around the first of October in the area of Pistolet Bay), they would have completed their voyage in approximately one hundred days. With every other day on the outward voyage set aside for exploration, even with a normal amount of stormy weather, they should have reached the vicinity of Moise Bay in the Gulf of St. Lawrence, approximately 360 miles from Leif's camp, after the middle of August. It was in the vicinity of Moise Bay that they came upon the grain shed.

Their description of the landscape along their course corresponds to the coast behind the rocky islands along the shore. The woods come down quite close to the sandy shores of the bays and fiords. In 1537, Cartier, like Thorvald, tied up his ship and explored to the west in his small boat. The harbor of Blanc Sablon (White Sands) still retains the name Cartier gave it because of its white sandy beaches.

On their return home to Greenland, the men of Thorvald's crew told the Greenlanders that there was a country west of Vinland where people raised grain, undoubtedly a country of farms and villages. Knowing that the Celtic Irish had been in both Iceland and Greenland, the Norse Greenlanders may have suspected that it was the Celtic Irish who were living in this civilized country to the west.

Thorvald remained in Newfoundland that year with most of his men, but there is no information in the sagas about his activities until the next summer when he "went eastward with his ship and to the north of the land."

Sailing out of Pistolet Bay, Thorvald went eastward through the sound and then turned north up the coast of Labrador, according to my interpretation of the saga account of his voyage. Off a cape along the coast, his ship was driven by a strong gale on shore and damaged so seriously that his voyage had to be delayed until he and his crew had mended the broken keel under the ship. Having repaired his ship, Thorvald and his men "raised up the keel here on the ness and called it Kialarness."

Even without the descriptions given later in the saga, it is possible to identify the place where the ship was wrecked. As far up the Labrador coast as Cape North, the steep rock-bound cliffs of the coast are screened by equally rocky and precipitous islands. A ship driven by a storm on these rocks would have been damaged beyond repair.

There was, however, one place along the coast where Thorvald's ship could have been blown ashore without being damaged beyond repair and could have been refloated. This place is Cape Bluff, the most prominent headland on the southern Labrador coast. One hundred miles north of Belle Isle Strait, the great projecting Cape Bluff stands wide open to the North Atlantic. Close by is a short sandy beach. Driven up on this beach, the sturdily built but flexible Norse vessel might have landed with little more damage than a broken keel. From the forest west of the beach, the crew could have obtained the timber for a new keel.

Leaving Kialarness, Thorvald turned west and sailed for a long distance into a fiord which was surrounded by a thickly wooded country. Somewhere on the shores of the fiord, a long distance inland from the sea, he caught sight of an Eskimo village. The only fiord north of Cape Bluff which extends to the west through wooded country for a long distance is Lake Melville. Near the end of the lake and almost 140 miles from the sea is Carter Basin, where there was an Eskimo village when the Hudson Bay traders made their first records. This village was one of the last sites to be abandoned by the natives when they moved to the coast.

The Eskimo village sighted by Thorvald was located on or near a river which flowed from the east to the west and emptied into a bay. Near the mouth of the river between the bay and the fiord was a headland so situated that a person standing on it could look up the river and see the low dirt-covered houses of the village. The Eskimo village near Carter Basin was in the neighborhood of the Kenemich River. From Epinette Point, a headland lying between the lake and the bay, it is possible to survey all the country around the basin. The only river along the Atlantic coast between Belle Isle and Port Manvers that flows from east to west is the Kenemich River. It was here that Thorvald was to die.

As he was passing Epinette Point, Thorvald saw three small mounds, which he recognized as natives' boats turned bottom side up on the shore with men asleep under them. Apparently, Thorvald landed on the north, or lake, side of the Point. Then spreading his men apart far enough to completely surround the Eskimo asleep there and to cut off their escape, he crossed the Point and seized all but one. Evidently an Eskimo kayak was drawn ashore unnoticed by the Norse, for one of the Eskimo woke up, gave the alarm, and escaped in a kayak.

The Norse killed the remaining eight men, and after a short time, they fell asleep, exhausted. But their sleep was ended by a shout warning Thorvald to leave the area with his men as soon as possible if he "would save his life." Immediately many leather boats came into the fiord headed for the startled Norse. The Skraelings (Eskimo) "shot at them for a little while and then fled as hurriedly as they could."

> Then Thorvald asked his men if they were wounded. . . . They replied that no one was wounded. "I have got a wound under the arm," he said. "An arrow flew between the side of the ship and the shield under my arm and here is the arrow. As this will probably be my death, I now order that you prepare to go back as soon as possible, but that you shall take me to that headland that I thought to be the most habitable. It may be that a true word came out of my mouth that I might dwell there for a while. There you shall bury me."
> Now died Thorvald, and they did all according to what he said.

Returning to Vinland, Thorvald's companions spent the winter there, gathering wood and wineberries, which they took home with them when they returned to Greenland the next spring.

The ranking family of Greenland could not allow the death of Thorvald, Eric's son, to go unavenged. Leif, the elder brother, would be the proper leader of an expedition to seek revenge. But he could not go, for he had succeeded to the chieftainship after the death of Eric. And so to the other brother, Thorstein, fell the responsibility of heading the war party.

Only in describing this next voyage do the sagas mention that weapons were taken along on a voyage and that the vessel was manned by a powerful crew: twenty-five "tall and strong men." They took with them "nothing more than their weapons and provisions." The accounts of Thorstein's voyage in the two sagas differ in some details, but they are in substantial agreement on the journal of the voyage. The luckless Greenlanders on this expedition tossed about hither and yon on the high seas, and returned home at the beginning of winter, exhausted. Their voyage had taken them within sight of Iceland and probably beyond that island, for they reported seeing birds from the Irish coast.

14

The
First Settlement
in
Vinland

Credit for establishment of the first settlement in Vinland does not belong to the prestigious family of Eric. It belongs to his fellow Norseman, Thorfinn Karlsefni of Iceland. Karlsefni's venturesome decision to explore land south of Leif's camp near Pistolet Bay at the north end of the Newfoundland peninsula, instead of land north of the camp as previous expeditions to Vinland had done, paid off with his finding an ideal site for a settlement along his way southward. The site selected by Karlsefni is now known as the Sop's Arm area, 130 miles more or less south of Leif's camp. Located on the east coast of the Newfoundland peninsula almost at the southern end of White Bay, Sop's Arm is a beautiful circular inlet from the bay.

After Thorstein's return from his ill-fated voyage, miserable conditions in Greenland threatened the survival of the settlements. Planning and organizing a new expedition to Vinland and vengeance for Thorvald's death therefore had to be postponed. The winter following Thorstein's return, an epidemic of bubonic plague struck the colonies. Spreading by sea from England, where it had been raging since 987, the epidemic decimated the population and paralyzed the economic life of the settlements. Even Thorstein, the logical leader of an expedition

120

of revenge, was a victim of the plague. (As described in the sagas, it was similar to the Black Death which struck three and a half centuries later.)

Then, one autumn, two merchant ships arrived in Ericsfiord, each carrying a crew of forty. One ship was owned by Thorfinn Karlsefni, a member of a prominent Icelandic family. The other was the property of two partners also from Iceland, Thorhall Gamalsson and Bjarne Grimolfsson. The crews of these ships were exceptionally large, too large for an ordinary trading voyage. The purpose of the expedition, it must be surmised, was at least in part military.

When the ships arrived near Brattahlid, Leif and his neighbors came out to greet the visitors. Trading immediately became brisk. The Greenlanders exchanged fox and wolf skins, cattle hides, whalebone, walrus ivory, dried fish, and other native products for manufactured goods which the traders had brought from Iceland. In accordance with custom, the foreign traders gave substantial presents to Leif, the ruling chief of the district, and to his family. Also according to custom, Leif extended an invitation to both crews to make their winter quarters at Brattahlid, where there were many commodious warehouses in which they could store their cargoes of merchandise.

The visitors were delighted with the hospitality and entertainment extended to them during the winter. On the long winter evenings, their Greenland hosts told stories of the newly discovered countries to the west, describing the vast hardwood forests and incredible wealth of these lands, and undoubtedly fascinating their merchant guests from Iceland.

The Greenlanders and their Icelandic visitors decided to go to Vinland and establish a settlement there in the spring. Half of the men for this voyage were recruited in Greenland; the remainder of the total complement of 160 men was provided by the crews of the two Icelandic ships.

Two conflicting records of this joint voyage have been preserved in two sagas, one composed in Greenland, the other in Iceland. The Greenland saga relates the story of the voyage as the skald learned it from both the Greenlanders and Karlsefni, the Icelander who owned one of the ships. The Greenland saga is now in manuscript form in the library of the University of Copenhagen. The Icelandic saga, in its original form, has disappeared. Parts of that saga, however, are still extant in a historical romance written centuries after the voyage by Hauk Erlendsson, a descendant of Karlsefni. In this romantic account of the joint Greenland-Iceland voyage, the author has apparently altered the true account to make it appear that his ancestor, Karlsefni, was the real discoverer and explorer of most of the lands west of Greenland!

In order to give his ancestor credit for the discoveries, Hauk invented a story that Leif had been blown to some place on the Atlantic coast on his return from Norway and had called this place Vinland. To establish this, he inserted in his copy of an Icelandic history a reference to his ancestor of three centuries before as "Karlsefni who found Vinland the Good." Hauk's distortion of the facts regarding the voyage is revealed by several glaring blunders. He omits the discovery of Bjarneyjar (Resolution Islands) by Bjarne Herjulfsson, although he states that Karlsefni went to Bjarneyjar. He does not mention Vinland in his account of this voyage to Vinland except inadvertently in the beginning and at the end when he states that "there began to be much talk . . . that Vinland should be explored" and that "Karlsefni then left Vinland." He relates the incident of Thorvald's death as occurring on Karlsefni's side trip up into the country of the Eskimos, when in fact Thorvald had died on a voyage years before.

Unfortunately for historical accuracy, the Hauk narrative has been accepted in modern times as an authentic record of this voyage of Greenlanders and Icelanders to Vinland, and so has replaced the conflicting, but true, account given in the Greenland saga. Acceptance of this partly fictional Hauk* story has made it impossible up to now to unravel the true record of the coming of the Norse to the American continent. Considering the fact that the Hauk account was written around 1300, long after saga time, and so was not contemporary, I have used only those parts of Hauk's story in my reconstruction of the Vinland voyages which are not in conflict with more authentic records, in particular the Greenland saga.

During the winter in Greenland, Karlsefni married Gudrid, Thorstein's widow. In preparation for the expedition to be undertaken in the spring, he outfitted his ship. So when spring came, joined by his fellow Icelanders, Bjarne Grimolfsson and Thorhall Gamalsson, with their ship and men, he was ready to set out for Leif's camp in Vinland.

---

* Since the Hauk account is known as the *Icelandic saga,* it will hereafter be referred to as the Icelandic saga. Material from both editions of the narrative will be used: the unabridged edition, known as A.M. 557, and the abridged edition, A.M. 554.

As the third ship—that of the Greenlanders—joined the expedition, the trail of blood vengeance reappeared. For in this ship were Freydis, sister of Thorvald and Thorstein, and her husband. Since her brother Thorstein had died in the epidemic and her other brother, Leif, was unable to go, it had become her duty as the sister of Thorvald to avenge his death. Also on this expedition went Thorhall the Hunter, a Greenlander sent along by Leif as one of the leaders of the group. Thorhall was at home in the wilderness, for he had hunted and fished many summers for Eric the Red and Leif, whom he served as a steward in the winter.

The Greenland saga naturally places emphasis upon the plan to settle Vinland, because the Greenlanders involved were farmers, while the Icelanders were traders. The Greenlanders took with them many cattle. Leif offered to lend, though refused to give, his housing in Vinland to Karlsefni. And so the joint Icelandic-Greenland expedition set sail and arrived at Leif's camp without serious mishaps or delay.

As the route to Leif's camp had been described in the previous sagas, the Greenland saga does not give it. However, because this is the first expedition to Vinland led by an Icelander, the Icelandic saga gives quite complete details of the route.

Evidently Karlsefni and his men followed (with one exception) the same route as Leif. They first went north up the Greenland coast until they were near the Western Settlement. Then, probably on the advice of Leif, instead of following Leif's course to "the land which Bjarne found last"—the Baffin Land peninsula north of Frobisher Bay—they sailed directly to Bjarneyjar (Resolution Islands). After reaching Bjarneyjar, the saga relates that they sailed south for two days, landing then in a country where they found large, flat stones and saw many fox. They named this country Helluland. Sailing for two days more, bearing from the south to the southeast, they landed again, this time in a heavily wooded country with many wild beasts, which they named Markland. After stopping at an island southeast of this land, they sailed a long time until they came to a cape.

About 100 miles south of Cape Chidley lies a bay called Kangalaksiorvik. The mouth is wide open and its north shore is sandy. On the south side of the cape are endless acres of flat stones, reaching away to the snow-capped Torngat Mountains. Two days' sailing south of the Resolution Islands would have brought the expedition to this bay, which, in the opinion of Sir Wilfred Grenfell, is the place where Karlsefni first landed. The description of the place where they made their second landing is very indefinite, but the next two days' sailing would have placed them somewhere near Nain.

> After a voyage of two days, they sailed near the land and saw that it was a headland. They kept close to shore with the wind on the starboard side and left the land on the starboard side of the ship. There were places without harbors, long strands, and sandy beaches there. . . . Then they rowed to the land and found there on a headland the keel of a ship [Thorvald's] and they called the cape Kialarness and they called the strands Furdustrandir because they were so long to sail by. Then another bay extended into the land, and they steered into the bay.

The first headland was probably Cape Harrison. Rounding this cape and following the coast, they would have come to the long strands and beaches of Porcupine Beach, the only continuous sandy beach along the northern Atlantic coast or the Gulf of St. Lawrence that could not have been passed by the Norse boats in a short time. Cape Bluff is the most prominent headland along the southeastern coast of Labrador and almost the only one open to the sea. Thus it may have been the Kialarness of the sagas. South of it are several large bays where Karlsefni might have landed. After passing Kialarness, "another bay extended into the land and they steered into the bay."

Upon sailing past Furdustrandir, Karlsefni put ashore two Scots, known to be fast runners, who had been given to Leif by King Olaf Trygvvasson of Norway. Leif loaned the Scots to Karlsefni, who took them along on the voyage. He put them ashore with instructions to investigate the country to the south and report back in a day and a half. When they returned to the ship, one of them was carrying a bunch of wineberries and the other an ear of wild barley.

The country southwest of Cape Bluff could not have been attractive to the Norse, and there must have been indications that there were Eskimos in the vicinity. Both the wineberries and the barley would have been found in this area in the spring. According to Grenfell, the berries are as edible and juicy immediately after the snow has disappeared as when they are first buried by it in the autumn. The wild barley heads remain intact through the winter unless they are stripped by birds. As spring advances, the grain gradually drops off the stalks and a new crop is self-sown.

Leaving Sandwich Bay, Karlsefni probably sailed well out to sea and gave the dangerous rock coast a wide berth. Sailing in toward

Belle Isle Strait between Labrador and the north end of Newfoundland, he would have come directly to Belle Isle, less than 40
miles northeast of Leif's camp at Pistolet Bay.

> They stood with their ships into a bay. At the mouth of the bay
> there was an island around which there were strong currents. There-
> fore, they called it Stream Island. There were so many eider ducks
> there that it was scarcely possible to step between the eggs. They
> sailed through the fiord and called it Straumfiord and carried their
> goods ashore and prepared to stay there. They had with them all
> kinds of cattle. It was a pleasant country and they neglected every-
> thing except the exploration of the country. There were mountains
> nearby. . . . . There was an abundance of grass.

Karlsefni had reached the locality of Leif's camp. Straumfiord
and Stream Island are quite suitable names for the strait and the island,
Belle Isle. In the strait there is a very unusual movement of the currents, predominantly tidal and complicated by a flow called the "dominant." To get through the strait, it was necessary for the captain of a
Norse merchant ship to select a time when the currents were favorable.
To avoid the strait, the usual route for vessels going to Vinland, judg-
ing from an old Norse map, was down the east coast.

Karlsefni and his men remained at Leif's camp through most of
the winter, exploring the land around. It was a harsh winter, for which
they were unprepared. So before spring came, they joined their Greenland companions who had moved to Belle Isle.

On their arrival at the camp, both Leif and Thorvald established
an orderly routine for their crews. Leif divided his crew into two
groups, one to explore and the other to work at the camp. Similarly,
Thorvald sent only part of his crew to explore. The camp was at the
end of a narrow peninsula, and so after it was frozen in a severely cold
winter, the forests in which the campers could hunt and the waters
where they could fish would have been very limited. Survival of the
members of the expedition depended upon their hunting and fishing.

Probably because he was not aware that in the north end of Newfoundland the forests and waters were barren of game and fish during
harsh winter seasons, Karlsefni neglected to obtain in advance enough
game and fish for the winter. If he had been camping in an area farther
south (in New England, for example), he would have found good
year-round fishing and the best game in the winter. In the locality of
Leif's camp, however, the fish, plentiful near the shore in summer,
leave the shallow waters of the bays and straits for the deeper waters

of the ocean after cold weather sets in. The caribou migrate south then, and the bears hibernate. Consequently, when winter came, Karlsefni and his crew did not have enough food.

Thorhall the Hunter, the Greenlander sent along by Leif, evidently was aware of the hazards of winter life in the area, for he took his men out to Belle Isle, a few miles to the north of Leif's camp, where there is good fishing in open waters all winter. Later the Icelanders, probably urged by Thorhall, also moved out to Belle Isle. The Greenland saga reports that they soon had "no want of food," for "a whale was driven up there, both large and excellent," which they cut up for food.

Finally spring came, and with an abundance of food on hand, they made plans for the future. Thorhall the Hunter decided to go north around Furdustrandir and Kialarness to explore the land. Karlsefni, however, decided to go southwest because he thought that there were larger tracts of land in the south.

Thorhall was not a member of Karlsefni's group. He was on a separate mission, which was, of course, to avenge the death of Thorvald. Accompanied by nine men, he sailed north past Furdustrandir and Kialarness, but was driven off his intended course by westerly gales which carried his ship to Ireland. Merchants reported that he and his crew were beaten and made slaves, and that Thorhall lost his life there.

Blown out to sea by a sudden storm, Thorhall evidently lost his sail overboard. With only nine men on board, about all he could do was to drift in the Atlantic current east to Ireland. He would not have had enough power to keep his ship away from the shore. At that time, the Irish were in control of most of their west coast, and they immediately killed any Norsemen shipwrecked there, or made them slaves.

Karsefni, however, followed his hunch that there was desirable land to the south and sailed in that direction. His decision to explore to the south resulted in the establishment, under his leadership, of the first settlement in Vinland on record.

> He sailed southward along the coast with Snorre and Bjarne and their people. They sailed for a long time until they finally came to a river which flowed down from the land into a lake and then into the sea. There were great shallows at the mouth of the river so that it could only be entered at high tide. Karlsefni and his people sailed up to the mouth of the river and called the place Hop. They found there self-sown barley wherever the ground was low. Wine trees were

found where it was higher. Every river there was full of fish. They
dug pits on the shore where the tide rose highest, and when the tide
fell, there were *flatfish in the pits*. There were great numbers of wild
animals of all kinds in the woods. They remained there half a month
and enjoyed themselves and kept no watch. They had their cattle
with them.

Karlsefni had sailed south from Straumfiord (Belle Isle Strait)
along the east coast of the Newfoundland peninsula until he reached
the present-day Sop's Arm, a landlocked harbor. When he turned his
ship into the northern entrance to Sop's Arm, he saw on his right a
rocky mountain coming steeply down to the sea. On his left was Sop's
Island in the circular inlet. The word *Hop* in Old Norse means "a
small landlocked harbor." From the south at the end of White Bay,
Corner Brook River "flows down from the land into a lake and then
into the sea."

At low tide Karlsefni and his men could sail well into the mouth
of this river before being stopped by shoals. These shoals now form
low mounds about 30 feet high on each side of the river mouth. The
hills sloped sharply down to the river on both sides, but beyond the
south end of the lake they could see a wide, pleasant valley. The land
there is low and level, and excellent site for the houses of the Icelanders, who were fishermen.

No snow fell during their winter there, and their cattle fed in the
open. Early one morning they saw nine leather boats approaching and
"staves were brandished from the boats with a noise like reeds shaken
in the wind and swinging with the sun." The sound of double-bladed
paddles striking the water, flicking a few drops each time they came
out, resembled the sound of the wind rustling dry weeds or straw in
the roof thatch of a house. The motion of the paddles in the air, dip-
ping first to one side and then to the other, would, to a person to whom
the sight was unusual, give the appearance of revolving. The motion
puzzled the Norsemen. A pole swinging with the sun meant nothing to
the Eskimos, but to the Norse it was a sign of peace. So they displayed a white shield. The strangers came on land. They were
swarthy, evil-looking men with bushy hair, broad cheeks, and very
large eyes. After looking over the Norse, they returned to their boats
and rowed away to the south.

This incident happened at the time of year when the Eskimos
would have been returning from seal hunting on the outer island of the
east coast of Newfoundland. It was their custom to split up into small

parties and go up the small bays and rivers to catch salmon. The Eskimos had come up the river and across the lake before the Norse, who had not been on guard, saw them. They were so close to the shore that the Norse could hear the water dripping from their paddles. The behavior of the strangers was typical of Eskimos who had been in touch with white men. After looking the Norse over carefully, they turned around calmly and went back to hunt up another fishing place.

That autumn they probably returned to Labrador and reported the presence of the strangers they had seen. For the next spring many Eskimos out on their regular seal-hunting voyage swarmed into White Bay. They, too, had apparently traded with white people before, for they brought raw furs with which to trade. This time the Norse were not surprised. They had posted a watch on a point overlooking the bay. Early one spring morning they saw countless leather rowboats coming around the headland. Karlsefni again displayed the white shield and the Eskimos came ashore, offering to trade their peltries and pure gray skins for Norse swords and spears. Karlsefni and Snorre refused to give them any weapons, but did trade cloth for the pelts and skins. Apparently fascinated by Norse red cloth, the Eskimos traded a single pure gray skin for a strip of red cloth to tie around their heads.

So the trading went on for a time. When the cloth became scarce, the Norsemen cut it into thin strips the width of a finger, but the Eskimos gave as much, and even more, for these small strips.

At first, most of the trading was done by the Icelanders, who, being merchants, had a supply of trade goods. The Greenlanders, being farmers, had very little to offer in exchange. As the meager stocks of the Icelanders were exhausted, the trading began to fall off. A sudden snorting and bellowing of a bull interrupted the bargaining. Greatly alarmed, the Eskimos tried to force their way into the Norse houses for safety from what they apparently thought was a serious threat. Some tense moments must have followed as the Norse beat back the terrified natives. The situation soon eased, however, when some Greenland farmers' wives offered butter in exchange for furs. To the Eskimos, any form of grease was a delicacy, and so they promptly resumed trading.

Greatly concerned by this visit, during which a virtual horde of Eskimos had almost precipitated a serious incident, the Norse set to work constructing palisades around their houses. The ensuing months of vague apprehension provided at least one occasion for light-hearted celebration. For Gudrid, wife of Karlsefni, gave birth to a son,

Snorre—the first recorded birth of a white child on the American continent.

At the beginning of the next winter, the Eskimos, as expected, returned—in even greater numbers than before. The news about the strangers and the report that they had desirable goods to exchange for raw furs had spread far and wide. The Eskimos, however, were to be disappointed. The Icelanders had traded off all their wares, and the Greenlanders could offer nothing except a limited amount of milk and butter. When the Icelanders did not come out to trade, the Eskimos threw their packs of furs over the pickets into the stockade. The correct response for the Icelanders, if they had anything to trade, was to place it outside. If the Eskimos were not satisfied, they would not take it. The Norse were then supposed to return the Eskimo furs. When they failed to do so, one Eskimo tried to grab a Norse weapon. The Norsemen promptly killed him. That meant war.

The Eskimos, however, had come on a peaceful trading mission and were not prepared for a fight. According to one saga, ". . . they fled hurriedly, leaving their garments and goods behind them." From the wording of the saga, it would seem that the Norse rounded up the Eskimos and stripped off their fur garments besides taking their pelts.

During the time when the Eskimos were trying to trade with the Norse, a curious incident occurred. While Gudrid was sitting inside by the cradle of her son, Snorre, a short woman wearing a narrow black garment and a ribbon over her light-brown hair entered. She was pale and very large-eyed. The stranger approached Gudrid and asked, "What is thy name?" "My name is Gudrid, but what is thy name?" was the answer. "My name is Gudrid," replied the stranger. Just then an Eskimo was killed by one of Karlsefni's men and in the ensuing noise and confusion the stranger disappeared.

The Gudrid who had come with the Eskimos may have been a Norsewoman from a ship which had landed in Labrador and lost its crew. While the men were probably killed, it is likely that the women were kept by the Eskimos.

The Labrador Eskimos were as vindictive in revenge as the Norse. They undoubtedly would have attacked the Norsemen when they saw that their valuables could not be obtained by peaceful trading. But when one of them was killed and all their furs stolen by the Norse, even the clothes they were wearing, war was inevitable. The scanty one-sided saga report of the subsequent battle between the Eskimos and Karlsefni's men reveals careful planning by both sides.

> "Now we must needs take counsel together," said Karlsefni, "for that I believe they will visit us a third time in great numbers and attack us. Let us now adopt this plan. Ten of our number shall go out upon the cape and show themselves there, while the remainder of our company shall go into the woods and hew a clearing for our cattle when the troop approaches the forest. We will also take our bull and let him go in advance of us." It so happened that the lay of the land was such that the proposed meeting place had the lake upon the one side and the forest upon the other. Karlsefni's advice was now carried into execution.

This plan of battle produced a perfect setting for the Eskimo attack. There is a level area on the east side of Corner Brook Lake near the mouth of the river, exactly like the spot which the saga describes as that chosen for the battle. The picket of ten men whom Karlsefni sent down to the cape to keep watch must have been Icelanders, for the Icelandic sagas describe the approach of the Eskimos from the south into the bay and the description is obviously that of an eyewitness. The Eskimo plan of attack succeeded. They struck so hard and fast that, the saga reports, the Norsemen never knew what happened to them.

> Now was there battle, and were slain many of the Skraelings. . . . There came a great multitude of them in boats approaching from the south. . . . All the poles were turned from the sun, and they all howled very loud. . . . Karlsefni and his men displayed red shields. The Skraelings ran out of their boats, and a fight ensued. There was a fierce shower of missiles, for the Skraelings had war slings.

By keeping up constant and vigorous volleys of arrows and darts, the Eskimos forced the Norse to hide behind their shields. Then came a surprise which startled the Norse. The Eskimos threw at the Norse ballista—very large, nearly black, bell-shaped objects on poles, from which they were hurled. When a ballista hit a shield, the shield broke in pieces with a loud crash, and the man behind the shield went down as though he had been pole-axed. The men behind him were then exposed. All fighters at the places where the wall was broken must have been killed instantly. The only way that the Norse could save themselves was by running away. And so, seized by fear, Karlsefni and all his men fled up the riverbank. When they came to some jutting rocks, they halted. Freydis shouted to the fleeing Norse: "Why do you run, stout men as you are, before these miserable wretches whom I thought you would slaughter like cattle? And if I had weapons, me thinks I would fight better than any of you." Pursued by the Eskimos, she also fled.

The Norse had been decisively defeated. Fleeing in a state of demoralization, they did not stop to help their women, even pregnant Freydis. Running back up the valley, they crossed the shallow river and clambered onto the rocky slope at the base of the cliffs on the east side of the river. The cliffs were so high that the Eskimos could not attack from the rear. Standing above the campsite with a steep rocky slope in front of them, the Vikings were in an improved position. Here also they could look down on the settlement and watch the movements of their victorious enemies. While observing the actions of these enemies, they saw an astonishing incident: to defend herself, Freydis took up a sword lying at the side of a dead man. Then, as the Eskimos came toward her, she drew out her breasts and dashed them against the naked sword.

The Eskimos do not lack a sense of humor. When they saw this frantic woman slapping her breasts with a sword to frighten them, while the great Norsemen were huddled against a protective cliff, they must have roared with laughter and gone back calmly to the camp to gather up the loot. Having taken a full measure of revenge for the murder of their comrade and the stealing of their packs, they were now in possession of all the goods of the Norsemen. Attacking a cornered enemy with his rear protected offered little, if any, advantage at this point. So, as their custom dictated, they withdrew, leaving the defeated and frustrated enemy behind.

Despite his satisfaction with the site of his settlement, Karlsefni decided it would be wise to leave it and return to his home in Iceland because of the constant hostilities from the natives. So he left the beautiful land, Hop. Sailing north close to the coast, Karlsefni and his men saw five Skraelings (Eskimos) asleep near the sea. They killed them and then sailed on to Straumfiord (Belle Isle).

Thorhall the Hunter evidently had planned to return to Leif's camp after his voyage of revenge for the death of Thorvald. When Karlsefni arrived at the camp and learned that Thorhall had not returned, he decided to go north in search of the Greenlander. After his defeat by the Eskimos in the land at Sop's Arm, Karlsefni realized that it had been unwise for Thorhall to go to the Eskimo village where Thorvald had been killed with only nine men. Now that Thorhall and his crew had not returned after a year and a half, the Icelander feared that the Greenlander and his crew had been killed or at least captured by the Eskimos. He would not have dared to return to Greenland without ascertaining their fate and attempting to rescue or avenge them. Knowing where Thorhall had planned to go and the course to follow to get there, Karlsefni set out with one ship and its crew, leaving the other ships and men at the camp to await his return.

Sailing north to Kialarness, they bore to the west and reached a country that was "a wooded wilderness as far as the eye could see, with scarcely any open space." After sailing a long time they turned into the mouth of a river that "flowed down from the land from east toward the west."

Karlsefni had reached the place for which Thorhall had been headed when he was blown out to sea: the mouth of the Kenemich River near the site of the slaying of Thorvald by the Eskimos. Apparently the Eskimos lured Karlsefni into an ambush here, for the Icelandic saga describes an encounter with an Einfoeting as follows: One morning when Karlsefni and his men were in their boat, they saw a shining object in the woods above, running down to the riverbank. It was an Einfoeting (one-footer). The stranger shot an arrow at Thorvald Ericsson, who was at the helm of the boat. Thorvald pulled the arrow out, saying, "There is fat around my belly. We have hit upon a fruitful land, and yet we are not likely to profit from it." He died soon afterward. Karlsefni and his men tried to catch the stranger, but he escaped.

Thorvald, however, had actually been killed several years before. Karlsefni's expedition to the land of the Eskimos was for the purpose of finding Thorhall the Hunter, who had gone there to avenge the death of Thorvald. This obvious contradiction is another confirmation of the suspicion that the Icelandic saga is pseudohistory composed partly to glorify the ancestor of the author (Hauk). "They then sailed back toward the north and thought they saw the land of the Einfoeting. Nor were they disposed to risk the lives of their men any longer."

Thoroughly defeated by the Eskimos, Karlsefni and his men rowed across Lake Melville to get as far away from Eskimo land as they could before turning east to return to Vinland. In ambushing the Norsemen, the Eskimos of southern Labrador evidently used the same method that they used centuries later with the Indians. Vaino Tanner states, "A single kajac man would lure the Indians to follow him out to an island where a large number of his fellows lay in wait. They took the Indians' canoes away and killed their owners." [1]

Explorers have reported that on approaching a shore inhabited by strange Eskimos, they have observed them dancing on one foot. Norsemen who first noticed this unusual custom gave the Eskimos the name Einfoeting (one-footers). Dancing on one foot with the other raised high in the air was an Eskimo signal that an enemy was approaching or that a bear was in sight. Five centuries after the time of Karlsefni, Donnacona, king of the Iroquoian Canadas, told Cartier that he had been in the "land of the one-footers." [2] Three centuries after Cartier's time, Sir John Richardson, the naturalist of the second Franklin expedition, saw the Coronation Gulf Eskimos giving the same signal. [3] The area south of Coronation Gulf is named Einfatingialand on the Thordsen map described in Chapter 16.

It was in this area nine hundred years after Karlsefni's expedition that Diamond Jenness, the Canadian archaeologist, saw Eskimos using the one-foot dance as a signal. He stated that the "two animals that are considered the most dangerous, polar and brown bears, have a special signal. The hunter capers first on one foot, then on the other, waving his arms or his coat above his head. [4]

Knowing that he could not rescue Thorhall if he were alive or avenge him if he had been killed, Karlsefni and his crew sailed back south to Leif's camp. They spent the third winter there and then returned to Greenland. On this return voyage, they stopped in Markland, where Karlsefni kidnapped two boys whom he carried off to Iceland. After Karlsefni taught the boys to speak Norse, they told him that their mother's name was Vaetilldi, their father's name was Vaegi, and that in their country people lived in caves and holes.

On his return to Greenland, Karlsefni "brought back with him much wealth in timber, wine berries and peltries." Bjarne Grimolfsson, the captain of the remaining ship, was driven out into the Atlantic Ocean by a storm while on his way home from Vinland. Blown south into waters where the mischievous shipworm, the teredo, was very active, his ship sank. Part of the crew escaped in the aftboat, but Bjarne was never heard from again. "The boat came into Dublin and there these things were told."

Like many explorers of his time, Bjarne Grimolfsson was a victim of one of the most terrifying hazards of seafaring: the shipworm that paralyzed seamen with fear by gnawing on their ships until they were honeycombed with holes. In a letter written on his fourth voyage in 1503, Columbus said he was forced to abandon a ship in the harbor of Porto Bello because it was so damaged by the gnawing of the teredo that his crew could not keep it afloat despite their efforts to bail out the seawater with pots, kettles, and pumps.

Evidently discouraged by their heavy loss of men in their attempt to establish a settlement in Vinland, the Icelanders thereafter directed their expeditions to Vitramannaland, the agricultural land west of Vinland which Thorvald had reached but had not entered. The Greenlanders, however, immediately undertook another voyage to Vinland. Leif's sister, Freydis, and her husband went in one ship and two Norwegians went in another. They found Leif's camp without difficulty or delay, the Norwegians arriving there first.

Freydis and her crew occupied the *skala* Leif had built. The Norwegians built new housing for their crew. There was much quarreling between the Greenlanders and the Norwegians all that winter. Eventually, avaricious Freydis, taking advantage of the prevailing ill will between the two crews, persuaded the Greenlanders to kill the Norwegian men and take their property. Seizing an ax, she murdered the Norwegian women herself when her countrymen refused to harm them. With no Norwegians left to bear witness to her crime, she was not punished for it after her return to Greenland.

15

Later
Viking Migrations
to
Vinland
and the
American Mainland

It will be recalled that Leif's camp in Vinland was used both by the expedition led by him and by later expeditions primarily as a makeshift base of operations. Elsewhere in Newfoundland on at least seventeen locations, archaeologists have found stone and iron tools and weapons indicating prehistoric occupation by Scandinavians. Among the many sites on Sop's Island which I excavated, a number were occupied in the eleventh and the twelfth centuries.

The rate at which the northeastern point of Newfoundland is rising has been determined, and so it is possible to estimate the approximate date of each site by its height above high tide. The sandy beach at Sop's Island in 1150 is now about 32 feet above the sea. Consequently, all sites above it were habitable before A.D. 1200, and those below it could not have been occupied until after that date. Because of the steady rising of the land, since 1500 there have been no usable landing places or safe anchorages where these sites are located. Some Micmac Indians, attracted by the fertile ground, made an attempt to settle there about 1870, but left, moving to a cove about 2 miles away. They still have gardens on the sites. Viking occupancy came to an end early in the fifteenth century, and Eskimo campsites began to appear in the vicinity during the sixteenth century.

The inhabitants of these eleventh- and twelfth-century beaches were primarily seamen and fishermen. Their large weapons show, however, that they were also hunters of big game: caribou, bear, seal, walrus, and whale. Seals are especially abundant in the White Bay area. Then, as now, great herds came down on the Arctic ice and early in March gave birth to their young at the north end of the bay. Armed only with a club, a hunter can go out on the ice and in two or three days procure a year's supply of seal skins and seal oil. By the end of March, the young seals are strong enough to abandon the ice floes and take to the water.

The hunters scarcely have time to try out the seal oil and prepare the skins before the fishing season begins. First come the herring, then salmon and trout, followed by capelin, squid, and, for a short time, mackerel. The Viking settlers would have been able to supplement the wide variety and abundant supply of fish with fresh meat from the harbor seal and the whales, which then as now frequent White Bay. On land they could choose from an equally wide variety of berries and fruit: red and black currants and the white magna tea, all excellent for making wine, as well as gooseberries, strawberries, blueberries, raspberries, partridge berries, plums, prickly pears, and wild cherries.

The newcomers to Vinland in the eleventh and the twelfth centuries were probably Danes from Ireland, who at that time were confronted with a compelling reason to leave Ireland in search of new homes. For their power in Ireland, which had endured for a century and a half, had been shattered recently by their final defeat by a provincial Irish king. Faced with virtual or actual enslavement if they remained in Ireland, they were prepared to take great risks to escape such a fate. Where could they go?

Norway had just extirpated the last of the Vikings and was at war with the Danes. Scotland was now an independent Christian kingdom which would not admit the pagan Danes. England, and in fact all northwestern Europe, was then being scourged by the plague, and under no conditions would allow pagan Vikings in large numbers to enter. As their power in Ireland waned and finally vanished, important news about newly explored lands overseas was reaching the harried Danes. They were hearing about Vinland, the land which Leif Ericsson had discovered—about its green pastures, its great forests swarming with game and rivers and fiords teeming with fish. Vinland, so they would learn, had numerous sites available for settlement and none of the disadvantages of the other countries in the New World: Greenland, Iceland, and Vitramannaland. Greenland was already fully occupied, and as the last expedition of Greenlanders to Vinland showed, many settlers there were trying to find new homes. Iceland was overcrowded and rocked by earthquakes. Vitramannaland was inhabited, according to reports of traders, by civilized people who did not allow strangers to settle there. Gudleif, the Icelandic trader who landed in Vitramannaland in 1019, spent the following winter in Ireland, and while there, he may have told the Vikings about the hostility of the settlers in Vitramannaland to strangers, explaining that foreigners landing there, with the exception of traders, were enslaved or executed.

The troubled Danes in Ireland had many ships, they knew the route to Vinland, and so to Vinland they probably went—in such large numbers that they were able to overrun the Eskimos of Newfoundland so easily that they enjoyed a practically peaceable occupation. (The conclusion that the Danes from Ireland settled in Newfoundland is based mainly on circumstantial evidence added to archaeological findings described later.)

That Vinland was an island and that Danes were living there was reported to the historian Adam, canon of the Cathedral of Bremen, by the king of Denmark, Sweyn Estridssen (1036–1076). Mute though Church records are concerning migrations to Vinland, these records do reveal that there was a Vinland, for they state that the Church sent at least two missionary bishops to Vinland between 1053 and 1121. To overcome the stubborn resistance of the many Vikings in Iceland, Ireland, and Greenland, who were still pagans in the middle of the eleventh century, the Church apparently undertook an especially active missionary campaign.

It may have been in recognition of the fact that the Scandinavians in Vinland then were from Ireland that Archbishop Adelbert, in 1053 or 1054, selected as the first missionary bishop to them a certain Jon, reportedly originally from Ireland. After preaching the gospel in Iceland for four years, Jon was consecrated as a bishop and sent "to Vinland to convert its people and finally sealed his mission there by torture and death." [1] Bishop Jon, the first known Christian bishop of America, was also the first known Christian martyr of the New World.

Just how long Bishop Jon endured persecution by his pagan charges in Vinland is not known. It is known, however, that another bishop was sent to Vinland seventy years later. This second bishop was Eric Gnupsson, who had served in Greenland as a missionary for six years and then as regionary bishop. Consecrated a second time in 1121 by Adzer, bishop of Lund, Denmark, Eric departed for Vinland the same year, according to the annals of Iceland. The last record of a voyage to Vinland is the brief report of Eric's setting out on his mission in 1121. With the exception of the rune on the Kensington stone (1362), this record is also the last contemporary reference to Vinland extant.

The Danish Vikings from Ireland found the Sop's Island harbor site more desirable for their activities as seamen and fishermen than Karlsefni and his Greenland companions had found it for farming. Needing natural meadows to provide wild hay and pasture, Karlsefni had gone to the southwest corner of the Arm, 8 miles from the sea, where he found a salt-water lake into which he could sail at high water. There he found a valley open to the north and northeast winds and at its southern end a natural meadow, where he built his settlement.

But the Danes stayed out on the easily defended island harbor sites, accessible only by water. There on a gravel beach they built their dwellings well above high tide, facing the landlocked circular harbor. Their boats could be drawn up on the broad sandy beach, then at sea level, for inspection and repair. While working on their boats, they must have dropped the iron boat spikes and nails that I dug up there nine hundred years later.

Across Sop's Arm is another sandy beach at about the same height above the sea as this beach. There my crew dug up a Viking ax and a large iron chisel. The thin flat blade of the ax had been strengthened by cladding[2] a sheet of carburized iron on each side of the soft iron blade. Carburized or cladded nails will not be found often on Viking sites. In assembling their ships, the Vikings used soft boat rivets and clinch nails. In their later models, however, such as the Gokstad boat, they fastened the plank to the keel with hard nails.

Sometime after A.D. 1200 there was a change in the occupancy of the settlement on Sop's Island. The evidence of this change is a considerable increase in the number and variety of the small stone tools and triangular tiny arrowpoints and the numerous iron clinch nails and rivets which I dug up on the lower beaches. Another indication of a change in occupancy after 1200 is the remains of the housing on the sites of this later settlement. These remains are of longhouses—wide, substantial wooden structures with long central hearths such as were in general use in Greenland, Iceland, and Norway after A.D. 1200.[3] In and around these wide longhouses there and similar ones at Englee, 60 miles north of the Sop's Island site, I found more iron tools, nails, and rivets than Danish archaeologists dug up in thirty years of excavation in the Norse ruins of Greenland. Most of these iron artifacts were scattered about the soot-blackened floors of the longhouses or in the cinder beds of the long hearths. They were closely associated, both inside and outside the houses, with stone artifacts—indubitable evidence that the inhabitants of these sites used both iron and stone tools. The remains of these longhouses with central hearths and the quantity of iron artifacts dug up in and near these dwellings suggest that these later occupants of Sop's Island were also Vikings.

The movement of new settlers into Vinland at that time, it appears, was again intimately related to events in Greenland and Iceland. The prosperity of Greenland was coming to an end during that century. A decline had set in which continued until the entire white population of the island disappeared sometime within the next two centuries.

Misled by promises of increased prosperity, the Greenlanders abolished their republic in 1261 and became subjects of the king of Norway. Norway had become an absolute monarchy, and title to all property in the country, as in Norman England, was vested in the king as head of state. Taxes, tithes, and the royal monopolies were followed by complete subordination of the individual to the state. All property was ultimately confiscated by taxation. In addition to the royal taxes, every household paid tithes to the Church. The state and the Church were so closely allied that the burdened Greenlanders held the Church responsible for conditions and renounced Christianity. By 1342, according to the annals of Bishop Gisle Oddson for that year,[4] they were in open rebellion and were apparently using every opportunity to escape to Newfoundland. This region, as they probably knew, was then being vacated by the Danes who were migrating to the mainland of America.

The Icelanders were in worse straits than the Greenlanders. Great sections of their country had been devastated by a series of volcanic eruptions and earthquakes (see Chapter 16). The horror was compounded in the middle of the fourteenth century by a violent outbreak of the bubonic plague on the island (see Chapter 18). During these decades of disaster and disease, many Icelanders probably fled from their island homes to the free countries in America, about which they had heard in detail.

The earthquakes which almost tore Iceland to pieces undoubtedly shook Greenland. The volcanoes in Greenland probably erupted as violently as the Icelandic volcanoes, sending forth similar enormous bursts of poison gases. It is not surprising, therefore, that about 1340 the royal governor of Greenland was informed that the entire West Settlement had been vacated. The settlers had probably fled to America.

Fortunately the wide longhouses built by the Norse during this period enable us to follow the emigrants to the places of their final settlement. Some went to Newfoundland. There on the raised beaches occupied at that time are sites of these longhouses, which are distinguished by their greater width of 35 feet, almost double the width of the eleventh-century Norse longhouses.

In 1535, Cartier found the Iroquoian Indians in Hochelaga, near present-day Montreal, living in these wider longhouses, which were similar in almost every detail to the Scandinavian houses of this later period. In 1615, Champlain found Iroquoian tribes living in these later-type longhouses in settlements hundreds of miles farther inland.

The earliest refugees from insufferable living conditions in Greenland evidently sailed up the St. Lawrence River to the junction with the Ottawa. Finding the St. Lawrence Valley fully occupied, they followed the Ottawa route to Lake Huron. Others followed and finally occupied the country between Hochelaga and the western end of Lake Ontario. Cartier and Champlain found them there. From a merger of these Norse of Greenland with the natives on the American continent came the Hurons, the Tionontati, the Neutrals, and possibly the Eries. The Senecas and the Cayugas joined the Mohawks, the Onondagas, and the Oneidas to form the League of the Long House.

Once the Greenland immigrants had reached Lake Huron, they were in direct communication by water with the ancient copper-mining people of the Lake Superior area. The desire for new lands and new homes far from famine-stricken, war-ravaged Europe probably lured immigrants from Norway and Sweden as well as from Iceland and Greenland. Evidence of infiltration by these peoples, in addition to the remains of longhouses of this later type, includes Norse loan words in the Iroquoian languages and culture traits common to both the Iroquoians and the Scandinavians.

With less actual evidence in hand, I am tempted to speculate concerning the likely migration of Scandinavians southward into Virginia and inland at least as far as Tennessee. The stone graves and remains of wattle houses in the drier climate of this state strongly suggest a one-time Danish occupation. And the remains of primitive iron-producing furnaces of both the Celtic and the Norse type uncovered in Virginia by James Howe and me in 1949 (described in Chapter 3) indicate that Celts and Norse were in that state before the arrival of the English colonists.

A century and a half following the defeat of the Danes in Ireland and the probable subsequent migration of many of them to the New World and settlement in Vinland, the Norman conquest in A.D. 1170 placed the welfare of the Danes who remained in Ireland in greater jeopardy than ever before. Expelled by the Normans from inside the walls of the five great cities that they had built, deprived of all civil rights and finally of their lands, they had either to get out of Ireland or to become serfs of the Normans, bound to the land and sold or traded with it.

Newfoundland was now crowded. The people of Vitramannaland were still bitterly hostile to the Danes in Ireland. The Celts and their Christian allies had by then spread south along the Atlantic coast as far as Virginia, possibly merging with the natives along the way and forming with them the Algonquin tribes who were living in that area in the fifteenth century.

The Danes by now may have been scouting around for additional territory, for they appear to have sailed south along the coast to Virginia. Moving up the James and the Roanoke rivers to the head of navigation, they evidently settled in the cooler uplands where they found ample bog iron ore.

Finding this country preferable to Newfoundland, later immigrants from Ireland, following the first movement to Virginia, may have passed by Newfoundland and settled in the newer country. With increasing immigration from Ireland, the Danish settlements may have expanded into Tennessee, where the Danish-type stone graves and wattle house remains can be seen.

After the Scandinavian civilization in the New World collapsed in the Black Death epidemics, the survivors may have merged with their native subjects to form the two Iroquoian tribes who occupied large areas in Virginia and the Carolinas—the Nottaway and the Tuscarora. (See Chapter 18 for an account of the Black Death and the return to the Stone Age.) Although the Tuscarora later joined the five Iroquoian tribes of New York State, they always kept about the same difference between their dialect and that of the Mohawk as there is between the Danish and the Icelandic. The dialects of the northern Iroquoians have tended to merge, while the Tuscarora tongue has retained its original form.

16

Pre-Columbian
Charts
and
Maps
of the
New World

Ancient maps and sailing charts, only recently deciphered, reveal that long before Columbus, peoples from other continents crossed the Atlantic, reached this continent, and explored and mapped extensive areas of the land that was to be America.

These documents show the coasts and the inland waterways of pre-Columbian North America and even chart the ancient transoceanic sailing routes. As a whole, they outline an area extending from the Bering Strait to the eastern end of the Mediterranean. It has been believed by modern geographers that most of the Arctic coast shown on them was not explored—in fact, not even known—prior to the sixteenth century. Yet in themselves, the maps and the charts are documentary evidence of longtime communication between the ancient trans-Atlantic world, perhaps even the ancient trans-Pacific world, and this continent, including contiguous North Atlantic and Arctic coasts.

During my beginning service in the Transportation Corps during World War II, I served as a first officer under a Captain Myrdal, a Norwegian navigator whose forefathers had been skippers since the time of Eric the Red. On our voyages in the Atlantic, the Caribbean, and the Pacific, I learned under his guidance the technique of the ancient navigators of the Polar seas. This knowledge helped me read and transliterate to a modern projection the ancient charts of a long-forgotten maritime civilization—charts that had made it possible for navigators to cross the Atlantic centuries before Columbus and to sail along unlighted shores without compass, log, or chronometer and under these conditions still be able to determine their longitude at any time.

Knowing that the Celts and the Vikings did not have the compass, I realized, as an experienced navigator, that they would have had navigation charts drawn for use without the compass to reach areas overseas where their artifacts have been found. It was very improbable that master mariners would have risked their vessels and the lives of their men on oft-repeated voyages without accurate charts to guide them. And so when I came upon some scrawls that seemed to be crude outlines of sea and land areas, I decided to find out if they could possibly be charts for the guidance of ancient voyagers. The problem before me was, of course, to find the projection on which they were drawn.

After years of study, I found the unusual projection on which the maps and charts were drawn and deciphered them. They depict accurately the waters and the land areas of the North Atlantic and the northern part of North America as they were centuries ago. Such priceless navigation aids would have been made and preserved only by a maritime people who used them regularly, who presumably copied and recopied them and handed them down from father to son for many generations.

The ancient maps of the Mediterranean area called *protolanos* were cherished and copied by many generations of mariners. Many of these ancient maps and charts which I deciphered were platted by the same methods and on the same grid formed by the meridians of longitude and the parallels of latitude as those famous Mediterranean portolanos.

In most cases, my interpretations of the ancient maps and charts have been verified by the Hydrographic Office of the U.S. Navy, where map experts gave me great assistance. One of these cooperative cartographers, M. I. Walters, has described our work as follows:

> Captain Mallery was introduced to me by the Head Engineer of the Hydrographic Office shortly after World War II with the request that I check with him an old map which he had. . . . I procured from our files a number of present-day charts and together we examined the map in question, which on first sight seemed to be like a hobgoblin and of no real value. However, we began to check various

islands, capes, and peaks and this old map showed astounding accuracy in presenting the land and water areas in their exact locations. This was ten years ago.

From that time on, Mr. Mallery has made a great many visits to the Hydrographic Office and each time he was brought to me for the purpose of rendering whatever assistance I could in his old map studies. . . . The deductions and conclusions which he has reached I consider of the utmost importance in solving some of the secrets of our world history and its peoples, the extent of its water areas and the demarkation of its coast lines. . . . Where present-day charts are inaccurate or lacking in survey information, he has been able with the use of these old maps to supply missing data and correct errors. . . . These maps go back 5000 years and even earlier. But they contain data that go back many thousands of years previous to that.[1]

Midway in my research on the old charts and maps, I discovered that the grids marked on them were incorrect. After deciding that these incorrect grids had probably been added much later by persons other than the original draftsmen, I removed them and worked out what I consider to be correct grids. During this time it became obvious that each map or chart was an assembly of several charts and/or maps of contiguous areas and that the separate charts or maps combined to produce a single map were not all drawn to the same zero point.

Modern navigators were not able to determine longitude accurately until long after the latest of these maps and charts, according to their *known* history, were drawn. With the exception of the very crude method of estimating the run of a ship, known as dead reckoning, no means of finding the longitude of a ship at sea was devised until the introduction for practical purposes of the lunar problem in the eighteenth century. Because of the complicated calculations required by this method, longitudes of comparatively few of even the principal ocean ports and landmarks were determined. Until the invention of the practical chronometer about A.D. 1750, navigators were unable to find longitude by simple calculation. Consequently, except for the portolanos and the charts derived from them, European charts drawn in the historical era prior to the eighteenth century were very inaccurate. Therefore, the fact that the relative longitudes of hundreds of identifiable points are platted with remarkable accuracy on the old maps and charts recently deciphered presents a dilemma.

The various geographical areas shown are placed in a conventional sequence: the Atlantic coasts of Europe on the right side of the maps; the Arctic coast at the top; Greenland at the upper left-hand corner; and the Atlantic coast of North America on the left side. Strange as it may seem, the upper right-hand corner of the maps corresponds to the Arctic coasts of both Europe and Asia.

Reproductions of several of these charts and maps with my interpretations have been deposited with the Bureau of American Ethnology, Smithsonian Institution, and with the Library of Congress. They are presented here with analyses and details of their history.

The first ancient map presented here is the so-called Friseo map. It is a reproduction of a copy made in 1605 by Christian Friseo of a sailing chart originally plotted centuries earlier. Friseo's copy was published by the Danish government. A legend at the top of the map in Latin tells us the following about the origin of the map. "Greenland and nearby regions toward the north and west from an ancient map drawn in a crude manner many hundred years ago in Iceland in which they were then known lands." (See Fig. 16-1.)

The original map was probably drawn before A.D. 1200. On his copy Friseo added notes and trapezoidal grid which were not on the original. After removing these notes and grid, I added correct meridians and parallels for the four separate sailing charts and land maps which in combination compose the map. The following areas are shown on the map:

1. The Arctic coast of Alaska and Canada and the Canadian Arctic island between Baffin Bay at 74° west longitude and Cape Prince of Wales in Alaska at 158° west longitude. The island named *Narvei* is Victoria Island.

2. Greenland, Newfoundland (named *Promontorium Vinlandia*), the Gulf of St. Lawrence, and the seacoasts of Nova Scotia and Maine. This chart, as drawn, warns ships headed for Maine, Nova Scotia, or the western end of the St. Lawrence Gulf to avoid Belle Isle Strait by taking the long way around Newfoundland.

3. Baffin Island, Labrador, and the northeastern coast of the Gulf of St. Lawrence. Apparently ships bound for the gulf sailed through Belle Isle Strait. The zero point of this map is located on a map of Iceland which is part of chart 4.

4. The sailing routes from the west coast of Spain to Ireland, Great Britain, thence to Iceland via the Faroes, and to Norway via the Shetlands. This navigation chart is very ancient.

The original ancient map which Friseo copied had apparently been deposited in the diocesan archives of the cathedral in Skalholt,

Iceland. In 1630 a fire destroyed the archives, but copies of the map which survived were evidently made before the fire and preserved elsewhere. Many documents of historical value were probably lost in the disastrous fire of 1630, most likely records of the Church in America.

Another original ancient map and chart that undoubtedly went up in the flames of that fire was copied in 1579 by Sigurdr Stephansson, a student and later a headmaster in the diocesan school at Skalholt. A copy of Stephansson's reproduction, make by Thord Thorlaksson, survived elsewhere and is presented here (see Fig. 16-2). This Stephansson map has been presented hundreds of times in books dealing with early Scandinavian history, but it remained undeciphered—in fact, an enigma—until I found the key to interpreting it in other ancient maps.

The Friseo and Stephansson maps and charts are drawn to different zero points, but they are both correct delineations of the Arctic coast of North America and of inland areas. On them the Vikings placed Old Icelandic names they gave to areas which they explored and, in some cases, settled. Certain features common to both sets of maps and charts are specific documentary evidence of the one-time presence of Vikings in these areas. One of these common features is the designation of Newfoundland as *Promontory of Vinland the Good,* clear identification of the island as the site of the Vikings' Vinland. Another feature common to both the Friseo and the Stephansson sets is the naming of Labrador as *Markland,* an indication that the Norse knew Markland and may have explored and settled the area. Confirmation of the presence of the Vikings in Markland (Labrador) is provided also by the port records of Reykjavik, Iceland, for the year A.D. 1347.[2]

On both Friseo and Stephansson charts, Victoria Island is given the Icelandic name for *Norway Island, Norvei* on the former and *Narve Oe* on the latter. This is an important documentary detail, for it is supporting evidence that residents there, though they were Eskimos, were descendants of the Norse. The Arctic explorer Vilhjalmur Stefansson reported finding blond Eskimos on Victoria Island whom he believed to be descendants of the Norse.

The legend on the Friseo map is one of two authentic records indicating that maps of North America plotted long before Columbus were preserved in Iceland. The other such record is a published statement of the eminent Icelandic historian Bjorn Jonsson describing the Thordsen map, which is analyzed in Chapter 9. (See Fig. 9-1.)

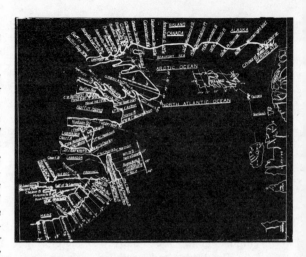

Fig. 16-1. The Frisco map of the North Atlantic and Arctic. Copied by Christian Frisco from an ancient drawing discovered in Iceland, this map of "Greenland and nearby regions toward the north and west" was published by the Danish government. The original chart was probably drawn before A.D. 1200. The notes and trapezoidal grid added by Frisco have been removed. The correct meridians and parallels for four of the charts have been added.

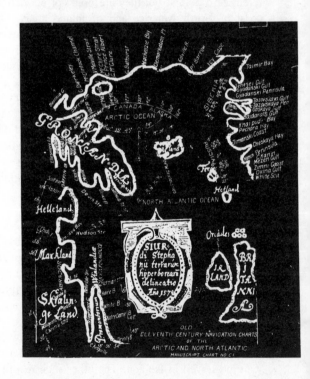

Fig. 16-2. The Stephansson map, which is also a combination of several separate maps and charts, nine in number, drawn to four zero points.

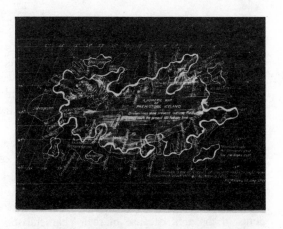

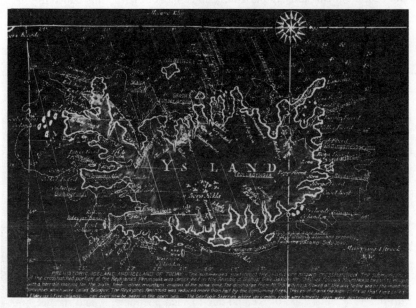

Figs. 16-3 and 16-4. Ancient maps of prehistoric Iceland. The accompanying maps of prehistoric Iceland were probably drawn before A.D. 700. Heavy black lines are part of the originals. Broken lines mark the present coast of Iceland. Stippled parts indicate the areas now submerged. Volcanic action and glacial debris have covered some of the submerged areas. Dotted lines mark the present 100-fathom line. The grid showing the latitudes and longitudes has been added by the author.

Like the other ancient maps and charts, the Thordsen map is a combination of several separate maps and charts of contiguous areas. It is a map of the inland waterways of eastern Canada, some of which were not correctly plotted on modern maps until nearly two hundred years after Father Thordsen deposited the ancient map in the archives of the cathedral in Skalholt, Iceland.

This section of the Thordsen map presents specific evidence corroborating the saga story of Viking penetration of this continent. The area marked Einfatingialand is now the home of Eskimos, including the Copper Eskimos. The term *einfoeting* is Icelandic for "one-footer" and was apparently chosen by Icelanders as the name for residents of the area because of their characteristic dance on one foot. Both Sir John Richardson and Diamond Jenness describe this dance in their accounts of the life of the Copper Eskimo.[3]

There is additional specific evidence of the validity of the saga story in other Old Icelandic names on this map. It will be seen, for instance, that the southern part of central Canada is named *Einhyrningaland,* which is Icelandic for *Land of the People of the One-Horned Ax.*

Together, the Friseo map, the Stephansson map, and the Thordsen map contain seventeen separate charts and maps of areas of North America and of routes to them from Ireland, Great Britain, Norway, and Siberia.

Another dimension is added to the documentary value of the ancient maps and charts as a whole by the two maps of Iceland reproduced in Figs. 16-3 and 16-4. In particular, these two recently deciphered maps reveal with special emphasis the great changes in the size and contour of Iceland through the centuries—changes which were consequences of such natural phenomena as the advancement of the glacier, the eruption of a volcano, or the shock of an earthquake. There is confirmation in historical records of great changes in the outline of the land mass of Iceland due to such phenomena, and so the recording of continuing alterations in the size and contour of the island on these maps points up their great age and in doing so tells us that there was an advanced civilization in the North Atlantic area centuries earlier than geographers and historians have considered conceivable.

Both of these maps were plotted on the same unusual projection or grid and with the same accuracy as the Thordsen map and the portolanos of the Mediterranean which the famous Swedish geographer Baron N. E. Nordenskiold named *Homeric* maps because he believed that they were much older than the famous, inaccurate Ptolemaic maps. The maps of Iceland were probably drawn originally before A.D. 700. The older of the two (the larger in the reproduction) was found along with other maps in the Faroes in 1508. Presumably, Bishop Henry of Garda, Greenland, took the maps with him when he was transferred from Greenland to the Faroes in 1394.

Comparison of the larger old map with a modern map of Iceland shows that the island has sunk about 300 feet since the old map was made. The heavy lines are the outline of the original map. The unshaded portion shows the outline of present-day Iceland, and the shaded areas are the sections of the island now under water. Dotted lines mark the present 100-fathom line.

The catastrophe that struck Iceland, devastating the Reykjanes Peninsula (marked 2 on the map) and sinking the maritime provinces, which were the first areas of Iceland to be settled (marked 4 on the map) is described in the annals of Bishop Gisle Oddson for the year A.D. 1342 as follows:

> Mt. Hekla began to erupt with a horrible roaring for the sixth time . . . other mountains erupted at the same time. The discharge from Mt. Trolledynja flowed all the way to the sea in the maritime provinces which were called *Selfogur*. *The Reykjanes Peninsula was reduced more than half* by the consuming fires. Traces of it and the high cliffs at that time called Eldeyjar . . . can even now be seen in the open sea. The Geirfugle Skerries . . . were destroyed. In southern Iceland, Sidujokul and many other mountains erupted. Whole provinces were devastated. More than half of the Reykjanes Peninsula disappeared, and the Island Eldey, forty miles west of the present Reykjanes, blew up. The maritime provinces of Selvoge, which had endured unchanged for thousands of years, gradually sank into the Atlantic. They were completely submerged before 1607.[4] and now lie fifty fathoms or more below the sea level. The present-day shoals called *Eldeyjarbodi* and the fishing banks Eldeyjar Banks mark the spot where Eldey once stood, and the Iceland fishermen still keep alive the memory of the lost provinces of Selvoge as they set their trawl lines on Selvoge Bank.[5]

The other ancient map of Iceland (the smaller one) shows the outline of the island as it may have been some time before the visit of the Greek astronomer Pytheas in 330 B.C. On this map, as on the larger map, heavy lines are the outline of the original map; the un-

Fig. 16-5. Donald Macbeth, Captain Mallery, Mrs. Porter, and Tom Porter examine copy of ancient map in December, 1953. Macbeth and Porter were official archaeologists for the Ross County Historical Museum. (Photograph by Leland Puttcamp.)

shaded portion gives the present-day outline of the island, and the dotted lines mark the present 100-fathom line. Submerged areas are indicated on this map by stippling.

The evidence in these two maps that Iceland has been sinking for thousands of years has been corroborated by the modern explorations of the Norwegian North Polar Expedition under Frithiof Nansen.[6] Nansen concluded that the Faroes and Iceland were once connected by a basaltic plateau emerging above sea level at a period when the shore line stood on an average 500 meters lower than it does now. The Faroe-Icelandic ridge now extends beyond Iceland to Greenland, and the southern end of Greenland is also sinking.[7]

The Celts and the Scandinavians were among the users and the preservers of these navigation aids which mapped the New World long before Columbus. It is obvious that the people who made them possessed knowledge of astronomy and celestial navigation far in advance of that of fifteenth-century Europeans. There is some evidence that some of these charts and maps must have been drawn at least one thousand years before the invention of a practical chronometer in the eighteenth century enabled modern European navigators to compute longitude. The longitude of a thousand or more points on the coasts and in the interior of North America, Europe, and Asia is platted on them with an accuracy not attained by European cartographers until the eighteenth century.

17

The Long-Lost Gunnbiorn's Skerries

In their efforts to reconstruct the saga account of Vinland voyages and settlement in pre-Columbian America, scholars have been frustrated mainly because they have overlooked the tremendous changes in the natural features of the Greenland-Iceland area due to disruptive natural phenomena. Unaware of the consequent sinking of land and the forming of undersea shelves as the surface of the earth shifted under the weight of glacial ice, they have not realized that some landmarks on the Viking trail have even vanished under ice and water. So completely obliterated have some landmarks been that modern geographers and historians, unable to locate them, doubt that they ever existed, and consequently doubt the validity of the saga story.

The principal vanished landmark was a group of rocky islands known as Gunnbiorn's Skerries, located midway between Greenland and Iceland. The Skerries are shown on the oldest map of Greenland in this location (see Figs. 17-1 and 17-2), but they do not appear on any modern map. The fact is that there are no islands today in the location of the Gunnbiorn's Skerries of Viking time—no Gunnbiorn's Skerries. The main Skerries known to the Vikings are now hidden from sight, partly under the Greenland glacier and partly under the

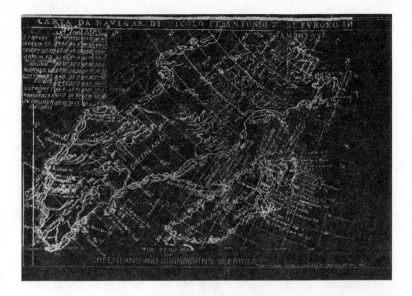

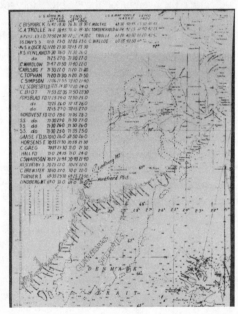

Figs. 17-1 and 17-2. Greenland and Gunnbiorn's Skerries as shown on the Zeno map. Although most of the areas shown on the map are still covered by glaciers or are under water, more than thirty places or fiords have been uncovered as the glacier retreated.

waters of Denmark Strait. All that remains visible of the original group are a few northern islands shown on present-day maps and bearing modern names.

For more than one hundred years before Eric the Red landed in Greenland, the people of Iceland knew that the Skerries were out in the sea to the west. For centuries thereafter, they heard of Gunnbiorn's Skerries as the halfway point on the route from Iceland to Greenland. When voyagers, sailing directly across Denmark Strait, picked up the rocky islands, they knew that they were on the direct route and had covered half the distance between Iceland and Greenland, for their sailing directions stated: "From Snaefjeldness in Iceland from which point this passage to Greenland is the shortest, the course is two days and two nights due west, and there you will find Gunnbiorn's Skerries halfway between Greenland and Iceland." [1]

Sometime after Greenland was settled by the Norse, the advancing Greenland icecap covered the central and southern Skerries. Sinking under the weight of the glacier, the southern Skerries finally became submerged in Denmark Strait, where they still form a plateau underseas. The original outline of the southern Skerries, now hidden from sight under the waters of Denmark Strait, can be made out from the soundings recorded on the latest U.S. Hydrographic Office and the British Admiralty maps. [2]

For an interval lasting centuries, beginning about nine thousand years ago according to geologists, [3] the Arctic region had a warm climate. Known as the *Climatic Optimum,* this warm era came about as a result of the pressure of the weight of glaciers in the northern part of the North Temperate Zone. Being depressed in this area, the earth took the shape of an oblate spheroid flattened at the poles, and the bottom of the Arctic Ocean sank almost 2,000 feet at the pole. Into this depressed area, the Japan Current and the Gulf Stream poured the warm waters from the tropics through both Bering Strait and Davis Strait. This influx of warm air raised the temperature of the Arctic region so high that the forest line of North America advanced 500 miles north of its present position.

As the Arctic became warm, the glaciers disappeared, the weight of the ice was removed, and the shell of the earth began gradually to resume its former spherical shape. The land of the Arctic regions rose and the bulge in the equatorial region, which had been produced concurrently with the sinking of northern areas, began to disappear. As the land rose, Bering Strait and Davis Strait became so shallow that eventually the two warm currents no longer flowed through them. The climate of the Arctic gradually became cold again.

As this internal movement of the earth was taking place, gigantic cracks developed along the North Atlantic coast and through Denmark Strait into the Atlantic Ocean.

Just when the different stages in these geological and climatic changes took place is not known. Ice was reported seen in Iceland only twice in the eleventh century and three times in the twelfth century. After 1200, however, winters became more severe and increasing quantities of ice floated down into the fiords of the island. By 1274 ice approached so near the shores that polar bears were landing there, and the next year twenty-seven bears were caught on drift ice. In another four years it was possible to travel with horses many miles from shore on the ice, and the sea remained frozen for the first time until late summer.[4]

By 1340, the Skerries must have been completely covered by the advancing glaciers, for at that time Ivar Bardasson, steward of the diocese of Garda, Greenland, wrote: "Anyone sailing from Iceland must shape his course from Snaefjeldness in Iceland . . . for a day and a night he will sail due west, but must then steer southwest to avoid the ice that adheres to Gunnbiorn's Skerries."[5]

The temperature of the sea waters and of Greenland and Iceland declined as the rising land along the Arctic coast cut down the warm currents flowing north through Bering Strait and Davis Strait. Although grain had been grown in northern Iceland until the end of the twelfth century, by the end of the fourteenth century it could no longer be grown in the southern part of the island.[6]

The north end of Greenland was rising,[7] and the south end was sinking.[8] Earthquake after earthquake accompanied by violent submarine explosions and many volcanic eruptions rocked Iceland in the thirteenth and the fourteenth centuries.[9] In 1340 came the series of volcanic eruptions and earthquakes. (See the preceding chapter for account of the devastation of the Reykjanes Peninsula of Iceland and the sinking of the maritime provinces as related in the annals of Bishop Gisle Oddson in A.D. 1342.) Great tidal waves swept the shores of the North Sea as the southern Skerries slid into the widening abyss created by a gigantic submarine crack or fault in the surface of the earth along a line passing northeast and southwest through Denmark Strait.[10]

By 1456, most of the main island of the Skerries had disappeared.[11] Only one mountain peak then showed above the water of Denmark Strait. Located on the southeastern shore of the island, this peak at one time had towered almost 1,000 feet above the shore of the strait. In 1476, Didrik Pining, sent by the king of Norway to put an end to the pirate raids in Greenland waters, made his headquarters on this mountainous island, which he named *Hvitserk*.[12] (After a long and noteworthy career in the service of Norway, part of the time as governor of Iceland, Pining became a pirate and from Hvitserk preyed on the ships passing the island.)

With the deepening of Denmark Strait, the cold east Greenland current poured through the widening channel, carrying vast quantities of Arctic ice. This ice chilled the Greenland climate and formed a great ice barrier which severed communication between Greenland and Europe. Because of that ice barrier, Greenland was lost to the world for longer than a century.

The vanished remnants of Gunnbiorn's Skerries are shown on several Amsterdam maps of that area, published about A.D. 1600. The sunken south end of the main island, near the center of Denmark Strait, according to a notation on one map, was by then 25 fathoms (50 yards) under water. Sixty-five miles long and 25 miles wide, it was a shoal named *Gombar Skaare*.[13] By 1932, the highest point of this shoal was 60 fathoms (120 yards) below sea level![14] On the Amsterdam map, a group of islands named *I. Gombarma* appear northeast of the shoal, and for a century these islands appeared on maps of Denmark Straits with names that are variations of "Gombar."

As recently as 1753 and 1756, numerous volcanic eruptions and earthquakes in western Iceland were accompanied by great inundations in Ireland, England, Holland, and Germany.[15] Ten years later the final chapter in the history of the Skerries was written by a French navy officer, Captain Kerguelen, who reported:

> Being in that part of the seas and on the precise spot where formerly were several islands under the name of *Goubermans,* I sounded and found one hundred and fifty fathoms of water, muddy water mixed with herbs.
>
> The sketch of these islands was taken by some Danish engineers who drew the map of Iceland. The islanders relate that *they formerly consisted of nine,* that they were no more than four leagues from the mainland, and that *they were swallowed up during an earthquake.* What is certain respecting them is that there now remains no vestige of them, their former residence being that part of the coast where now is the deepest water.[16]

One of these islands, named *Suga* on a Dutch map of Denmark Strait, and another west of it are still shown as submerged peaks on British Admiralty Chart 515.

It may be assumed, however, that corroboration of my theory regarding the existence of the one-time Gunnbiorn's Skerries under the icecap of Greenland has come in more recent times—as late as 1951, in fact. For on October 26 of that year, an Associated Press news dispatch announced that a French expedition reported that Greenland is really three islands bridged by an ocean.

Several months before this announcement, I had published my findings in *Lost America*. (See Chapter 22 for an account of the findings of the French Polar Expedition under Paul-Emile Victor.)

18

The
Black Death:
Return
to the
Stone Age

By 1450 or thereabouts, the great copper-mining, metalworking, and mound-building civilization of the Ohio Valley and the Great Lakes region had disintegrated. A century later when Cartier and other explorers reached America, the Celts, the Norse, and the Danes had vanished from the New World. The Iroquois with their Stone Age culture had taken their place.

The one-time settlements of the displaced white warrior peoples had to be inferred centuries later from the indirect evidence of artifacts, masonry, ancient maps, cultural similarities, and the records of the sagas. Despite their prowess in seamanship, their intrepidity as voyagers, and their military capacity, the white groups were either exterminated or dissolved.

All that can be reasonably inferred about their pre-Columbian settlements in America is consistent with attributing their total disappearance to onslaughts of the worldwide epidemic of bubonic plague in the mid-fourteenth century and the subsequent merger of the surviving settlers with the neighboring American aborigines.

That epidemic of the plague-ravaged Europe, killing at least one-fourth of the population between 1346 and 1351, came close to causing a definitive break in the continuity of civilization. In its worldwide course, the epidemic first appeared in China and India, swept through the Mongol empire, hit the seaports of the Mediterranean and the Atlantic coasts, and then crossed the continent to northern Russia. If, as is likely , the insidious pestilence also crossed the Atlantic on ships carrying frightened, infected refugees from northern Europe, it had a devastating mortality effect in the densly crowded communal dwellings of the white settlers of North America.

Known in England as the Black Death, because its victims turned a ghastly deep purple, the fourteenth-century epidemic was one of the many recurrent attacks of bubonic plague throughout the ages, attacks which have depopulated continents, brought about the disintegration of sturdy nations, and wiped out their cultures. There were at least six outbreaks on the continent between 1294 and 1346.[1]

Bubonic plague—the pestilence—is essentially a scourge bred by civilization. Beginning as a rodent disease, it is transmitted to man from rats diseased by fleas. Not yet eliminated, the plague is still with us, surviving mainly in tropical areas with large rodent populations. A form of the disease, ordinarily not fatal, is endemic at all times among the rodents of India and of Manchuria, Astrakhan, and Yunnan. It has spread to wild rodents throughout the world, where occasionally it is manifested in isolated cases or limited epidemics. Early in this century, it again killed more than one million people in one year, mostly in India. Wild rodents of the Rocky Mountain region are plague-infected, and sporadic cases of bubonic plague have been noted as far east as North Dakota.[2] In sparsely populated areas and on deserts, the rodent population is held down by lack of food. As a country becomes urbanized, grain and other food supplies are brought into towns and cities where they are stored for concentrated populations. Thriving on these foods and on large quantities of garbage and refuse, the rats propagate rapidly and the disease spreads like brush fire through a resulting dense rodent population.

Also conducive to the development of the plague, if it is already present in endemic form among the rodents, is a protracted and severe curtailment of the food supply for any reason, such as war or drought. The resistance of both rats and humans is then seriously decreased because of malnutrition, and if bubonic plague is present in endemic form, it is likely to become virulent.

The first warning of an oncoming epidemic is the death of great numbers of rats. In India, when the residents of a village see that the rats are dying, they flee from the locality immediately, for they know that an epidemic threatens. Throughout history the deadly pestilence has been prevalent in India, and the source of many worldwide epidemics can be traced to that country.

The bubonic plague appears in three forms: the bubonic, the pneumonic, and the septicemic. In the first and last stages of the disease, it usually assumes the bubonic form. At the outset it may be so mild as to be mistaken for a severe cold or fever, only a small proportion of the cases proving fatal. In the closing years of the epidemic, it again is mild.

As the pestilence becomes more virulent, deaths are more frequent, usually occurring about the eighth day after the appearance of the first symptoms of the disease. Fortunately, many people survive its attacks at this stage and are thus rendered immune. It is when the epidemic reaches the pneumonic or septicemic form that it is transformed into the really malignant killer it can be, spreading with great rapidity and causing death within one to four days. At this stage, infection results from the inhalation of airborne droplets from the infected lungs of a victim, much as the common cold and some forms of tuberculosis are spread.

A typical plague epidemic, in the first three months, may exterminate 20 to 50 percent of the population of a densely settled country. Becoming sporadic, it may then kill from 15 to 40 percent of the survivors, and, finally, after ceasing completely for five or ten years, it may strike again, wiping out from 10 to 30 percent of the survivors. Plague epidemics have not only decimated populations and wrought immense social and economic changes; they have brought down seemingly stable governments as well.

The survivors in a stricken nation sometimes escape, leaving their country almost uninhabited. Prior to the development of the art of writing, transmission of the accumulated knowledge in the arts and crafts—the culture base of a society—was oral. When a nation or even a whole race was brought down by plague and many of the survivors abandoned their settlements, only knowledge that was common to all adults would normally be preserved. The specialized arts and crafts might be lost both because the class which had mastery over them was annihilated by disease and because these refinements were not necessary in the intense struggle for survival in a new habitat. Long periods, even centuries, might elapse before a stricken civilization could recover the ground lost by the onslaught of pestilence.

During the Middle Ages, bubonic plague was largely a seaborne disease, particularly in the case of the Black Death. The preeminent role of maritime trade in the spread of the disease is illustrated by the way in which it reached Russia. Appearing in China and India in 1332, it spread westward slowly by the caravan routes. Fourteen years later it struck the Black Sea port of Caffa (now Feodosiya), then an outpost of traders from Genoa. At the time Caffa was being besieged by Mongols, whose empire had been suffering the pestilence. During their attack on Caffa, the Mongols threw the cadavers of their victims of the plague into the city, thus infecting the defenders of the city and causing a heavy death toll among them. The survivors of this bacteriological attack left Caffa, returning by sea to Genoa. Soon thereafter the pestilence spread rapidly to Sicily, some ports of Italy, and Marseilles. Then it ravaged the papal seat of Avignon, Spain, Belgium, England, and Austria, and soon reached all Scandinavia, Germany, and Poland by way of the North Sea and the Baltic. It did not reach Russia until a few years later (1351), probably by way of the inland waterways from the Caspian and the Black Sea.

It is reasonable to assume that the plague was carried to western Europe on ships with a cargo of infected rats and fleas in which the Genoese returned to Genoa from Caffa. A contemporary Flemish chronicler, Matthias Neuwenburgensis, tells of three death ships which reached Genoa in January, 1348, with infected crews and cargo. The sailors evidently landed and introduced the disease, but were forced back on their ships, which were then driven to sea with fiery arrows. This same process was repeated in Greece, Tuscany, Marseilles, and Languedoc until all areas were infected. It came to a stop only when all members of the unfortunate crews were dead: "many galleys . . . found drifting about the sea with their cargoes but with no living soul aboard."

Records show that there was bubonic plague in Iceland in 1346,[3] the year that the Black Death first appeared in the Black Sea area. One possible explanation is that the 1346 Icelandic pestilence was a sporadic outbreak, a forerunner of the Black Death. After securing a foothold in Iceland and Greenland, the plague would undoubtedly have been carried across the North Atlantic to the American continent. It is logical to assume that fugitives from the epidemic would have sailed for plague-free Markland, carrying the infection with them. While rats could easily have been trapped, killed, and thrown overboard from small undecked vessels, these rodents were not a necessary element in the process of infection. Insect parasites would have moved directly from man to man on the crowded ships. Fleas, securely lodged in furs and cargo, would have been another reservoir of infection. Once the crew landed in a Vinland settlement, the rodent population there would have been stricken by plague and the disease would have spread rapidly from rats to fleas and from fleas to men.

In 1347, the year after pestilence struck Iceland, a small Greenland ship was wrecked in the outer harbor of Reykjavik, Iceland. This vessel, which had been returning from Markland, was blown off its course. The crew of seventeen went on to Norway and were then carried back to their home in Greenland by the royal merchant ship *Knaaren*. Either this ship or others from the British Isles may have carried the Black Death to the New World, thus serving as the executioner of Viking civilization in early America.

There were other possible carriers. Numerous vessels with entire crews who had perished while on board were drifting about in the Atlantic. Any of these death ships running ashore in America could have brought the plague to the mainland, for, except in areas under rigid government control, it has long been a universal custom to board and loot abandoned or wrecked ships.

Although scourged by the Black Death and by later epidemics of the plague, Iceland did not go down. For a long time after the widespread severe epidemic of 1402–1404, the monasteries on the island remained empty. All the learned men at the bishop's seat in Skalholt, except the bishop himself, died in the plague. Even the schools were abandoned. Farms lay uncultivated. Entire families died out or disappeared. It was about this time that the settlers vanished from the Western Settlement in Greenland. When the report that only one-third of the population of Norway had survived the Black Death reached Iceland in 1349, many Icelanders and Greenlanders probably fled to America. The settlers in Iceland might have abandoned their island too if British traders had not continued to come there. Overrun by Hanseatic armies and pirate hordes, Norway was unable to come to the assistance of Iceland. In effect, the plague destroyed Greenland and would probably have destroyed Iceland also if the island had not been in continuous contact with the British Isles.

When the pestilence again struck Iceland in 1402,[4] carrying away two-thirds of the population, many of those fleeing by sea from this scourge may have set sail for Vinland, carrying disease and death with them. In view of the heavy mortality and almost total disintegration of the social and economic life of Iceland, no records of any such expeditions would have been preserved.

My detailed examination of a Newfoundland beach for remains of Scandinavian settlements has turned up evidence, though indirect, in support of the theory that settlements there were destroyed by the plague. Since the land there has been rising at the rate of 4 feet every century, it is possible to date various artifacts by their location in relation to the advancing shoreline. Proof of Norse occupancy during the period 1250 to 1400 exists in the form of artifacts, but there is no evidence of any settlement for any period subsequent to 1400. These settlements probably became plague-infested either during the era of the Black Death or as a result of the later widespread plague epidemics which almost depopulated Iceland. The settlements would then have been abandoned and the survivors would have fled into the interior. In America the plague reappeared among the Mayas in 1519,[5] and an outbreak among the Hurons in 1636 was a contributing factor in the destruction of that nation.[6]

The Black Death may have had a bearing on another puzzle of American archaeology—the Kensington Stone, which some scholars think was carved by a party of Goths and Norse while they were facing ambush by Indians and death near Kensington, Minnesota. The date on the stone is 1362. The answer to the question of why this small party ventured so far into the American interior by boat may be that pestilence in the shore settlements drove them westward in search of a disease-free area.

Onslaughts of the plague in Celtic or Viking settlements in North America would undoubtedly have been more devastating to these sedentary white people living in crowded communal houses than to the wandering woodland Indians or even to the more settled tent-dwelling tribes. With their accumulated stores of grain, the white settlements would have been more hospitable to large rodent populations and consequently have offered conditions favorable for the swift propagation of the pestilence. Without such stores of food, the Indians by contrast would not have been hospitable to infected rodents, and so for them the hazards of infection would have been far less.

Since the record of the movement of the Black Death in Europe and Asia shows that sea traffic was a more effective and swifter carrier of the epidemic than land travel, plague infection would have spread more rapidly among Vikings herded together on ships with no possibility of escape than among Indians moving by land. Persons stricken while traveling by land could drop out or be expelled from the group, fend for themselves, and probably die. No rat population would accompany such treks. With the plague-stricken isolated or abandoned, there would have been comparatively little possibility for massive flea-to-man infection.

The toll of pestilence would have borne upon the members of the community who had specialized skills as heavily as upon the general population. When families with a mastery of special arts were extinguished by the plague, their knowledge and skill would die with them, particularly with the absence of written records. The slashing of the artery of trade and communication with Europe would have deprived the American settlements of a continuing source of stimulus, of new blood, of knowledge, and of know-how. In time, techniques of smelting and fashioning metals would be lost, and there would be a regression to the use of stone tools. Thus, with its greater impact on the more complex culture of the white settlers than on the life pattern of the Indians, the pestilence would have altered the balance of power between the two groups.

The foregoing is, I believe, a reasonable explanation in general for the disintegration of the pre-Columbian Norse settlements on the continent of North America. It is conceivable that at some stage in the regression to the Stone Age, the diminished and weakened populations of these settlements merged with their neighbors, the American aborigines, who still retained their Stone Age culture. Such an eventual merger of Vikings and Indians may have been a major part of the process of the cultural degeneration of the Viking survivors. After the white settlements in the Ohio Valley and the Great Lakes region had been almost depopulated by plague, the woodland tribes north of the Great Lakes probably moved down and occupied these settlements. It is likely that the surviving but weakened Norse already merging with aborigines pressed to the south and the northeast. Those who reached the south may have formed the Cherokee, the Caddoan, and related tribes. There is reason to believe that those who went northeast to the areas around the Great Lakes (Lake Erie and Lake Ontario) merged with more recently arrived Norse and formed the Iroquoian peoples. Later the Iroquois pushed west and reoccupied northern Ohio.

Authorities have readily admitted that the origin of the Iroquois and their culture is obscure. The conclusion that they were a merger of American aborigines and early Scandinavians is compatible with the findings of scholars:

We do not know the origin of the old Iroquois culture, which shows relationships with both southern and northern Indian types. We suggest the Iroquois were an amalgamation, a mixture of several culture types.

The old Iroquois culture [late prehistoric period] was dated 1350–1600 A.D. and covered the northeastern United States, principally the Great Lakes region and New York.[7]

19

The
Rise
of the
Iroquois

The Iroquois are one of the many Indian tribes whom scholars generally group together under the name *Iroquoian* [1] on the assumption of
blood relationship. The Iroquois are outstanding among American Indians, particularly for their highly organized society, which formed a
defensive and offensive league for mutual protection. Other tribes, as
white settlers moved in on them, shifted from one reservation to another, but many Iroquois are still living on land that was the home of
their ancestors when modern white men first came to this continent.

It is impossible to find out where the Iroquois came from, for apparently nobody knows. Information concerning the origins of all prehistoric American Indians is based largely on speculation. While ethnologists have placed the original home of the Iroquois in the West
or the Southwest, the Iroquois themselves insist that they came from
the North and the Northeast.* About one thing, however, not only

---

*For reasons which will become clear later, the entire Iroquoian people are
here divided into three groups: the first, the Iroquois, includes the Seneca, the Canada,
the Mohawk, the Oneida, the Onondaga, the Cayuga, and the Susquehanna; the second
includes the Nottaway and the Tuscarora; and the third, the Wyandot, includes the
Hochelaga, the Huron, the Tionontati, the Neutral, and the Wenco.

ethnologists but virtually everybody except the Iroquois seem to be in agreement: the ancestors of all American Indians came from Asia by way of the Bering Strait sometime in the obscure past.

For more than a century it has been generally believed that there was no cultural contact between Europe and this continent before Columbus landed on our shores and that man migrated to North America prior to the arrival of Columbus exclusively by way of the Bering Strait. These two beliefs have spawned the basic interpretations, or rather misinterpretations, of pre-Columbian American history and ethnology. And yet the only sound basis for these beliefs—commonly known as the Bering Strait theory—is the obvious physical resemblance of certain North American Indians to the Mongols.

But the Mongols also resemble the North American Indians! There is no more reason to infer that the Mongols migrated from Asia to America than to suppose that their original home was in America and that the migration was from there to Asia.

There is some evidence supporting the latter hypothesis. The homeland of the Mongols is in northeastern Asia. Throughout early history they almost invariably moved westward and southward, leaving behind them a trail of artifacts and cultural evidence of the great migration periods.

Reindeer, significantly, were tamed for domestic use in Asia, but not in America. If Asiatics had come to America, would they not have brought the institution of reindeer traction with them? If the movement was in the opposite direction, the use of reindeer might have developed in Asia after the migration from America occurred. Dog traction, on the other hand, appeared in northeastern America around A.D. 1000, spread across the continent to Alaska, and later showed up in parts of northeastern Asia west of the reindeer-using areas.[2] Undoubtedly there has been some migration via Bering Strait from Asia to America and vice versa, but the principal movements in either direction have been by water along the sea routes and inland waterways.

When these speculations first came to my mind several decades ago, I knew nothing of the numerous archaeological expeditions and the hundreds of thousands of dollars that had gone into the fruitless attempt to bulwark the Bering Strait theory. Nor did I then realize the total disinterest of archaeologists and historians in the search for evidence that Europeans penetrated this continent in pre-Columbian times. At that time I was searching for evidence of a merger of the Indians and the Scandinavian settlers, with the resulting consequence of the emergence of the Iroquois. My first need was to learn all I could possibly find out about the Iroquois and related tribes.

According to their own traditions and also according to archaeological and ethnological evidence, the Iroquois developed in the St. Lawrence Valley as a result of the absorption by the native tribes of an invading race from the north and the northeast. Attaining a dominant status in the valley, these invaders superimposed many of their culture traits on the native culture.

A systematic analysis of Iroquoian culture reveals many culture traits identical with corresponding culture traits of the ancient Scandinavians. The conclusion that the invading race was the Viking is inescapable. Once the dark skin of the western Iroquois is accounted for as their heritage from the dark-skinned aborigines who absorbed the northern invaders, their strong physical resemblance to the Vikings becomes patent. Sieur de Roberval, the first governor general of New France, described the Iroquois whom he saw in the St. Lawrence region in 1542: "They are a people of goodly stature and well made; they are very white, but they are all naked, and if they were appareled as the French are, they would be as white and as fair, but they paint themselves for fear of heat and sunburning." [3]

It is their cultural heritage, however, rather than their biological inheritance which identifies the Iroquois as descendants of the Vikings. This cultural heritage includes a highly developed science of warfare, comprising a system of defense and attack sufficiently organized and implemented to block a mighty nation and thereby alter the destiny of a continent. The Iroquois learned from some unknown source the technique of erecting elaborate timber fortifications and of establishing a highly organized society with a defensive and offensive league for mutual protection.

The earliest definite reference to the Iroquois is in Cartier's account of the Indians he met on his first expedition to the New World in 1535. Following a route suggested to him by Breton fishermen, the French explorer had sailed through the Strait of Belle Isle, across the Gulf of St. Lawrence, and had landed in Chaleur Bay. Here he met a party of the Canadas, one of the many Iroquoian tribes, who then occupied the area north of the Gulf of St. Lawrence and both sides of the St. Lawrence Valley as far as Quebec. [4]

The Canadas were on a fishing trip and were fittingly dressed—or rather, undressed—for this pursuit during hot summer weather. Their nakedness and their method of greeting Cartier apparently gave him the idea that they were a simple, guileless, uncultured people whom he could easily use for his own purposes. In underestimating them he made a serious mistake, his first in a series that ultimately cost him success in his undertaking in this continent.

In their canoes the Indians paddled fearlessly up to the sides of Cartier's vessel and received presents of knives, beads, and other trinkets. Lifting up their hands to heaven and singing and dancing in their bobbing canoes, they demonstrated their welcome to the strangers and their thanks for the gifts. In commenting on their appearance, Cartier wrote: "These people may well be called savages, for they are the sorriest folks there can be in the world . . . they go quite naked except for a small skin with which they cover their privy parts and for a few old furs which they throw over their shoulders."[5]

Although they gave the French a friendly welcome, the Canadas wisely kept their young women hidden in the woods when Cartier came ashore. Interestingly enough, they may have had good reason also to distrust the great symbol of Christianity; for they protested Cartier's raising of the cross, a ceremony by which he officially claimed the country for the king of France.

As Cartier set out in his ship for France, Donnacona, the tribal chief, accompanied by his two young sons and his brother, followed the French explorer in a canoe and continued to expostulate against the imperial gesture. Pretending to offer them an ax, Cartier lured them to the side of his ship and then seized the two sons. To all indications he took them back to France for the purpose of learning their language. In Cartier's record of this voyage, there appear several short vocabularies of the language of the Canadas, whose tribal name he gave to the New World territory he had penetrated.

In 1536 Cartier returned to the Gulf of St. Lawrence on his second expedition. Guided by the two captives he had taken to France the year before, he sailed up the river to the village where Donnacona, chief of the Canadas, lived. This village, Stadacona, was near present-day Quebec. There he learned that the Canadas were the subjects of a powerful Huron tribe who had their capital, Hochelaga, farther west on the St. Lawrence. With some of his men, he then set out from Stadacona in a small boat for the land of this ruling tribe.

After several days' journey on the river, the French explorers went ashore near the present site of Montreal. Here they were not far from the capital of the Hurons, who were the Iroquoian tribe ruling the lower St. Lawrence Valley. As they landed, a throng of Indians came from the forest-shrouded village of Hochelaga to meet them, unafraid and obviously delighted with their arrival, bearing fish and bread made from corn as gift offerings. The more than one thousand Indians gave the French a wild feast and dance of welcome that lasted well after nightfall. At dawn the friendly hosts led their strange visitors toward the village.

Emerging from the forest, the band stood suddenly on the threshold of a splendid countryside. Ahead of them, towering above the broad open fields of ripening corn, rose a steep-sided tree-covered mountain, which Cartier, deeply impressed by its beauty and grandeur, named Mount Royal (Montreal). Below in the yellowing corn fields lay Hochelaga. All that could be seen of the village was its enclosing palisade: tree trunks set in three rows sloping to the back, each piling above the other like a stepped pyramid. Only one gate gave entrance to the settlement. Over this gate, behind the protecting outer walls of the palisade, were galleries for defense, well stocked with piles of stones ready to be used as ammunition.

Led by their guides through the narrow gate, the French soon met Agouhanna, the chief ruler of the tribe. Completely paralyzed, he was carried in and placed before them on a large deer skin. He immediately gestured to them to indicate that, by touching his useless legs, the French leader might cure the paralysis. This seemed to be a magic idea; hordes of sick people poured in on Cartier—the blind, the lame, the impotent, all seeking his supposedly healing touch.

Cartier received an exceedingly warm welcome. His men in return handed out presents they had brought—knives and hatchets for the men, beads for the women, and rings for the children.

Accompanied by his sailors and Hochelagan guides, Cartier left the settlement and was led by the Indians to the summit of Mount Royal. There spread before him was a view of the land for 30 miles around, including the St. Lawrence River and the Ottawa River far off to the west.

Picking up the silver chain of the captain's whistle and the gilded copper dagger handle of one of his sailors, the Indians told the French with signs that such metals came from the Kingdom of Saguenay, a country far up the great river where the Agoianders lived. The Agoianders, they continued, were a hostile tribe, heavily armed and armored and continuously at war with all other tribes.

It was with such warm hospitality that the Indians welcomed Cartier on this voyage of 1536, his second to their land. The Canadas had shown the same eagerness to please him on his first voyage. Then Cartier had made the mistake of kidnapping the two sons of the tribal chief. When he returned to Canada after this trip, he made another mistake even more unfortunate than the first: he kidnapped nine tribesmen and their chief, Donnacona, lord of the Canadas. This act of treachery proved disastrous when the captives died in France, for their deaths were to start a blood feud which would alter the imperial fortunes of France and help to shape the destiny of the as yet unborn United States.

In 1537 the New World had become a dynamic factor in the expanding economy of Europe; the coffers of Castile were growing fat with treasure from that New World; the magnificent Spanish infantry had developed into the finest in the world, while the Spanish fleet was rapidly seizing control of the seven seas. Financed by the flood of American gold, the astute Charles V, emperor of the Holy Roman Empire, ruler of the Netherlands and parts of present-day France, king of Castile and Aragon, Naples, Sicily, Sardinia, parts of northern Africa, and the Spanish possessions in America, was still expanding his dominions.

The aim of Charles was to consolidate his far-flung empire, extend it to the new-found Philippines, and then pass it on to his blood relatives as the perpetual heritage of his family. All these circumstances were vitally affecting the few remaining independent peoples of Europe, especially the French and their king, the grandiloquent Francis I, who was Charles's most powerful and only dangerous rival.

Enviously watching his rival's growth in wealth and power, Francis was still smarting from the crushing defeat inflicted on him by Charles at Pavia, a defeat which almost destroyed the French kingdom. Only a fear-incited coalition of England, the Italian states, and the papal forces had saved Francis from becoming a helpless vassal of Spain under Charles. His kingdom was saved, but his Italian possessions were lost. So it was with fear and envy and hate that Francis watched the wealth of the New World flowing into his rival's treasury, inspiring Charles with the desire and supplying him with the means to make himself the master of Europe, the Americas, and the Indies.

The discoveries which Cartier had made appeared to open a way for France to obtain a share of the treasures of the New World. So, on Cartier's return to France, he received a royal welcome at the court of Francis I. The king listened avidly to the explorer's report of the silver and gold of Saguenay and the copper of Sagne. Inspired by the recent

Spanish discovery of Peru, Francis decided to send out an expedition to conquer and colonize Canada and secure its reported treasures. This third expedition set out from France in two sections: the first under the command of Cartier and the second under the command of Roberval, who was designated by Francis to be governor general of Canada.

On arriving at Stadacona, both expeditionary parties found the Canadas definitely hostile. Their opposition, crippling though it was, did not prevent first Cartier and then Roberval from attempting to go up the St. Lawrence past Hochelaga toward the Kingdom of Saguenay. Cartier's attempt failed, and he returned to France. Roberval, more determined, did get past the second rapids of the St. Lawrence. However, after losing many of his men, he, too, gave up and returned to France. The first French effort to colonize America had been defeated. No record of precisely what happened is extant, but the experiences of Cartier and Roberval must have become generally known. Almost forty years were to elapse before even one trading vessel sailed up the river as far as the Saguenay.[6]

The French apparently had not known about the great rapids of the St. Lawrence River. Although boats could not be rowed up the rapids, they could be towed past the hazardous points if there were no hostile attacks from the banks. From time immemorial these banks had been in the possession of the Onondagas—the largest and most powerful of the Iroquoian tribes when the French appeared.

Strongly entrenched in hilltop forts situated around and above the great sault, these Iroquoian were able to prevent anyone from going up the river.[7] They held that position for almost a hundred years after the third and last expedition of Cartier; and, as long as they held it, the French colonists could not get beyond Montreal. The only alternative was a circuitous route via the Ottawa River to Lake Huron. But this route was so difficult that few Europeans dared to traverse it; therefore little freight could be moved over it, and no European settlement could easily be established in the West. So nearly impregnable was the Iroquoian stronghold that the French never even attacked it, though its capture would have enabled them to extend their colonial empire far into the interior of the continent.

If Roberval's expedition had been successful, one French colony after another would probably have been established while French merchants pushed up the St. Lawrence and built trading posts in the Great Lakes area. Consequently French factories would have been able to expand the manufacture of trade goods for the vast inland empire. Under these circumstances France might have entered upon a career of colonial expansion giving her complete control of the continent between Florida and the Arctic Ocean, including the still-unknown and unsettled fertile lands along the Atlantic coast.

Circumstances involving settlements of other Europeans in America were propitious at that time for France to promote her plan of making the continent a New France. Spain had made no attempt to expand north of Florida. England was discouraging emigration to Newfoundland; it was not until nearly sixty years later that she sponsored her first settlement in America—the feeble, short-lived Roanoke Island colony in Raleigh's Virginia. During this period France could have developed colonies throughout the country that later became the United States. But North America became predominantly English because Cartier had lost for France her opportunity to establish the empire which Francis I had envisioned.

When the Dutch bought Manhattan Island from the Indians for a few trinkets and a jug of rum, they obtained little more than a few square miles of land. But they also acquired a reputation for fair and honest dealing with the Indians which permitted their peaceful entry into the Hudson Valley, where they established settlements far up the river and its tributaries. The English continued this policy of fair dealing with the Iroquois when they took over the Dutch colony, and their peaceful relations with the friendly Indians greatly facilitated the English penetration of America.

Had Cartier pursued a like policy and maintained friendly relations with the Canadas and the Hochelagans, they would probably have joined him in a war on their traditional enemies to the south and west. With the Canadas and the Hochelagans as allies, the French could have seized the banks of the sault from the Onondagas and freed it for navigation. A fortification at that point with friendly Indians in possession of the country to the east would have permanently opened the St. Lawrence River for navigation. Had Cartier known that after the death of Donnacona and his tribesmen in France, payments to their kinsmen would have stayed the impending hostility, he might even then have saved a fabulous empire for his king. The Iroquoians, to avoid blood feuds, required that the killing or causing of death be recompensed according to a definite scale based upon the rank of the person killed. Not familiar with the Iroquoian code, Cartier did not make the required payments. The deaths of Donnacona and the nine tribesmen had, therefore, under the code, to be avenged. For France the cost of Iroquoian vengeance proved high indeed!

20

The
Links
of
Culture

The links that tie one culture to another rarely change throughout the ages. By means of such enduring links archaeologists can trace the trading routes of the Phoenicians or the modern spread of American five-and-ten-cent wares. A variety of things—tools, weapons, metals, shards of pottery, fragments of textiles, paintings, carvings—all contribute to the anthropologist's knowledge of a culture and its probable origin. These artifacts are usually found on the direct route of an expanding society, such as village dumps, graves, and abandoned homesites. In addition, lying on each side of this route in such locations—perhaps, at the place where an ancient hunter might have traded an extra hatchet for a necklace of amber beads for his wife—will be found scattered items of the artifacts and culture of the main civilization.

Evidence of Viking influence permeates the culture of the Iroquoians in many areas in addition to the science of warfare which gave them mastery over the French colonists in the St. Lawrence Valley. Similarities are discoverable in the folk arts of the two peoples, in their housing, and in the affinity of their languages. Yet historians, believing that the Scandinavian impact on pre-Columbian

America was inconsequential, have disregarded this massive evidence of one-time mingling of the Vikings, or their descendants, and the Indians.

The Decorative Arts

Individuality in folk art expressed in decorative motifs is a common characteristic of cultures such as the ancient Scandinavian which developed in more or less isolated countries. The relative isolation of both the Northmen and the Iroquoian makes highly significant the fact that these two people used in their folk art the same two decorative motifs—and used them almost exclusively: the chevron and the interlined chevron. Wherever the Vikings went, they left an almost invariant brand of their influence—the chevron—on the art of the countries they conquered. The chevron was a characteristic motif of their primitive decorative art, most frequently used in the ornamentation of their weapons and pottery. Long centuries after the Vikings had been absorbed by their subject races, the chevron survived as one of the most commonly used motifs of the folk art of the British Isles, Scandinavia, France, Germany, and Italy in the Old World. The same motif appears on ceramic remains in the areas of America which were occupied by Iroquoians in pre-Columbian times. This chevron, common to both Norse folk art and Iroquoian art, is one of the many links connecting the Iroquoians with the Norse. No other Indian group used the chevron consistently.

The chevron is a zigzag line. Sometimes the zigzag was filled in with parallel lines, and sometimes the parallel lines were used without the zigzag lines, particularly on cruder pottery. The chevron with the parallel lines is here called the interlined chevron. In its most elaborate form, the chevron was a group of parallel zigzag lines. Known as the Norman chevron, this most highly developed form was used on columns and over the arches of many famous cathedrals. To the pagan Vikings the chevron seems to have been a religious symbol, developed from the circle and the ray, which had its origin in the worship of the sun.

Although the chevron was largely replaced in formal Norse art by the imported Dyre or formalized animal ornament, it was used for many centuries in Viking folk art long after its religious significance was forgotten. Domestic workers used it almost universally on their homemade household utensils and farm implements.

Figures somewhat similar to the chevron have occasionally been found in the decorative art of other people; but no people so frequently used the chevron with and without diagonal lines as almost exclusive motifs in their folk art as did the Norse and their primitive descendants, the Iroquoians.

It is the conclusion of a noted ethnologist, W. H. Holmes, that the early occupation of the lower Susquehanna by the Iroquoian Indians could be proved by the ceramic remains of the area if history were silent on the subject! He contrasts "the archaic rectilinear decoration of the pottery with the graceful and elaborate designs of the pottery" of the Indians of the South and the West, mentioning in particular the following characteristics of Iroquoian pottery: the lack of curved lines and curved ornaments common to other American Indian ceramics and the formal designs on Iroquoian pottery consisting of "straight, incised lines and indentations or notches." [1]

Another ethnologist, Dr. Matthew W. Stirling, director of the Bureau of American Ethnology, Smithsonian Institution, stated to me that the rim decorations consisting of the chevron design on the pottery found in northeastern North America have always been an enigma to archaeologists because they cannot be derived from the great ceramic areas of the South and the Southeast.

Canadian archaeologist W. J. Wintemberg found the chevron used so frequently as a motif of Iroquoian pottery, particularly in the extensive deposits along the St. Lawrence River, that he called it the pan-Iroquoian chevron. [2]

A figure formed by indenting three small circles so as to form a triangle occurs very frequently in Scandinavian pottery. Called the Scandinavian Triad, it was the symbol of the three principal gods of ancient Scandinavia. This symbol was often used in the Iroquois pottery found in New York State. It occurred so frequently in the St. Lawrence Valley that Wintemberg made a special note of it. [3]

The close relation of Iroquoian decorative art to early Scandinavian art has been remarked upon by W. M. Beauchamp in his *Earthenware of the New York Aborigines*: "A strong resemblance has been noted between the rude pottery of our land and the early ware of Scandinavian, Celtic, and Teutonic peoples. Not alone does this appear in general form, material and ornament, but in the remarkable feature of the dark hue within and the comparative brightness of the exterior." [4]

At Gardar in Greenland, a famous Danish archaeologist, Poul

Norlund, found steatite pot fragments decorated only by incised circles on the top and around the sides of pots.[5] Similar pots with almost identical decorations were found by an American archaeologist, Junius Bird, in the Hopedale area of Labrador, directly across Davis Strait from Gardar.[6] Since there are forests of large spruce and juniper in the Hopedale area and the pots seem to be of Norse origin, they were probably brought over from Greenland and used for cooking food for the Norse lumberjacks cutting timber. These ceramic remains (and Norse iron boat spikes found nearby) are the first direct and tangible evidence that the Hopedale area was the Greenlander's Markland.

Venturesome young Vikings in the New World who had learned handicraft from their parents probably introduced their Indian brides to these domestic decorative arts.

The Norse Wergild System and the Iroquois Equivalant

The Iroquoian code of compensation for injuries or death, as described in Thwaite's *Jesuit Relations,* was almost identical with the

Fig. 20-1. Ancient pottery decoration.

Viking code—the law governing the payment of *baug*. The ancient law of "an eye for an eye, a tooth for a tooth, and a life for a life" was almost a religion with the ancient Norse. To take revenge was not only a right; it was a sacred duty imposed upon the injured man if he lived, and, if he died, upon his kinsmen. The bloody feuds thus begun were so destructive that it became the custom to atone for injury and even for murder by payments called *baug*. This custom was called the *wergild*. The old Norwegian Gulathing Law, initiated about A.D. 950, fixed precisely the amounts of *baug* to be paid for certain injuries and for murder. These payments were assessed against the relatives of the slayer, each of whom had to pay a stipulated amount to the corresponding relative of the slain man as well as to his son or father.

Under the code, the amount of payment to be made was based on the rank of the injured or slain person. For example, if the slain man was *odal*-born (the possessor of an inherited right in the family lands), a head *baug* of ten marks or thirty-two cows was paid to the son of the slain man by the slayer. A *baug* of five marks was paid to the brother of the slain man by the brother of the slayer. Likewise, the slayer's cousin paid four marks to the slain man's cousin, and so on down through the family according to the closeness of the blood ties, to the fifteenth degree of kinship. Payment had to be made in gold or burned silver or certain chattels: horses, but not mares; sheep, but not goats; *odal* land, but not purchased land; a good ship, but not a damaged one; new cloth for a man, but not for a slain woman; male thralls, but not bondwomen. There was a stipulated price, also, for the slaying of a stranger, which varied according to his nationality.

The murderer was tried before the local council, the *Althing*. Where there were extenuating circumstances, only the *baug* was assessed. If the crime was particularly odious, the offender might be either outlawed or exiled from the district or the country for a term of years or for life. It was the duty of the relatives of the slain man to kill him if he was outlawed or if he returned to the district or country before the end of his term of banishment. If the relatives caught him before an offer of atonement was made, they killed him. In the event that he was outlawed, no atonement was paid until he died. Then the relatives of the injured or slain man collected the *baug* from his kinsmen. The Norse *wergild* system was a rather effective way of ensuring the execution of criminals.[7]

While the Iroquoian custom of punishment for crime was in general almost the same as the Viking, the method of levying the assessments on the clan or the community is not known. From Jesuit observers we learn that all the people of a country were involved in making amends for the offenses of individuals. The Jesuits reported that the assembled people decided what presents should be given to the "tribe or to the relatives of him who was slain" for the purpose of restraining the taking of vengeance.[8]

The Jesuits felt that this proceeding was very mild but more effective in repressing violence than the custom of personal punishment in France. They explained that if a man was slain, it was not the assassin who gave presents to the relatives, but the village or the nation, and that the presents given depended upon the "quality or the condition of him who was put to death." However, if the assassin met relatives of the slain man before amends for the offense were made, he was "put to death in the field. . . ."[9]

Like the Norse, the Iroquoians had a fixed scale of atonements graduated in terms of the status of the person slain. Forty presents were demanded for the slaying of a Huron woman by a Huron man—ten more presents than for the slaying of a Huron man. The explanation given for the greater amends for the death of a woman was that women cannot easily defend themselves and their lives are worth more because they people the country. To prevent wars between nations and to preserve trade, even more amends were exacted for the slaying of a stranger.[10]

Among the Iroquoian tribes, the individual in tribal law did not exist outside the *obwachira,* the uterine kin, in which he was born. A blood feud always involved groups of persons, the *obwachira,* not individuals. The amount of compensation for slaying a person was determined by the law of atonement, thus reducing the impulse for excessive revenge.[11]

The Longhouse

Instead of a horde of improvident, unorganized Indians, Cartier found at Hochelaga a highly organized society; orderly, well-kept plantations and granaries; and three-story fortifications to protect the giant communal houses of the village from outside enemies. Nowhere in his native France, except in its castles and palaces, were there dwellings comparable in size to those of the Huron Indians in Hochelaga—half a hundred great two-story houses set row on row around a large central square.[12]

Communal dwellings have been in existence since primitive families first banded together for mutual protection in permanent buildings occupied jointly by related families. Through the ages these houses have usually been circular; if they were rectangular, their width was only slightly less than their length.

The early Scandinavians up to the twelfth century[13] and the Iroquois throughout colonial history[14] lived in dwellings which were different from all other communal houses. They were long, narrow, one-room, one-story buildings with passageways and long central hearths running lengthwise through the building. The only lighting came from the fire on the hearths and through openings left in the roof to permit smoke to escape. There were no windows. A single door at each end usually opened onto a porch where the communal stores were kept.[15] Platforms built along each side of the passageway provided seats during the day and sleeping quarters at night in all the longhouses. Space under the platforms was used for storage; weapons and clothes were hung on the side walls or suspended from the roof timbers.[16] Varying in length from 50 to 300 feet, the early houses were seldom over 20 feet wide.[17]

In the twelfth century the Scandinavians modernized their homes by subdividing the interior. Now wider, the long central halls had bays along the side which were cut up into separate rooms for the individual families, with doors opening into the hall. Also higher, these new dwellings had lofts over the entrance doors and occasionally a tower for storage, the *skemma*. Twice as wide as the older type, this new-type house with windows and separate rooms was generally used in Scandinavia by A.D. 1200.[18]

None of these changes was ever adopted by the Iroquois. Their longhouses were always the narrow one-room, one-story longhouses.[19] On the other hand, nearly all the Wyandot longhouses were about as wide as the new-type houses of the Scandinavians.[20] Some inland Huron houses had windows high up on the sides for lighting only.[21] Others had separate rooms with doors.[22] Some houses of the Neutrals (a Huron tribe) had towers like the Scandinavian *skemma;*[23] and at Hochelaga Cartier found dwellings of the Hurons that were similar to the thirteenth-century Icelandic house described by G. W. Dasent, who noted that, inside, these houses were divided into a long narrow center and two much lower side aisles. In the center, which was supported by rows of pillars, were long hearths and openings in the timber roofs for the smoke from hearth fires to escape. Doors opened into the sleeping quarters in the low side aisles. Above some halls, there were more sleeping chambers or lofts.[24] Cartier's description of the houses at Hochelaga differs only in minor details from Dasent's description of these Norse homes in Iceland. Cartier found that there were about fifty houses in Hochelaga, each about "fifty paces wide, all made of timbers and covered with great pieces of bark and strips of timber as broad as tables, well and carefully tied together." He describes the interior of the houses as having many chambers and a large space in the center with a ground floor, where fires were built and people gathered. Lofts above provided storage for corn, a most important staple in the nourishment of the residents.[25]

All longhouses in America and Scandinavia were built with wood frames and covered with bark, except in those parts of Scandinavia, Greenland, and Iceland where timber was scarce.[26] There the side walls were built of stone or stone and turf, and the roofs were covered with sod or thatched with straw or grass. Many of the later longhouses, both in America and in Scandinavia, had lofts for storage.[27]

The existence in Viking times of an unbroken line of the older, windowless, one-room longhouses extending from Sweden to Greenland was established by Scandinavian archaeologists. Explorers and missionaries have described a continuous line of the same type of longhouse in use by Iroquois and related tribes.

The existence of these early-type longhouses in these locations indicates a movement of Scandinavians into the country south of the St. Lawrence River prior to A.D. 1200. They apparently merged with the natives, and their descendants, the Iroquois and related tribes, continued to use the old Norse *skala* as late as 1800.[28]

Sometime after A.D. 1200 a second wave of Scandinavians came up the St. Lawrence. Unable to pass the Iroquois who were then controlling the head of the river, they detoured into Canada via the Ottawa River. There Scandinavians merged with the natives to form the Huron and other Wyandot tribes whose descendants continued to use the more modern-type longhouse introduced by this later wave of Scandinavians.[29] Evidence of this second immigration is in the existence of a continuous line of the newer-type longhouse or *skala* from the Baltic Sea to Lake Huron. My discovery of these later-type longhouse sites in Newfoundland filled in the gap in this line from Greenland to the American continent.

Norse Loan Words in Iroquoian Vocabularies

Equally important as connecting links between cultures are loan words in a language. The terms borrowed from a foreign language indicate a contact, direct or indirect, at some time with the people who spoke that language. These loan words indicate also quite clearly the nature and the extent of the intercultural exchange. In the Iroquoian language there are many Viking words of importance which tell the linguist that there was a close and longtime contact of the two peoples.

It was in Cartier's vocabularies of the Canada language that I found the first link connecting the Iroquoians with the Norse. A comparison of the Canada vocabularies with the earliest Norse vocabulary which I could find disclosed many Canada words derived directly from the Scandinavian. Some of these loan words are listed below, with the identifying root *italicized*.

English	Old Norse	Canada
cape	*kápa*	*caba*ta
eight	*átta*	*adda*give
fire	gni*sta*	az*ista*
	gne*isti*	as*ista*
forehead	*enni*	hetgu*eni* or
		etg*eny*
go	sin*na*	qua*signo*
ice	*isa*	can*isa* (snow)
testicle	e*ista*	xi*sta*

Soon thereafter I found in the languages of other Iroquoian tribes a number of words with roots identifying them as loans from the Old Norse language. Some of these words are listed below.

English	Old Norse	Iroquoian	Tribe
day	*dagr*	kiven*dagi*	Oneida
fat	*smjörugr*	*ior*esen	Mohawk
juniper	*einir*	an*ein*ta	Huron
near	*naerri*	*niyarea*	Mohawk
only	*einga*	ku*engwa*	Onondaga
seed	*auki*	*ook*uhnuh	Mohawk
slow	*seinn*	*saien*	Mohawk
snake	*nadr*	i'*nad*du	Cherokee

The detection of loan words by comparison of vocabularies is an accepted, time-tested, accurate method of gauging the nature and extent of contacts between peoples. A leading authority on the English language, Otto Jespersen, states:

> It is possible to read whole chapters of the cultural history of the English nation out of successive strata of important loan words. Before the migration from the continent, came *mint, manger, pound, inch, wine, dish, cook, kitchen.* Then came words connected with the Christian religion, *pope, bishop, nun, shrine.* Then we have Scandinavian words, *law, by-law, thrall, crave, egg, skirt,* etc. The Norman French words show the conquerors as the refined and ruling upper class, *crown, reign, duke, court, judge, jury, beauty, flower, dinner.* And finally we have learned words from the classical tongues after the revival of learning, *intellect, abstract, educate, biology,* and innumerable others. In the same way we are able to draw inferences from loan words with regard to the nature of prehistoric contacts between various races, e.g., Scandinavian and Baltic words in Finnic.[30]

Finding a sufficiently close resemblance between these few words of the Iroquoians and words with equivalent meaning of the early Norse to justify my continuing along this path, I decided to study comparative language factors on an exhaustive scale. The first step was to compile short vocabularies of approximately forty words for the various Indian tribes in the northeastern section of North America: the Iroquois, the Eskimo, the Algonquin, and the Micmac. Then equivalent vocabularies were assembled for all the European peoples who reportedly reached America before Columbus: the Scandinavians, the Irish, the Britons, and the Basques. Upon discovering that the only language that showed a direct connection to the Iroquoian was the Scandinavian, I compiled much larger vocabularies of the two languages.

As research progressed into the oldest Scandinavian language, the ancient Icelandic, it revealed more and more words resembling those of the Iroquois. Inasmuch as there was a possibility that many Iroquoian words similar to the Icelandic might have been obtained through English contacts, it was essential to explore all the vocabularies of the oldest Iroquoian languages made by French missionaries long before the Iroquoians had come in contact with the English. Iroquoian words in the vocabularies later recorded by the English appeared also in these vocabularies compiled by French missionaries.

Many Viking words showed up in Iroquoian vocabularies. Next arose this question: Are many of these Viking words in other Indian languages? In order to determine a satisfactory answer, equivalent vocabularies of the other Indian languages of northeastern America were compiled. With few exceptions, the Viking words appeared only in the Iroquoian languages.

Confident that the prehistoric Indians and the Vikings had indeed met and mingled, I assembled complete comparative vocabularies of all Iroquoian words available either in manuscripts or published works in America and in Europe. My next move was to live with the Indians on their reservations and study their languages. With the help of an eighty-six-year-old Mohawk Indian who had married a Tuscarora, I collected vocabularies of the Iroquoian dialects as they are spoken today. Upon completion of my work, I had assembled vocabularies of the Iroquoian languages from the time of Cartier in 1535 down to 1941.

The final step was to determine the origin of the Iroquoians, if possible, by comparing their languages with the languages of other peoples of their time and earlier. With fifteen hundred English words as a basis, every known Iroquoian equivalent of these words was listed and, in addition, a fair sample of equivalent words in the ancient languages of northern Europe, Siberia, the islands of the Pacific, and in the important Indian languages of North, Central, and South America. This assembly of nearly six hundred comparative vocabularies revealed that a significant percentage of the Iroquoian words were derived directly or indirectly from the Scandinavian language!

The Iroquoian language is similar to the old Norse language in several general details. A terminal *a* indicates plural in both the Norse and the Huron languages. The suffix *nnie* used to indicate plurality by the Onondaga tribe resembles the suffix *ini* used by the Norse to indicate plurality. Both the Iroquois and the Norse used *a* to denote nationality: *a ganniege* (a Mohawk) and *a Gronlandia* (a Greenlander).

A single root such as *ok, auk, auka,* and its derivatives had in both languages the same five uses: as a conjunction, *and;* as an adversative, *but;* in comparison, *as;* as an adverb of time, *when;* and as an adverb of repetition, *also.*

Since the beginning of their recorded history, the Iroquoian tribes have changed their religion many times. There is evidence in their vocabulary that their primitive religion was similar to the old Norse religion. *Niord,* the name of the Norse god for seafarers, appears as

Nioh, Neeyooh, and *Niyoh* in all Iroquoian dialects as the name for God. Likewise, *loki,* the Norse name for the devil, appears as *loki* in the Huron dialect and as *okee* or *oki* in the Tuscarora and other Iroquoian dialects.

A glance at the comparative vocabularies in Appendix C shows the sort of relationship I found between the languages of the Iroquoians and the Norse. The conclusion implicit in that comparison of selected words in the Norse and the Iroquoian languages is that the two people were in contact for a long time. Upon being confronted with this evidence, philologists countered with the argument that the two peoples could not be related because of the dissimilarities in their grammar. These same scholars, however, would not disown on similar grounds the conclusion of linguistic experts that the Canadas were Iroquoian because of the many Iroquoian loan words in their vocabulary!

As to the objections cited above, Viking invaders always quickly merged into the people whom they conquered, adopting the native language without changing materially its structure or inflections. History gives many illustrations of this circumstance, which should be taken into account in properly gauging the extent of a Viking invasion and conquests of a country by the changes in the language. A plausible explanation may be that the native language remained the language spoken in the home because the mother was a native, that the children learned the mother's language, to which they added a few words from the language of the father, who in the first generation was likely to be an invader.

Speaking the Danish language, for instance, the Vikings conquered the northernmost province of France early in the tenth century. Then, speaking French (with the exception of a few Scandinavian words relating to the sea),[31] as Normans they conquered England, southern Italy, and Sicily. However, England, Italy, and Sicily did not become Norman-speaking lands. Although the rule of the Normans continued in those countries for several centuries, the language they brought with them did not survive.[32] The Norman conquest did not cause a break or marked change in the development of the English language; apart from its vocabulary, English might have developed to its present form even if the conquest had not occurred. And in the Mediterranean countries the Norman language disappeared without a trace.

Like the Scandinavians, many other people have conquered and ruled alien lands for centuries and then disappeared, leaving the language of their subject peoples essentially unchanged. In Italy, for example, the Normans were preceded by the invading Lombards and the Greeks. Nevertheless, though the Lombards ruled in the North for two hundred years and the Greeks lived in the South for one thousand years, the only linguistic traces of their occupation are a few Germanic words in Italian in the North and some Greek words in the South.

A similar effect of foreign invasion on the language of a conquered people is seen in the Spanish conquest of the Mayans. Here also the only change in the native language was the addition to it of certain loan words, although the native ruling class had been replaced by a new ruling class of an alien race.[33] In North America, as in Maya, the language of the invaders finally disappeared, except for some loan words.

The basic structure—the grammar, prefixes, and suffixes—of the Iroquoian language are unquestionably derived from the language of the natives with whom the Norse merged. The marked resemblance of Iroquoian grammar to the Cherokee and Sioux indicates that the merger was mostly with tribes related to one or the other.

To determine by linguistic analysis the extent of the Norse infiltration into America, it is therefore necessary to examine the Viking loan words found in the Iroquoian language. Significantly, these words provide an adequate basis for challenging previously accepted dogmas of American history.

The trail which the Vikings traveled from their homeland in the Arctic led across Scandinavia and the British Isles, through the fogs of the northern seas to the western shores of the North Atlantic, on to Newfoundland, and beyond to the places of their final settlement in North America.

There they marked their wares with the Nordic chevron and the Scandinavian Triad, sign of the gods of ancient Scandinavia.[34] There they built longhouses and hilltop forts, ringing them about with stone and earthen walls, just as their ancestors had done in far-off Europe. There they buried their dead in stone-lined graves in stone and wooden tombs and covered them with earthen mounds, also in the manner of their ancestors; and there their descendants—the Iroquois—fought and won battles that altered the course of history.

21

The Kensington Rune Stone

The ancient Scandinavians made history, but they did not write it. Preoccupied with pirate raiding and conquering of distant lands, they did not have much time or inclination for the business of writing about their exploits. They did manage, however, to concoct a crude alphabet, partly from Greek letters. The symbols of this alphabet—called runes—appear mainly in brief records carved by the Vikings in stone or metal. For written accounts of their raids and conquests, historians must turn to the literature of the many countries which they conquered. But in their messages carved in runes and in their maps, sailing charts, and sagas, they have left fragments of their history which, properly fitted together, constitute a special kind of historical literature.

Warriors and explorers frequently marked the farthest point which they were able to reach by an appropriate inscription in runic letters on stone. Castaways and shipwrecked sailors, finding themselves faced with inevitable death, also left records of their end in runic inscriptions.

The only mementos of the farthest known Viking voyages are three runic inscriptions. One of these inscriptions turned up in the Old

World, and two in the New World. A runic message cut on a marble lion found facing the harbor of Athens, Greece, tells about the capture of Athens by the Vikings and their expedition into Armenia; and another inscription, on a stone found in Baffin Bay, records a Scandinavian voyage to a point almost 500 miles north of the Arctic Circle.

The longest of these three runic messages was carved on a stone which was dug up from under the roots of a tree on a farm near Kensington, Minnesota, in 1898. This stone marks the place where thirty Scandinavian explorers came to the end of their expedition in A.D. 1362. Marooned on an island in a lake located about 200 miles southwest of Duluth and surrounded by savages who had already slain ten of their companions, these hapless men left a message cut in runes on stone while they awaited death. Translated, their message reads:

> Eight Goths and 22 Norwegians on a journey from Vinland through the West. We had camp by 2 skerries [rocky islands] one day's journey north from this stone. We were out and fished all day. After we came *home* found 10 men red with blood and dead. A V M [Ave Maria] save us from peril. Have 10 of our party by the sea to look after our ships and 14 days journey from this island. Year 1362.

The finding of this stone by a farmer was well documented; the age of the stone and the character of the runic letters engraved on it were attested by competent authorities. It is almost impossible to forge a lengthy runic inscription on a dated stone without detection; for the runic alphabet was constantly changing, the forms of the runes varying in different countries and centuries. Despite all these circumstances, archaeologists refused for half a century to accept the Kensington stone as a genuine relic. One authority on Icelandic history, as late as 1936, dismissed it with the comment that "it is perfectly clear that the inscription is a modern forgery." [1]

The first mishap in examination of the stone was in dating it several centuries too early. Unable to translate the runic number symbols, experts assumed that, if the stone were genuine, only Scandinavians from the Greenland colonies who had gone on into the Lake Superior region by boat could have inscribed it. That assumption placed the date at some time during the eleventh or twelfth century. It was then generally agreed that, this being true, the inscription was an obvious fraud, easily detected.

During the eleventh or twelfth century, moreover, Swedes and Norwegians would not have been together on an expedition, because they were then enemies. The curious mixture of languages used in the inscription was believed to be, in itself, a blunder which showed up the unsuccessful hoax. Pointed out, also, were the facts that the stone was not found on an island and there is no lake within many miles of its resting place. Strongly weighing against the stone was the undisputed belief, almost a religion, that no white men had set foot in the interior of America before Columbus's discovery.

Completely discredited, the stone was discarded and sent back to the farm where it had been found. For many years it lay there in the farmyard, fortunately face downward. But it was not without persistent defenders. One of the most untiring—Hjalmar Holand—believed that the runic inscription was an important historical record, and he persisted in his effort to establish its authenticity. One by one, he proved false the suppositions which had sent the stone back to its finder.

First, the date was correctly determined to be A.D. 1362, following the discovery of the meaning of the runic characters for numbers. It was then conceded that a joint voyage of Swedes and Norwegians was not improbable at that time because Norway and Sweden were then united under one king. The Latin letters A V M in the inscription were explained by the fact that, by the fourteenth century, Latin letters were commonly used to reinforce Scandinavian runes. Finally, it seemed plausible that the place where the stone was found might, in 1362, have been on an island in a lake now dried up; for dried-up beds of former lakes between Kensington and Duluth indicate that there were more lakes in the area in the past.

After disposing of all evidence of forgery, Holand was confronted with the questions of skeptical experts and an unimpressed public. "How," these incredulous critics asked, "could Scandinavians have been in Minnesota 130 years before America was discovered? How did they get there, and what were they doing?" History gave Holand no answer to these questions, nor did any expert offer any. But Holand soon thought he had one, based, though it was, on the flimsiest of evidence: a recorded decree of King Magnus around 1350 authorizing one Paul Knutson to organize an expedition from the king's bodyguard to Greenland on the royal ship, the *Knaaren,* to bring the Greenlanders back to Christianity. The Goths (Swedes) and Norse who met disaster in Minnesota, so he believed, were members of this Knutson expedition who had gone west in search of the departed Greenland colonists. They had traveled in rowboats, so he figured, from Hudson Bay to Minnesota.

Pat though this explanation seemed, it lacked corroboration in records and circumstances. King Magnus had issued the decree, but he later evidently abandoned the plan for the expedition. For there is no other reference to Knutson or the expedition in the records of either Norway or Greenland.

Holand's ingenious story about Paul Knutson failed to explain the Kensington stone. It failed not so much because of disbelief in the Paul Knutson expedition, but because of the incredibility of the idea that thirty men had rowed two boats from Hudson Bay up the rapid Nelson River and the crooked Red River to central Minnesota in thirteen days. To have done so, they would have had to make four times the highest speed of the average Norse rowing boats of that day.

With its inscription cleared of forgery charges but with the explanation for its presence in mid-America invalidated, the stone remained on display in Alexandria, Minnesota—an enigma for another quarter of a century. And then, suddenly, in March, 1948, it was taken to Washington, placed on display in the Smithsonian Institution, and acclaimed by the director of the Bureau of American Ethnology as "probably the most important archeological object yet found in America." [2] The feeble testimony of the old Knutson story was hesitantly resurrected to answer the persistent questions: How did Scandinavians get to the mid-continent of America in 1362? What were they doing there?

But in 1948 the Knutson fable seemed more flimsy than ever. By then the exclusively-Indian-pre-Columbian-America theory needed substantial protection from rapidly accumulating evidence that there were Scandinavians—great numbers of them—in prehistoric America.

By 1362 Vinland appears to have included, in addition to Newfoundland, the St. Lawrence Valley, the copper-mining areas of the Great Lakes region, and the iron-smelting regions of the Ohio Valley. The sending of a small group from settlements anywhere in this greater Vinland to explore the West was not only possible; it was probable. From the message on the stone, it would seem that the expedition was traveling "from Vinland through the West" without any fixed objective, stopping to hunt and fish along the way. The starting point of such an expedition may have been a mining settlement on the Keewenaw Peninsula or on Isle Royale in Lake Superior; their aim may have been to find copper or bog iron ore.

The carver of the Kensington stone was probably one of the eight Swedes from Gotland, for he used the Swedish *resa* (journey) instead of the Norwegian *raisa*. The inscription was written in the pointed

Gothic runes which, widely reinforced by Latin letters, were used by cultured laymen in all Scandinavia during the Middle Ages. The use of the pointed Gothic runes and the Swedish *resa* confirms the runic message that there were Goths in the marooned party.

The ill-fated party would have done well to traverse 15 miles in an average day's journey on foot or by boat between Duluth and Kensington. At that time the average day's journey of Greenlanders in a six- or eight-oared boat at sea was about 20 miles. But rowing up narrow, winding streams or against the currents of the wider rivers of northern Minnesota, the voyagers would hardly have made over 15 miles per day. Thirteen days' journey inland from the sea where they had left their ships, they had halted and built camp near one of the small lakes north of the place where the stone was found. Undoubtedly the savages who had killed the ten guards left at camp while they had gone on a fishing trip had looted the camp and carried away all the supplies. The survivors would have had left only their fishing gear and the weapons which they had taken on their fishing trip.

Cut off as they attempted to flee south, they had been forced to take refuge on an island in a lake which has since dried up. Here, less than 20 miles from their abandoned camp and 200 miles from their ships, they were trapped in a trackless wilderness, surrounded by hostile savages. Knowing that there was no chance of escape or rescue and that their doom was certain, they carved a message in runes on a convenient stone as a record of their fate—an old custom of Viking expeditions. Near the summit of the divide between the Mississippi River and the Red River, there is even now a lake which may have been the location of their camp: Lake Christian, approximately thirteen days' journey southwest of Lake Superior and one day's journey north of the place where the stone was found.

Rune stones have been found scattered along the coasts of New England and Nova Scotia in various places: Hampton, Hampton Falls, Popham Beach, Sebes, Cheney, Yarmouth, and Aptuxent Trading Post. None of these stones has, as yet, received scientific recognition. In 1948, I found a rune stone marking a Scandinavian-type grave in a mound near the stone-walled fortress of Spruce Hill, Ohio. Nearby was a Scandinavian-type iron-smelting furnace. This stone and many of those mentioned above must now, because of the other evidence showing the one-time presence of the Scandinavians, be accepted as connecting links in the chain of evidence proving the prehistoric infiltration of Scandinavians into America.

22

The Zeno Map *of the* North

In 1558, a book describing the travels to the north two centuries earlier of two wealthy Venetians, Antonio and Nicolo Zeno, was published in Venice. This book is important to cartographers and historians because it introduced to the world an original copy of a map of the North Atlantic and Arctic areas which has been a subject of controversy for more than four hundred years. Known as the Zeno Map of the North, it has been praised as an authentic document by several eminent explorers and denounced as a fraud by ethnologists and archaeologists in general. (See Fig. 22-1.)

The author of the 1558 book was a descendant of the Zeno brothers, another Nicolo Zeno. He compiled the account of his ancestors' travels from letters preserved in the family archives, where he also found the map.

According to the published story, in 1380 the brothers set sail from Venice for the north in a ship of their own. Soon thereafter, Antonio died on an island south of Iceland named Friesland. The surviving brother, Nicolo, continued north to "Engroeneland." In his letters to his family, Nicolo described the marvels of Greenland, including a monastery and a church he visited there. He said that the monastery

Fig. 22-1. The Zeno map of the North.

and the church, which was dedicated to St. Thomas, were close to a mountain "which cast out fire like Vesuvius and Etna."

A hot spring near the monastery, he reported, warmed the buildings, the church, and the sleeping quarters of the friars. It even heated the water in the kitchen to the boiling point and the copper cooking pots sufficiently for baking bread "as in a well-heated oven." The same hot springs, Zeno explained, preserved covered gardens near the monastery from winter snow and freezing temperatures. In these gardens, according to him, the friars grew flowers, fruits, and herbs just as they are grown in season in temperate climates, and "the rough and wild people of these countries, seeing these supernatural effects, consider the friars as gods."

Zeno's sensational account of Greenland was accepted as fact when it was published in 1558, in the afterglow of the dazzling Age of Discovery. In time, however, the story was attacked by scholars as being incredible, and finally it fell into general disrepute. During four centuries, no sailor or cartographer could find such an island as Friesland, which was named in the story as the place where Antonio died and shown on the map south of Greenland. Their failure to do so was the principal factor in the discrediting of both the story and the map.

When I first came upon the Zeno map in my research, I surmised that it was probably an authentic map despite its reputation as a phony. It could be, I thought, an assembly of several charts of different contiguous areas, like many long-rejected maps that I had found to be accurate (see Chapter 16). Having a special interest in Greenland because of my work on several maps of that island, I chose the portion of the map showing Greenland for careful examination, with the hope of deciphering it.

The Greenland depicted differs radically from the Greenland known to the modern world. The land surface is shown free of ice, almost covered by mountains, crossed by open rivers, and divided into *three* islands! A fiord marked *Ollum Lengri* on a version of the map and a flat surface, which I concluded was a strait, extending westward between the mountains, divide the land which, now hidden by ice, we know as Greenland, a single island.

My belief that the map might be authentic was not shaken by the fact that it shows such an unusual topography for Greenland. For, as I have explained, the topography of both Greenland and Iceland has been drastically altered since the Middle Ages by erupting volcanoes, earthquakes, and icecaps. Consequently, an accurate ancient map would show both countries with contours unlike their modern contours.

So, assuming that the map was an ancient Norse sailing chart, I platted it on a polar projection. It then became obvious that the original map had been platted on a portolano projection. Drawing grids on a copy of the Greenland section of the map, I found even more than I had dared to hope I would find: all the points were platted with remarkable accuracy when compared to the same points on the latest U.S. Army maps! I was then certain that the rejected Zeno map was an accurate map of Greenland before it was covered by its present sheet of ice more than a mile thick.

The consonance of the points on the map with corresponding points on a modern map means that the original compilers of the Zeno map knew the shape of the earth, the science of computing longitudes and latitudes, the exact comparative longitudes and latitudes of many points in the North Atlantic, and that they had the sophisticated instruments for using this science. At the time of the Zeno brothers (1380), the computation of longitudes was an unknown science. Consequently, they could not have drawn the original map bearing their name. As I have explained in Chapter 16, until the invention of the practical chronometer, about A.D. 1750, navigators were not able to find longitude by simple calculation. Consequently, European maps and charts drawn prior to the eighteenth century were very inaccurate. What culture prior to 1750 could have produced an accurate map of Greenland—a map showing the subglacial topography of the country?

It came to my mind that Nicolo, the surviving brother, may have picked the map up in Greenland and sent it to Venice. It seemed probable that this map in its original form had been preserved since ancient times in Greenland, possibly in the monastery that Nicolo Zeno had visited, after the ancient civilization which made it had been destroyed or driven from its home. Of one thing I was certain: this accurate map of the North Atlantic was the product of a very remote, very advanced civilization.

If Zeno did not acquire the map in Greenland, he may have obtained it from Bishop Henry of Garda, the last resident bishop of Greenland, after Henry moved to the Faroes in 1394. It is known that Bishop Henry took with him to the Faroes many old documents that had been preserved in Greenland. The date of Zeno's return from his voyage to the North Atlantic was 1402.

In addition to Greenland, the Zeno map shows the coasts of the Scandinavian countries, Germany, Scotland, and the outlines of several islands, including the unknown Friesland and a large island marked *Islanda*. I have concluded that Islanda is not Iceland, as was commonly thought, but the vanished Gunnbiorn's Skerries, the Viking landmark on the route between Iceland and Greenland mentioned in the sagas. (See Chapter 17 for an account of the existence and the disappearance of Gunnbiorn's Skerries.)

I have concluded also that the small island on the map marked *Icaria* is, in fact, a map of Iceland, outlined as it was in a remote age before some of its coastal areas were submerged in the waters of the sea. It is shown on the Zeno map both out of scale and out of place, but in its contours it closely resembles the Iceland shown on several other ancient maps.

Like innumerable scholars through centuries, I have been unable to identify the island marked *Friesland*. It is certainly not unreasonable to suggest that in the time of the Zeno brothers (1380), there was such an island, and that since then it has been submerged in the waters of the sea, as portions of Iceland have been, or that it may be concealed by the Greenland ice sheet. The same fate may have befallen several other small islands shown on the Zeno map that are not in their respective locations there today.

In my study of ancient maps it became obvious that scholars studying them through centuries added grids, names, and other features to the original maps, often confusing later scholars. Fictitious place names are scattered around on the Zeno map, which research reveals were taken from an old Danish nursery rhyme. They were probably added to the original map by the Danish geographer Cladius

Clavus. Could some, or all, of the small islands on the Zeno map not yet identified have been added to the original map in the same way?

Sooner than I would have thought possible, confirmation of my analysis of the map (at least the portion showing Greenland) came from an authority in the science of determining subglacial topography by seismic soundings. The authority was Paul-Emile Victor, whose French Polar Expeditions explored Greenland from 1948 to 1951. An Associated Press news dispatch announced on October 26, 1951, months after I had published my analysis of the map, the following discovery of the Victor expedition: "A French expedition reported this week that Greenland is really three islands bridged by an ocean. . . ." In a letter to me, dated October 22, 1953, Victor said: "The analysis of our soundings confirms the preliminary announcement that Greenland is really three islands."

Under Victor's leadership, the French Polar Expeditions had charted the topography of Greenland—its mountains, flat lands, and valleys—by setting off charges of dynamite on the surface of the ice sheet and recording the time it took the waves generated by the charge to pass down to a reflecting material and back. The time for passage of the waves down and back told them what material was down there. The process is somewhat similar to determining the distance between two hills by timing an echo.

Victor's soundings revealed a passage westward across Greenland corresponding to the flat area between the mountains which I had pointed out as a strait dividing the land. They also showed the presence of a large fiord in a location corresponding to the location on one version of the Zeno map of a fiord marked *Ollum Lengri-Lengri,* longest of all.

In confirming my analysis of the Greenland portion of the Zeno map, Victor accomplished something of magnitude for cartographers, historians, and scholars in general: he restored to the Zeno map its original reputation for authenticity. In consequence, a multitude of baffling questions arise regarding the identity of the cartographers who drew the original map of the North Atlantic as it was untold centuries ago, maybe even before the Ice Age. Coming almost as an anticlimax to Victor's confirmation of the accuracy of the Zeno map, a later development strengthened this confirmation. When I asked Victor to explain the presence of a single mountain in the flat area crossing Greenland, he showed me his soundings, which proved the "mountain" to be an island!

23

My "Discovery" *of the* Piri Re'is Map

I first saw the Piri Re'is map—a reproduction of the surviving section—in mid-November, 1953, at the Hydrographic Office of the U.S. Navy. Head engineer Medina handed it to me with the comment that it was a very old map that geographers and cartographers had been trying for nearly twenty-five years to decipher. "Perhaps," he suggested, "with your knowledge of ancient sailing charts and maps, you can do something with it." It was all that was left, he explained, of a long-lost map of the world compiled in 1513 by Piri Re'is, a Turkish admiral. This copy of the surviving section, he added, was sent to the Hydrographic Office very recently as a gift from a Turkish naval officer.

Stealing a glance at the map in my hand while Medina was briefing me on its history,[1] I saw something on it that startled me: the hump of Africa and the eastern portion of South America positioned correctly in relation to each other. Such accuracy in cartography requires knowledge of geography and the science of longitude as well as sophisticated navigational instruments supposedly not available to any cartographers in the world as early as 1513. Whoever drew this map, I remember thinking, knew much more about the world—its size

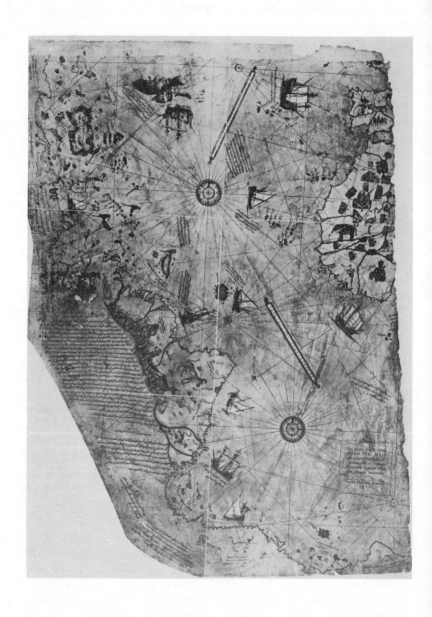

Fig. 23-1. The Piri Re'is map.

and shape and the size and shape and location of its land masses—than was known, according to historians, at that time or in any age before, including antiquity.

To me, however, the most puzzling feature of the map was its longitudinal accuracy, for I knew that experts in the science of navigation always maintained that there was no instrument for determining longitude until the chronometer was introduced in the eighteenth century, 250 years after Piri Re'is compiled his map.

Fascinated by the apparent contradictions posed by the map, I promised head engineer Medina that I would "see what I could do with it."

Very soon thereafter, I learned that the tattered map fragment has a recorded historical background going as far back as 1513, when Piri Re'is compiled his map of the world and included this section as a map of the Western world. Nobody seems to know what happened to the complete map, but it is known that the original fragment was found in 1929 in the Topkapi Palace Library, now a museum, in Istanbul by the director of Turkish National Museums.

The original fragment is painted in vivid colors on gazelle hide, dated in the Moslem year 919 (A.D. 1513) and signed by Piri Ibn Haji Mehmed, who is known also as Piri Re'is. Profusely illustrated, it follows the ancient custom of supplying information on areas depicted and warning signals for pilots to protect them and their companions from the treacherous hazards of the sea. It shows jagged coastlines, ships in the seas and along coasts, rocky places shaded in black, shallow waters marked by red dots and reefs pointed out by a cross, mountains in relief, and rivers traced by heavy lines. (See reproduction of the map on the facing page.)

The finding of this fragment with torn edges in 1929 caused great excitement worldwide, among such specialists as cartographers, geographers, and historians and also in the circles of general scholarly research. This excitement was so notable that it spilled over on the public, whose interest was engaged by the report that a map of the Western world drawn by Columbus had been found and, furthermore, that the map showed continents in correct longitudes centuries before the science of computing longitude was supposedly known!

In hundreds of lines of notes in Arabic script crowded into the margin of the map, Piri Re'is describes in the Turkish language areas depicted, relates dramatic legends concerning them, and names the sources he used in compiling his "map of the inhabited quarter of the world," saying in part:

> . . . The coasts and island on this map are taken from Colombo's
> map. . . . From about twenty charts and Mappae Mundi . . .
> charts drawn in the days of Alexander . . . which show the inhab-
> ited quarter of the world. . . . The Arabs name these charts Jaferiye
> . . . from eight Jaferiyes . . . and one Arab map . . . and from
> maps just drawn by four Portuguese . . . geometrically drawn, and
> also from a map drawn by Colombo in the western region I have ex-
> tracted it. By placing all these together on a common scale, I pro-
> duced the present map. . . . correct and reliable for the Seven Seas
> . . . considered correct and reliable by seamen.

The probability that at one time there was a world map compiled
by Piri Re'is had been known to scholars in Turkey and in European
centers of learning for a very long time, but it had been assumed that
the map had been lost. In the great libraries of Istanbul and European
cities, scholars had undoubtedly read a celebrated book titled *Bahriye,*
written by Piri Re'is in 1521, in which the author describes his compi-
lation of two world maps.

Partly biographical, *Bahriye* is a guidebook on navigation. It
deals with the science of navigation and describes currents, islands,
ports, and countries along the Aegean and Mediterranean shores. One
of the more than two hundred maps in the book is one drawn by
Columbus. In *Bahriye* and in a marginal note on the surviving fragment of the map found in 1929, Piri Re'is tells a dramatic story of ob-
taining the Columbus map from a Spaniard who was a family slave
and, before his capture by an uncle of Piri Re'is, was one of Columbus's sailors.

In the 1930s, at the time of excitement over the finding of the surviving section of the map, several studies of this section, sponsored by
top government officials, were published in Turkey and in the United
States. These studies and other scholarly analyses of the map failed,
however, to resolve the contradictions posed by it, or even to produce
evidence that it was, in fact, a map drawn by Columbus. So enthusiasm over "the Columbus map" and its mysteries died down. During
the next fifteen years or so, the once eagerly sought reproductions in
the libraries around the world were infrequently examined. Finally, the
public apparently forgot about the map, and nothing more was heard
about it.

My fascination with the map mounted when I saw on it some intimate details such as llamas in South America, ostriches and elephants
in Africa, and birds on islands, as well as South American rivers and
coastlines not yet explored or charted by 1513. Supposedly, informa-

tion concerning such details was not known to the outside world as early as 1513.

Crossing the map are many lines, not the usual grid of perpendicular lines, but radial lines from five centers in the Atlantic Ocean. Assuming that the map was a combination of several portolano charts of local areas, possibly not all drawn on the same scale and even imperfectly joined, I expected to run into some difficulty in identifying parts of it, and I did. Spain and a bit of France above Africa at the right were recognizable. But a variety of less distinctly outlined land masses above South America at the left were at first not identifiable. I soon concluded, however, that they could be the eastern shore of the United States, the Caribbean Islands, Greenland, and Iceland.

At first glance, the eastern coast of South America, as shown, looked very familiar, but at the southern extremity of the continent there was an obvious distortion of the coastline. It did not end as it does on modern maps. Instead, it tailed off in an unbroken line far to the east. Missing were two well-known features shown on modern maps of South America: the "tip" end of the continent at the southern extremity and Drake Passage, the sea below. Despite this strange distortion, I realized that here was a map of the entire Atlantic Ocean with its shoreline, its islands, and parts of four continents outlined far more accurately than on any other medieval map I had ever seen.

I again examined the land mass that I thought might be Greenland, this time with the Zeno map in mind. The idea came to me that an explanation for the unusual features of this land mass on this map—if it was truly Greenland—might be that the island was shown as it was before it was covered by ice. Noticing that inland Greenland was wider on this map than on the Zeno map, I decided that this map, if it was a portolano, was platted long before the Zeno map. That possibility carried with it another possibility: that the compilers of this map may have used instruments and source maps and other materials based on the science and the technology of a civilization antedating the Middle Ages—knowledge and skills lost to the Middle Ages.[2]

During this first systematic examination of the map, I glanced again at the strange tail hanging off the southern extremity of South America across the location where the Drake Passage should have been. Suddenly unwilling to dismiss this tail as a distortion, as scholars had done, I pondered several possibilities, rejecting each of them. Then an astonishing idea came to me: the long tail is the coastline of the Palmer Peninsula of Antarctica shown as it was before

Antarctica was completely covered by ice. Immediately I realized that the coastline not only of the Palmer section of Antarctica was shown but that the coastline of the Queen Maud section to the east was also shown free of ice.

Documented facts, however, contradict such fanciful thinking. First, the Palmer Peninsula, in fact the entire Antarctic Continent, was not discovered until 1818, three hundred years *after* Piri Re'is compiled the map; second, sections of the coast of Antarctica that the tail could possibly represent were not explored until 1948; and third, there was no detail on the map that could represent Drake Passage, the sea between South America and Antarctica.

So I decided to find out immediately as much as possible about the findings of scientific groups that had explored Antarctica. First I asked Captain Finn Ronne, who had explored the Palmer Peninsula in 1947–1948, about his findings. After examining the map and others drawn on portolano grids, Ronne made a very perceptive suggestion: the islands and coastlines east of the Palmer Peninsula on the Piri Re'is map might coincide in position with the mountain peaks appearing above the ice on maps of Queen Maud Land.

With Ronne's suggestion in mind, I enlarged the section of the Piri Re'is map showing the area east of the Palmer Peninsula, added a portolano grid, and brought the map to a scale in common with the Swithinbank map of Western Queen Maud Land published in the *Geographical Journal,* June, 1954. The position of the islands and the coastlines on the ancient map corresponded strikingly with the position of the mountain peaks shown on the modern Swithinbank map of Queen Maud Land. I felt encouraged in my belief that the Piri Re'is map was indeed a map of shores of Antarctica before they were covered by ice.

Certain that the torn old fragment of the Piri Re'is map could be tremendously important in my effort to reconstruct the past, I returned to the Hydrographic Office of the Navy with the map I had platted and with the suggestion that cartographers there check the latitude, the longitude, and the projection of the old map. The response to my suggestion was silence. Perhaps it was impatience that forced me to say with deliberate solemnity, "There is something on this map that nobody will believe coming from me. And they may not believe it coming from you. Columbus had with him a map that showed the coast of Antarctica before it was covered by ice."

In response to expressions of incredulity that followed my remarks, I added, "This old map shows bays and islands of the coasts of Antarctica now hidden under a mile of ice."

The Hydrographic Office checked the old map as I suggested, and they did much more. They constructed a Mercator chart of the Atlantic Ocean south of 45′ north latitude, and, bringing the Piri Re'is fragment to a common scale with it, placed the Piri Re'is coastline on the chart. In general, the two maps were in substantial agreement, particularly in regard to rockbound harbors and headlands. Most of the discrepancies between the old map and the chart can be reasonably attributed to changes in the coastline caused by silt moving down to the coastline from the interior.

My associates and I were astonished several times while working on the old map at evidence of a superior level of technical capability in remote times. Some of the discrepancies between the old map and modern maps were due to errors on the modern maps. One such case involved two bays on the Piri Re'is map in a location where modern maps show land. I persuaded several experts to check the seismic soundings in that location. They found the bays there. Modern cartographers had erred. The ancient map was accurate!

In the meantime I learned about the Norwegian-British-Swedish Expedition to the Antarctic Continent in 1949. Headed by John Viers, this expedition had made a seismic profile across the icecap of Queen Maud Land. I was excited about the possibility that this profile of the coast of Queen Maud Land as it really is under the ice might, just might, agree with what I had declared to be the coast of Queen Maud Land without ice on the old map. Specialists in the science of seismology and I, working together, were able to prove that geographical details on the map agree with that seismic profile: the topography (under the ice) of that part of Queen Maud Land agrees with the outline of the area on the map. The seismic soundings show that islands placed off the coast on the Piri Re'is map and bays placed between the islands are there today under the ice. Specifically, the location of the islands on the old map agrees with the location of mountaintops that, according to the seismic profile, exist under the ice today; and the bays are in locations where the profile shows below-sea-level areas today.

There can no longer be any doubt that this surviving fragment is an authentic map and that it was drawn in a very remote age before Antarctica was covered by the ice sheet, long before the time of Piri Re'is. For the Western world section of his world map, the Turkish admiral used a map charted by skilled cartographers of an unknown civilization far more advanced in scientific and technological capability than any civilization prior to his time recorded in history.

In some ways, authentication of the map, at least for the Antarctic section, compounded the dilemma, for it threw into sharper focus the remaining imponderable puzzle: the identity of that unknown civilization.

The charting of the map covering such a vast area as the Antarctic, Greenland, or the eastern portion of South America could be accomplished only by a civilization with experts in shipbuilding, seamanship, exploration, surveying, hydrography, astronomy, higher mathematics, detailed knowledge of the outside world, and certainly well-organized government. Individuals or small groups of explorers or adventurers could not produce such a map on their own. Only experimental technicians familiar with these various sciences and technological procedures and supported by a sophisticated, efficient government with economic resources could.

During moments of fanciful thinking, I have wondered if use of the airplane would have simplified the tremendous project that produced this map.

The problem of identifying the unknown civilization is involved with the problem of dating the glaciation of the Antarctic Continent, which has not been solved to date. All we have to work with is several contradictory conclusions. Geologists and other scientists have believed that glaciation at the poles is many hundreds of thousands of years old, possibly a million years or more. If they are right, the most recent date for the mapping of the ice-free coasts of Antarctica would have to be at least hundreds of thousands of years ago. Incredible!

There is, however, a recent study[3] that gives us some reason for assuming that the charting of the ice-free coasts might have been done as recently as six thousand years ago. This evidence is based on the analysis and the dating of cores taken from sediments at the bottom of the Ross Sea in the Antarctic in 1949. The study was the joint work of Dr. Jack Hough of the University of Illinois and Dr. W. D. Urry of the Carnegie Institution in Washington, D.C. Dr. Hough took the sediment cores from the sea bottom, and Dr. Urry, an authority in atomic energy, dated them by a process based on the ratios of radioactive elements in the cores.

These cores reveal, according to the two scientists, several periods of ice-free temperate climate in the Antarctic during the last million years. The most recent temperate period, they say, began about fifteen thousand years ago and ended about six thousand years ago, thus lasting nine thousand years.

From my years of research and work on the Zeno and the Piri Re'is maps, I have concluded, however, that glaciation in both the Arctic and the Antarctic took place much later than has been believed. This, I believe, is one of the most important implications of the Zeno map and the Piri Re'is map. (See Appendix D for a statement by Charles H. Hapgood describing a research project directed by him which confirms my claim regarding the Piri Re'is map.) Equally important, of course, is the evidence in the maps that during that period of an ice-free Arctic and Antarctic just before the most recent glaciation, there was a civilization as highly advanced as our own—probably a worldwide civilization. Support for this conclusion lies principally in the maps, which show exploration and intimate knowledge of the world, and also in thousands of stones engraved in the letters of the alphabets of many ancient and prehistoric peoples. These stones were buried in the soil of our country for centuries until they were dug up by farmers' plows throughout the eastern states and elsewhere.

24

The
Ancient
Worldwide Signary[*]

Peoples of the ancient world are speaking to us in messages recorded on the surface of rocks. Early American Indians tell us about their world in crude outlines of the human form, of animals, snakes, and natural objects cut into the surface of rocks with flint tools or painted on with sticks. Their messages in this high-decibel medium of fantastic scrawls are heard and are classified by experts as authentic Indian relics.

On many of these same rock surfaces, however, there are other messages that are not heard. They are transmitted by a less flamboyant medium: small abstract designs cut into the rocks in various positions around the Indian pictographs. Unlike the pictographs, these designs are not outlines of recognizable objects. They are merely expressions of shape. American experts have ignored them, believing that they are meaningless graffiti. On very rare occasions, an especially perceptive

---

[*] This chapter was written by Mary Harrison after Arlington Mallery's death. It is based on Mr. Mallery's ''rubbings'' of stones in the Strong collection, conversations with Mr. Mallery, and research by the author completed before Mr. Mallery's death and approved by him.

and sophisticated scholar has observed two characteristics of these small shapes: the recurrence of specific patterns among them and their resemblance to "letters" of ancient alphabets.

Fortunately, European and Middle Eastern scholars, unlike their American counterparts, have not ignored abstract shapes cut into the surface of rocks, cliffs, or walls if they were not obviously modern. Instead, they have studied them diligently, noticed the recurrent patterns, and identified them individually with "letters" of the alphabets of ancient cultures presumed to have existed at one time in or near the areas where they were found. Their findings have aided in the reconstruction of these alphabets.

The attitude of experts in general toward these abstract designs cut in the surface of rocks is shown in the work of Garrick Mallery, the foremost authority on Indian pictographs. During the 1880s, this Mallery of another century (of the same Mallery family) compiled monumental reports on Indian pictographs for the Bureau of Ethnology of the Smithsonian Institution. Although he used many illustrations of pictographs—drawings and photographs—to illustrate his research, he showed no interest in the small abstract designs appearing on some of these illustrations. In fact, in comments about some of these designs appearing on rocks from Idaho, Mallery dismissed them as probably "totemic characters . . . made to record the names of visitors to the locality." [1]

Since colonial days, amateur collectors of Indian relics have contributed items and often entire collections to the accumulation of many millions of Indian artifacts in our museums today. The young and the old living in the rural areas of the northeastern states combed the neighboring countryside for Indian points, axes, and hammers. They discovered the old Indian campsites and trails, and could go directly to them for an abundance of relics.

A boy growing up on a farm or in a rural village in earlier times had easy opportunities to become familiar with the natural elements and aware of the forces at work in, on, and among them. He learned about the properties of different kinds of rocks while observing the operation of quarries, the construction of masonry, and the building of roads. He saw how rocks could be trimmed, chipped, and polished with farm implements. And living in a world where life, and even survival at times, was dependent upon the soil and its condition, he became curious about the relation between the earth and rocks, about geology.

The late Dr. William Walker Strong, an outstanding collector of relics, described his boyhood on a farm almost a century ago with gratitude for opportunities like these.[2] He felt that they gave him special advantages in his lifelong search for the past. Born on a farm in the Susquehanna River area of Pennsylvania in 1883, Strong grew up there and on another farm in the area.

During his youth, he joined collectors in the community in the search for Indian relics. Henceforth, collecting was for him a major lifelong pastime. Following the procedure established by expert collectors, he kept only those items which they had classified as types of Indian relics, and he discarded all objects that were not of the classified types. In this way he built a collection of more than one thousand "approved" Indian relics.

In the meantime, Strong had completed his academic work for a doctorate in physics and had achieved recognition as a successful physicist. Maybe his success gave him a greater degree of self-confidence and a willingness to depend more upon his own judgment. At any rate, he decided to abandon the traditional procedure for selecting relics based on the judgment of the "experts." In the future he would not discard all of the objects that were of types not classified as genuine Indian relics. Some of these discarded objects might be very valuable, he reasoned, despite the opinion of the experts.

Among the discarded objects which he now decided to keep were hard iron stones with shaped "grooves" cut in them. He had seen such stones and had been intrigued by a discovery he had made: the "grooves" were in recurrent shapes. The recurrence of shapes perplexed Strong, but not the "experts." They explained that the "grooves" were of no significance because they had been cut by farmers' plows or by natural causes such as the weather or glaciation. But to Strong, it seemed improbable that the shaped "grooves" had been cut by farmers' plows, for plows could not cut recurrent patterns so precisely. The "grooves" could not be explained as the work of glaciation either, he concluded, because the latest glaciation had not reached the areas where the stones were found. The shaped "grooves" on hard stone, he felt certain, were the work of man.

Strong had seen soft stones with shapes pecked out on them, and he did not challenge their classification as Indian relics by some collectors. Extensive investigation, however, of Indian relic collections in museums around the country and much reading of the literature on the subject revealed that Indians very rarely cut "grooves" on iron stones, the hardest of stones.

Convinced by now that these new stones with the recurrent "grooves" were of great significance, Strong changed his objective in collecting from building an accumulation of Indian relics to building a collection of "grooved" iron stones, not yet fully convinced, however, that these new stones were not Indian relics as yet unrecognized by the "experts."

In not adhering "to orthodox ideas when the evidence seemed to lead him to other conclusions," Strong illustrated a point made a few years ago by the late Matthew W. Stirling, then director of the Bureau of American Ethnology, the Smithsonian Institution. In speaking about a researcher who chose unorthodox procedures, Dr. Stirling said: "It is the broad approach which, though often liable to error, is most likely to produce important new ideas. Botanists, astronomers, and physicists have been responsible for producing many of the most recent advances in archeology."[3]

Strong located sites in the Susquehanna area, from the upper Susquehanna to the Potomac, rich in iron stones and then went to work with the assistance of his son to build up a collection of the "grooved" iron stones. He soon placed another limitation on his selection process by restricting his collection to stones *with patination*. He added this requirement because he believed that it was possible to determine the age of the stones by the depth of patination and he had concluded that the "grooved" stones already in his collection showed, according to this index, an age of two thousand years. He hoped to have a collection of stones at least that old.

Between 1941 and 1953, the Strongs, father and son, collected more than one thousand hard stones with "grooves" of recurrent patterns and with patination establishing, according to his system of measurement, an age of at least two thousand years. At the time of his death in 1956, he was highly respected by amateur relic collectors as the owner of the unique and priceless Strong Collection of Gravured Stones.

To Dr. Strong, the mystery of the patterned grooves on his stones began to unravel when he discovered that the grooves were identical in shape with "letters" in not one, but many, ancient alphabets or signaries. He found the most frequent occurrence of identical shapes in the Phoenician alphabet.

Knowing about rumors of expeditions of Phoenicians to prehistoric America, Strong added another dimension to his research: extensive reading of the historical literature about these notable sailors, traders, and colonizers. Being familiar with the properties of rocks and stones, he concluded that the only ancient peoples who would have had the skill to select tempered Triassic diabase, the hardest of stones, for their gravures and the ability to saw and bore such massive rocks were the extraordinary Phoenicians.

In the writings of such ancient authorities as Aristotle, Xenephon, Diodorus Siculus, and Josephus and other sources such as the Old Testament and the work of Juan de Mariana, he found what he considered to be support for a theory taking form in his mind—that the Phoenicians had reached America in 370 B.C. and had occupied the Susquehanna area. Then, when he found the twenty-second letter of the Phoenician alphabet on a stone on the pathway to the kitchen of a friend's home, he was convinced that his "gravured" stones were relics of Phoenician occupation. The Strong collection of "gravured" stones became the Strong collection of Phoenician stones. (See Fig. 24-1.)

The "authorities" ignored the Strong theory, just as they had ignored the stones. When confronted with queries about the theory, they offered as explanation for the "grooves" the old standbys: "cut by farmers' plows" or "the result of natural causes such as weather or glaciation." A fresh, more ingenious idea was added: the action of tree-root growth on the rocks before they had hardened had cut the marks on the rock surfaces. This and any other explanation based on natural causes could not stand up if the findings of an examination by experts in 1961 of four rocks from the Strong collection are valid.

The report of these findings by the Topographic and Geologic Survey Department, Internal Affairs, State of Pennsylvania, reads in part: ". . . We consider that the grooves in the samples examined are not related to the type of rock nor to fractures within the rock. The presence of metal flakes in the grooves is strong evidence that the grooves were made, at least in part, with an iron or steel tool."[4]

When Arlington Mallery first saw the Strong collection in the early 1950s, he believed that they were authentic relics of an extinct culture, but he was puzzled by their resemblance to ancient Semitic writing, for he was not aware of any knowledge of Semitic settlements in prehistoric America. So he remained perplexed about the stones and doubtful about Strong's theory. His "discovery" of the Piri Re'is map a very short time later, however, made him conscious of possibilities that had not entered his mind before. Unknown ancient sailors and explorers had reached America, it was now certain, and some of them may have been in the Susquehanna area, he concluded.

Fig. 24-1. The complete Phoenician alphabet as inscribed on stones in the Strong collection and found "letter" by "letter" on many different stones by William Walker Strong. Presented to Arlington Mallery by William Walker Strong.

Fig. 24-2. Five inscribed stones in Strong collection showing daubing of "gravures" with white paint. (Photograph by Leland Puttcamp, 1953.)

Mallery recalled the legend on the Piri Re'is map in which the Turkish admiral claimed that among the sources he used in compiling his world map were maps drawn in the time of Alexander the Great. If Greek sailors of Alexander's time had maps showing the route to America, he reasoned, surely the Phoenician sailors also had maps showing the route to this continent. His interest in Dr. Strong's stones was reawakened. He decided to investigate them.

Accompanied by the well-known astronomer, the Reverend Francis J. Heyden, then the director of the Georgetown University Observatory, Mallery went to the Strong estate in Mechanicsburg, Pennsylvania, on October 10, 1957, to examine the stones again. On that day, he and Father Heyden made "rubbings" of 418 "grooves" on the stones by placing transparent paper over the stones and rubbing the "grooves" with a heavy pencil. He returned home with the "rubbings," hopeful that he would be able to identify each of them with a "letter" in one of the more than thirty ancient alphabets he had found in libraries.

Before Mallery could start his search for identical "letters," however, his health broke. Unable to do the heavy work such a study so involved with detail required, he gave me the "rubbings" with the suggestion that I search through ancient alphabets for "letters" in shapes identical with the shapes of the "rubbings."

The alphabets compiled by two famous authorities, Sir. W. M. Flinders Petrie, the English Egyptologist and archaeologist, and Sir Arthur Evans, an authority on pictographs and script of Crete and the Peloponnesos, were consulted first. Petrie had tabulated sixty ancient alphabets from thirty-four countries. He identified the nearly 1,000 "letters" in his ancient alphabets of the Mediterranean area as Proto-Phoenician, saying that they were older than the Egyptian hieroglyphics. Evans agreed with Petrie, but called those "letters" Proto-Egyptian. Petrie insisted that his tabulations be called *signaries,* not *alphabets,* explaining that it would be an anachronism to look on early signs as letters because the alphabetic stage of signs was probably not reached until later, about 1000 B.C.[5]

Ancient alphabets or signaries compiled by other authorities were consulted later. (For a list of all authorities consulted, see Appendix E-I.)

To conduct a search as comprehensive as possible for ancient "letters" identical with the "grooves" on the stones, twenty-eight ancient alphabets or signaries compiled by these authorities were chosen for the comparison. (See Appendix E-II for a list of the ancient alphabets selected.)

The "grooves" cut in the Strong stones, according to Mallery, and also in all the reproductions of other inscribed stones that he had seen, were cut by ancient flint engraving tools called burins that have been found in America and in Europe by the thousands. He explained that because of the peculiar shape of the "grooves," a tracing made on transparent paper with a crayon or a large lead pencil will show an accurate reproduction of the center of the "groove."

Dr. Strong, however, had covered the "grooves" on his stones with white chalk and white ink for photographic contrast (see Fig. 24-2). The white ink spread by capillary action, and consequently the tracings showed the "grooves" to be very broad and curved, in some cases not useful for a comparative study.

It has already been emphasized that "experts" question the authenticity of the stones. This fact together with the fact that archaeologists always reject surface finds that conflict with their theories convinced me that it was necessary to dig up some new stones in the Susquehanna area still in their original positions if I wanted to reduce the skepticism of such doubters. New stones would not be daubed with paint or chalk, and so would have "grooves" from which more accurate "rubbings" could be made. Expecting to go to Pennsylvania to get such stones, I decided to continue the current study with the Strong stones, but to limit findings to probabilities.

In nearly every major museum in the world and in publications of various scholarly institutions and groups there are drawings, photographs, and descriptions of ancient alphabetical "letters"—or signary —identical in shape with the inscriptions on the Strong stones. After examining many inscriptions reproduced in publications of accredited authorities, such as the Smithsonian Institution, the government, and universities, I decided to expand the study to include these inscriptions. I found in the Library of Congress, also, copies of "rubbings" from six hundred stones in the Strong collection that Dr. Strong had filed there. I added copies of these rubbings to inscriptions to be studied. Altogether—the reproduced inscriptions in publications and the "rubbings" from the Strong collection—there were now more than four thousand "letters" to be identified with "letters" in twenty-eight ancient alphabets or signaries. (See Appendix E-III for a list of publications in which the inscriptions were reproduced.)

A single glance at the "letters" inscribed on stones and other surfaces as reproduced in these publications shows an astonishing similarity of these "letters" on stones or other surfaces from widely separated areas of the world, and the world in this case is the ancient world! A sampling of "letters" from such far-apart areas as Peru, Argentina, California, Ohio, New Mexico, and Idaho is shown in Fig. 24-3.

This observation of the similarity of the inscribed "letters" from different areas is supported by the findings of the study, which show also an undeniable relationship between the inscribed "letters" and the "letters" of the ancient signaries. Among the 418 "gravures" on the stones in the Strong collection, "rubbings" made by Mallery and Father Heyden, I found 175 "gravures" identical with "letters" in the Runic alphabet, 173 identical with Iberian "letters," and 119 "gravures" identical with "letters" in the Phoenician alphabet. In addition, many other ancient signaries are represented among the "gravures" on these stones. Of particular interest is the presence there of 108 Egyptian "letters," 69 Pelasgic "letters," 60 Greek "letters," and 48 Etruscan "letters."

The table below gives the number of duplications of "letters" of ancient alphabets found among the inscriptions or "gravures" from

DUPLICATION OF "LETTERS" OF PREHISTORIC ALPHABETS IN NORTH AND SOUTH AMERICA

	Pelasgic	Egyptian	Greek	Iberian	Etruscan	Phoenician	Runic
Peru	13	24	19	32	13	23	13
Argentina	36	45	39	70	15	56	72
Pennsylvania, Maryland, and Virginia*	69	108	60	173	48	119	175
California	43	80	56	59	30	20	94
New Mexico	45	54	37	71	22	49	89
Idaho	9	10	8	13	2	14	4
Ohio	14	10	13	18	9	9	28
West Virginia	9	13	9	21	9	17	22
	238	344	241	457	148	307	497

*Inscriptions on stones in Strong collection from "rubbings" made by Arlington Mallery and Francis J. Heyden.

Fig. 24-3. Inscribed "letters" on stones in various locations of North and South America.

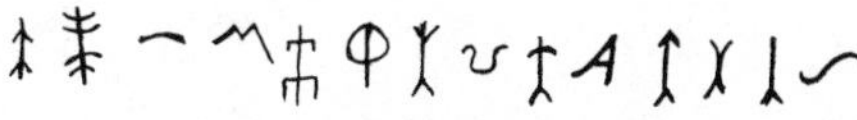

Idaho. [*Source:* "*Indian Rock Writing in Idaho,*" Twelfth Biennial Report of the State Historical Society of Idaho (*1929–30*), *pp. 35–111.*]

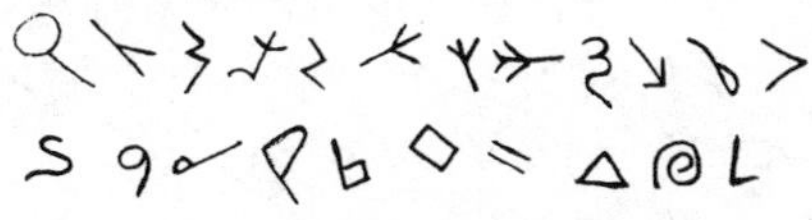

Lake Erie, Ohio. [*Source: Henry Rowe Schoolcraft,* Historical and Statistical Information Respecting the History, Condition, and Prospects of the Indian Tribes of the United States (*1851–57*), *Vol. 2, p. 88, plate 41.*]

California. [*Source:* University of California Publications in American Archaeology and Ethnology, *Vol. 24, No. 2 (1929), pp. 62–159, plates 22–57.*]

New Mexico. [*Source: Schoolcraft, op. cit., Vol. 4, plates 34C, 34D, and 35;* U.S. Senate Document 562, No. 64, plates 23–72.*]

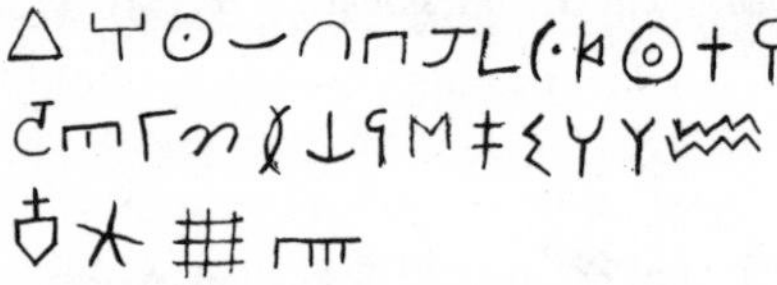

Yonan Pass, Peru. [*Source: T. J. Hutchinson,* Two Years in Peru (*London: S. Low, Marston, Low, and Searle, 1873*).]

Argentina. [*Source: Adan Quiroga,* Petrografías y Epictografías de Calchaqui (*Buenos Aires: Impresa de la Universidad, 1931, p. 502*).]

the "rubbings" made by Mallery and Francis J. Heyden and the inscriptions reproduced in publications. Approximately one thousand "rubbings" and reproductions were used in compiling this table.

The table above shows apparent duplications of "letters" from ancient Mediterranean and more recent European alphabets on American stones. The conclusion should not be drawn, however, that these individual languages or alphabets are in fact present on these stones in the percentages shown above. Many of the "letters" or symbols actually appear in several of the ancient alphabets, either representing the same pronunciation (value) or in many cases very different pronunciations (values).

Among the "grooves" on stones and the reproduced inscriptions, there are about three hundred different shapes or "letters," exclusive of diphthongs, script letters, and ligatures. Some of the ancient "letters" resemble letters in the English alphabet so strongly that it seems reasonable to assume that these English letters were derived from ancient signaries.

A comparative study of alphabets such as this study (which was concluded in 1959) requires the expertise of authorities in many disciplines. Only by the working together of such various experts can answers be found to the quandary produced by facts uncovered in this study—in particular, the presence on ancient rocks and other surfaces of engravings of shapes identical with units of communication among ancient peoples, and the duplication of shapes on rocks and other surfaces in areas very distant from one another.

Two probabilities enter the mind of this researcher: there was a worldwide ancient signary and there was worldwide communication among ancient peoples. Arlington Mallery believed that his research, particularly on ancient maps and iron smelting, proved that there was a worldwide civilization.

25

Conclusion

Rapidly accumulating evidence shatters the theory that there never was an Iron Age in pre-Columbian America. In fact, the extent of the metalworking civilization which existed then is only imperfectly indicated by the furnaces thus far discovered. The destruction of hundreds of pre-Columbian mounds and masonry sites by treasure hunters and earlier generations of archaeologists has obliterated much of the evidence of what was obviously industrial civilization.

My associates and I have only scratched the surface of the mass of material awaiting examination, but of this we are certain: civilization in this continent did not begin with the Stone Age Indians found here by Columbus. Back of these Indians was not a North America with a formless past. On the contrary, in the pre-Columbian era, a civilized Iron Age people lived here; and still farther back there was a greater civilization probably equal to the contemporary civilizations of the Old World, certainly in contact with those civilizations.

This conclusion is based on metallurgical and x-ray analyses of authentic pre-Columbian metal tools, information derived from ancient maps including the recently discovered Piri Re'is map, and the presence on this continent in various locations of stones bearing the signary of several ancient civilizations. It is also confirmed by archaeological explorations of the three high civilizations of Central and South America: the Aztec-Toltec, the Mayan, and the Peruvian. The relics of these cultures lie directly above the remains of primitive peoples. This circumstance reveals, as clearly as written records would, a fact of history: the immediate predecessors of these ancient American civilizations were primitive savages. The three cultures were already mature when they arrived. They must then have been offshoots of a parent civilization in a not too distant location.

The achievements of these ancient Americans in writing, astronomy, arithmetic, development of a calendar, chronology, and systematic historical records were equal to the achievements of the peoples of the Old World after thousands of years of consecutive development. Their attainments in the industrial arts and crafts, particularly in the construction of massive stone buildings and pyramidal structures, almost equaled the attainments of the Egyptians near the beginning of the first millennium B.C. The Aztec-Mayan paper was far superior in texture and durability to the Egyptian papyrus. The Peruvian textiles, considered among the finest in the world, were probably superior to the Egyptian in fineness of thread, variety of techniques, and range of color.

These ancient Americans were Bronze Age peoples using the same smelting technique as the Bronze Age metalworkers of Egypt. Certain of the Peruvian axes were facsimiles of the Egyptian. The Mayans possessed a knowledge of astronomy not attained by the Egyptians until Ptolemaic times. In arithmetic the Mayans possessed man's first positional arithmetical system, one involving the concept of zero. The Peruvians, like the Egyptians, had calendars with twelve months of thirty days each with five additional (holy) days. Yet not one of these three American civilizations has a historical record justifying a conclusion that its roots were in the locale of its discovery.

There probably was no great disparity in absolute achievement between these American civilizations and those of the Near East about 1000 B.C. There was, however, an enormous difference in rate of progress. In the Old World that period was a time of invention and steady growth—a growth that was continuous in one area or another. But in America, where the three cultures were apparently of foreign origin, civilization remained essentially unchanged. Empires rose and fell, art forms and social customs changed slightly, but the basic culture remained stationary.

The parent civilization of these three cultures may have been in North America. Ancient maps show that at some time in the far distant past, a highly developed maritime people lived in northern North America, a people whose knowledge of mathematics and astronomy may have rivaled that of the Mayans. The Mound Builder people in the Mississippi Valley, like the Mayans, quarried limestone, burned lime, and made concrete and pure lime mortar. Cylindrical seals like those of the pharaohs have been found in Ohio, Mexico, and South America. Corbeled arches were used in stone structures in North, Central, and South America.

A comparison of the Bronze Age cultures of the Old World and the New reveals that both had agriculture, agricultural implements, fertilizers, and irrigation canals; spinning with the loom, spindle, and whorl; domestication of animals; pottery, shaped, molded, and decorated; seagoing sailing ships made of plank; megaliths, pyramids, and other structures of brick and stone; writing, cylindrical seals, and paper; musical instruments, including the pan pipes; the beginnings of chemistry, of medicine, dental and cranial surgery, and mummification; arithmetic, astronomy, and navigation; the cartography of the ancient maps and portolanos; mining of ores and the metallurgy of copper and bronze; the reduction process of smelting bog iron ores; low-temperature iron welding; manufacture of steel by carburization in charcoal; plating of silver and iron on copper.

It is unlikely that two civilizations in not too distant locations with seagoing ships and so many cultural characteristics in common developed independently. It is reasonable to conclude that prior to the beginning of the Christian Era, there was in North America a civilization comparable to the contemporary civilizations of the Old World and in contact with them.

Appendix A:

Great Lakes
Copper Culture

Probably more than a hundred thousand pre-Columbian copper artifacts, mostly the product of the Great Lakes Culture, have been found in the northern United States and southern Canada. According to accepted theory, these artifacts were all hammered out of pieces of crude copper by Stone Age Indians. The theory is obviously wrong because many of the heavier pieces, many of the socketed axes and pentagonal chisels, have not been touched by a hammer except at the cutting edges. The micrographs of some of these tools show that they were *cast* from copper which had been melted in an open crucible and consequently were impregnated with cuprous oxide—proving that "alloying with oxide had occurred during the melting. . . . Such a product is considerably harder and more brittle than pure copper and has a characteristic red color." [1] The cuprous oxide causes small dots in the micrographs.

When, at the suggestion of Matthew Stirling, I examined the Perkins collection of copper tools in the National Museum, I noted that there were a number of castings in the collection. There are numerous similar castings in nearly every museum collection in America. Expert foundrymen who examined the Perkins collection of

the Wisconsin Historical Society declared that many of these specimens were cast in a mold.[2]

In the pentagonal chisels, there is additional proof of the effects
of cuprous oxide. Copper when molten absorbs a considerable amount
of gas.

> Some of the oxygen is trapped and combines with copper to
> form cuprous oxide. Most of it, however, escapes, especially from
> an open mold.
>
> The centers of the upper surface of some of these chisels were
> decidedly depressed or concave. This is caused by the decrease in
> volume (or shrinkage) of the molten metal upon solidification. It is a
> common phenomenon well known by all foundrymen and those con-
> nected with the melting and casting of metals.
>
> This concavity is more or less pronounced in many of the an-
> cient specimens and particularly so in the pentagonal chisels.[3]

To illustrate this action, a laboratory test specimen was cast from
Lake Superior copper. A cross section of the specimen shows this
depressed center.

The problem posed by the discovery of so many apparently cast
artifacts in the Great Lakes region was too important to be solved by
visual inspection alone. If only a few of these hundred thousand specimens were found to be cast, the conclusion would have to be that at
one time civilized people skilled in metalworking had lived in the
Great Lakes area. Such a conclusion would seriously weaken the
theory of a Stone Age pre-Columbian America.

So, at my request, James A. Ford of the American Museum of
Natural History selected three tools of a type which might have been
hammered from crude copper to be examined by the well-known New
York Testing Laboratories, Inc. The Laboratories made the following
report on the analysis of the three tools:

> A transverse section taken from each of the submitted speci-
> mens was prepared and examined at 100 magnifications to determine
> the type of material and the nature of fabrication. *The specimens
> were found to be forged from cast material.* [Italics added.] The
> microstructure of the axe and chisel consists of coarse-grained cop-
> per and in addition several annealing twins were detected in the
> structure. The above condition indicates that the tools were hot
> forged and the annealing twins were formed on reheating. The mi-
> crostructure of the spearhead consists of pure copper crystals or
> grains. This tool has been subjected to a greater degree of working at

a lower temperature than the previous tools, as indication of severe grain distortion is clearly detected in the structure.

SPEARHEAD:—100 Magnifications—Etched.

STRUCTURE:—Shows pure copper crystals or grains. The above structure is largely distorted due to subsequent working below the recrystallization temperature.

AXE:—100 Magnifications—Etched.

STRUCTURE:—Shows pure copper crystals. The dark parallel bands are annealing twins formed after reheating from the forging or working operations.

CHISEL:—100 Magnifications—Etched.

STRUCTURE:—Shows coarse-grained copper crystals. Several annealing twins are also detected in the microstructure.

X-RAY EXAMINATION:—The tools were radiographed using standard techniques. A review of the radiographs led to the following observations:—

#1—The three tools were originally cast.

#2—The copper chisel No. 20/6772 shows indications of piping in the interior. There were no indications of any washing of the mold material within the tool. Therefore, the mold was probably a stone mold.

#3—The axe No. 20/6804 and the spearhead No. 1922T both show indications of entrapped mold wash material. This would indicate that a clay mold was used.

SUMMARY:—The three copper specimens all show relatively low amounts of impurities with the exception of the phosphorous content of the chisel which is present in an appreciable amount. Metallographical examination indicates low oxygen content in all cases. The specimens are originally cast but apparently have been reheated and worked to some extent.

Following this report, six leading American museums furnished tools from the United States, Canada, Mexico, Guatemala, and Peru for testing. Various metallurgists who have examined the micrographs of these tools concur in the findings of the New York Testing Laboratories, Inc. that many of the specimens examined have been cast. Dr. George P. Ellinger, metallurgist for the National Bureau of Standards, said, after examining the submitted specimens, "The presence of cuprous oxide in the interior of the tools tested and the concavity caused by shrinking justify the conclusion that the vast majority of the ancient tools were cast."

It is almost axiomatic that a people who possessed the art of casting copper would not revert to cold-hammering single tools out of crude copper until the art of casting had been forgotten in a general collapse of their culture.

When additional radiocarbon datings become available, the relations of the prehistoric metalworking peoples of North America both to each other and to the peoples of other continents may be definitely determined. The available datings combined with a typographical study of the copper socketed tools of the pre-Columbian era indicate that the Great Lakes Copper Culture was the most ancient of the copper-working peoples of America and had a very early contact with Siberia and Peru. The open or semisocket is typical of all socketed tools of pre-Columbian North America and occurs occasionally in the coastal areas of Peru and Siberia but rarely, if ever, anywhere else. That fact indicates that this type of socket was the invention of the Great Lakes Culture, perfected later in the inland areas of South America and the Old World. Development of the socket in North America seems to have been arrested about 600 B.C. by the influx of the superior iron tools from the Hopewell areas.

The people of the Great Lakes Copper Culture, more or less isolated in the barren lands around Lake Superior, probably managed to survive and hand down the secrets of their craft until the Black Death epidemics of the fourteenth century. A few of the surviving artisans apparently carried on the copper-smelting industry until it was ended by the influx of European trade goods in the sixteenth century. The Knight of Elva, chronicler of the DeSoto expedition into the Mississippi Valley in that century, stated that DeSoto heard of a province to the north, named *Chisca,* where there was melting of copper.[4] Obviously, the copper was melted in crucibles and cast into shapes or sheets. No other use could be made of the molten metal.

Champlain was told that the Indians gathered copper in lumps and "having melted it, spread it in sheets, smoothing it with stones."[5] Unable to compete with the trade goods, the surviving copper workers probably merged with the woodland tribes.

The Vikings must have learned of the Great Lakes Culture early in the eleventh century when they arrived in the St. Lawrence Valley. The longhouses indicate that they finally reached Lake Erie and Lake Huron.

Like all ancient metalworking groups, the copper miners of the Great Lakes area kept very much to themselves, remaining on friendly terms with all surrounding peoples. They may have bartered their copper and their copper tools through the established trade channels by which the pre-Columbian Americans distributed their products from the Arctic to the Gulf and from the Rockies to the Atlantic. When European goods invaded their markets and took away their means of livelihood, they simply disappeared, as quietly and peacefully as they had lived.

Appendix B:

Ancient
Iron Production

Remains of prehistoric iron production, such as slag heaps, iron artifacts, and even hearthpit furnaces, are evidence of an ancient worldwide iron industry.

The principles of iron production were known, according to the Bible, as long ago as the seventh generation after Adam, and they were taught by Tubal Cain, "a forger of every cutting instrument of brass and iron." Both Aristotle and Pliny revealed knowledge of iron extraction, and in at least thirty passages of the *Iliad* and the *Odyssey*, Homer mentions iron, describing it as "difficult to work with."

The Celts were the first Europeans to extract iron from native ores. The first Iron Age in central Europe is known as the Hallstatt Epoch (1200–500 B.C.). Hallstatt, a village in Austria, was the site of the Celtic breakthrough in iron production in 1200 B.C. It is reputed that the native iron ores in that area were so exceptional that from them natural steel was produced.

The Celts were several related racial groups bound by a common culture and speaking dialects of the same language. After a longtime settlement in central Europe, they migrated both east and west, finding new homes in lands as far apart as Russia and Britain and Ireland. They took with them in their migrations their skill in iron production.[1]

Ancient iron smelting was a seasonal activity located near supplies of bog ore. It provided individuals and sometimes communities with iron, which though soft and impure, could be forged into shape. Bog ore is principally a combination of clay, loam, and hydrated oxides of iron. It forms in bogs, marshes, and lakes when iron carried by surface waters in solution as carbonate sulfate, or an organic compound, is deposited in basins rich in vegetable or animal matter. It usually has a high content of phosphorus and varies in sulfur.

The iron industry in pre-Columbian North America, Europe, Asia, and Africa apparently developed along similar lines from a common origin in antiquity. Diversification seems to have followed as improved methods were introduced by ironworkers in the more advanced societies in the temperate zones.

The stone-and-earth-walled fortresses on the hilltops of America, the ring-walled forts on the plains, the stone cists, the log-covered tombs, the stone-walled vaults, and the corbeled arches—in fact, every structure or fabric found in the sepulchral or memorial mounds in America—have a counterpart in the ancient forts and sepulchral mounds of Europe. And the mounds in America that American archaeologists have always identified as "sacrificial" or "altar" mounds resemble closely the furnace mounds of Europe.[2]

Moundlike heaps of slag, ashes, and other furnace refuse have lain on the hilltops of England, Belgium, and Scandinavia for centuries. The English slag heaps are the relics of a primitive iron industry that flourished long before the conquest of Britain by the Romans.

The pre-Roman iron industry of England must have operated on a large scale, for during the Roman occupation and at least a thousand years later, ironmasters reworked the slag remains of the ancient furnaces. In fact, the slag from the old hearthpits was the basis of the iron industry for many centuries, especially around Gloucester. As late as 1795, long after the replacement of the hearthpit by the blast furnace, half of the iron output was from slag and the other half from hematite.[3]

J. D. Swank, an authority on ancient iron, refers to these ancient slag (cinder) heaps in England and in Belgium:

> Heaps of iron cinder which antiquarians decided to be as old at least as the Roman occupation of Gallia Belgica have recently been found on the tops of iron hillocks in the provinces of Brabant and

Antwerp and in these cinder heaps have been found flint arrowheads and fragments of coarse pottery.

. . . Much of the cinder has been found on the tops of hills or mounds, a circumstance that leads to the belief that bellows were not employed in producing a draft, but that the wind was relied upon to produce a draft sufficient to smelt the ore in crude bloomeries, some of which were mere excavations with covered channels leading to the hillside in the direction of the prevailing winds.[4]

Believing that deposits of slag in Storegarden, Sweden, indicated that there was once a hearthpit thereabouts, John Nihlen states:

The owner of the farm found some pieces of slag on a hill about two hundred meters south of the farm. In a smaller pit there was found under the grass, one and one-half feet deep, a large amount of slag pieces, such as iron slag in chunks of glazed pieces mixed with or attached to pieces of hard-burned red clay.[5]

In an extensive deposit of slag on top of Spruce Hill in Ohio are several low mounds of typical hearthpit iron content of about 10 percent. Cutting a trench through this heap, I uncovered the edge of a 12-inch slab of clay, large pieces of slag, lumps of red-burned bog ore, charcoal, and glazed stone. On the side of the hill, there are ten stone-lined graves.

John Nihlen cut into a similar mound at Helgesgarden II, Essunga Parish, Västergötland, Sweden.[6] Not far from the mound were some ancient graves which had previously been identified as belonging to the La Tene III Iron Age period, which began about 100 B.C. and ended a century later. The soil surface of the furnaces in this area was identical with that of the graves. Slag from one of the furnaces contained 36 percent ferric oxide. Slag similar to this, but containing 30.7 percent ferric oxide, was found on a hill in southern Virginia, about 8 miles east of Oak Hill. Slag from the top of Farrell Hill, Ohio, 5 miles northwest of Spruce Hill, contained 28.2 percent ferric oxide.

European archaeologists recognized the moundlike heaps of slag, ashes, and furnace refuse as products of an ancient iron industry. Accordingly, they left the exploration of these heaps to metallurgists. Unfamiliar with metalworking processes, American archaeologists, along with other explorers and treasure hunters, did not know that identical remains in this country were the product of ironmaking. They destroyed many important sites and in their place left piles of dirt, superficially resembling the original mounds. The men who tore down most of the fire-hardened walls and foundations of the ancient civilization of the Ohio Valley, for instance, have made almost impossible the reconstruction of the story of the early industry and civilization of that region.

Identification and understanding of the pre-Columbian heaps of slag and furnaces in Ohio and in Virginia depend, because of this failure of American archaeologists, upon the work of European archaeologists and mineralogists. Their descriptions, illustrations, and diagrams reveal that their slag heaps and furnaces are counterparts of slag heaps and furnaces in this country, only recently identified as such.

The low basinlike hearths in America which have been called "crematories" are exactly like hundreds of hearths in the earliest European furnace heaps. These hearths are the furnaces which I designate as *Celtic,* the most primitive "furnace." Swank describes the discovery of a Celtic furnace in Europe similar to the Celtic furnaces recently found on Spruce Hill in Ohio and Oak Hill in Virginia. His account of the discovery mentions a "set" of hearths, one for calcining (preparing for smelting) the ore and the other for smelting the calcined ore.

> In the year 1870, a set of iron-smelting hearths of Roman and Celtic times (beginning of the Christian era) was discovered near Huttenberg, Austria. The calcining hearth is fitted with a layer of charcoal one and one-half inches thick on which a ten-inch layer of clay forms the inside lining of the hearth. This lining was found burned by the action of the fire to a depth of four inches. The depth of the hearth is two feet and its diameter is five feet. The second, or smelting, hearth is placed at a distance of sixteen feet from the former and is three feet deep and four feet wide. The lining consists of a layer of six-inch clay and quartz and is uniformly spread to a thickness of twelve inches. This lining is burnt and glazed to a depth of three inches at the inner side, thus recording the high temperatures reached in this hearth during the smelting operation.[7]

This European furnace operated with about the same efficiency as the Virginia Oak Hill pit. In Ohio it seems to have been the practice to calcine the ore on a flat hearth, as in Mound Number 3 of the Turner group (Little Miami Valley), or in small piles in the open field, as on Spruce Hill.

In Sweden, John Nihlen found a slightly smaller Celtic furnace of the same type but with stone walls. It was in a low gravel ridge forming an island around the surrounding bog. A gravel pit had been opened in the ridge.

While the gravel was being dug, pieces of slag were found here and there, none of them collected in heaps nor visible on the surface. . . . It was about three feet wide in the upper part and narrowed slightly downward, being cup-formed at the bottom. The sides were made of round or flat gray stone which were laid in clay which also covered large parts of the inside. Probably the lining was not entirely over the stones. The bottom of the furnace . . . consisted of a four-inch layer of hard and partially burned clay. It could almost have been taken out. In the cup-formed lower part there still remained a four-inch layer of small balls of slag, bog ore, and charcoal. The depth of the furnace was about three feet. . . . it has been a simple earth furnace without a blast intake, built of stone and clay and with a thick bottom of burned clay.[8]

Celtic-type pit furnaces quite similar to this Swedish furnace were found by archaeologists of Harvard's Peabody Museum in the Miami Valley of Ohio in 1890, who failed to identify them as furnaces.

Ancient furnaces with flues for conducting air into the smelter and conveying heated slag and iron out, like those in Ohio which I call *Nordic,* have been uncovered by Nihlen in Sweden and by others in Belgium and in Greenland. In his account of his excavation of the mound in Sweden already referred to, Nihlen tells the details of his discovery in this mound of such a furnace. He describes the so-called Helgesgarden II mound as being:

. . . forty to fifty feet in diameter and ten to thirteen feet in height. It was situated immediately south of a gravel ridge on the border of a bog which is now cultivated. The heap, after investigation, showed an interesting and well-preserved bog-ore furnace, the first one that had been heretofore found in the province [Smaland]. The pile did not contain a compact mass of slag like in the sepulchral mounds, but it contained throughout the greatest part soil, pieces of slag, burned lumps of clay, charcoal and stones.[9]

During the excavation, Nihlen cut a trench about 3 feet wide straight through the heap approximately north-south. Just below the surface he found pieces of slag, charcoal, and both burned and unburned clay. And then, about as deep as a spade could go, about in the center, he found flat stones laid in order. Enlarging the trench and digging deeper, he came upon a circle of stones

which turned out to be the top of a melting furnace, the upper rim of the stones being ten inches under the surface. These stones were standing on edge and were flat inside. The arrangement was fairly regular with a diameter of two and one-half feet. The sides were comparatively vertical with a slight leaning toward the outside. The depth was two and one-half feet. The bottom consisted of a hard-burned four-inch thick layer of clay. . . . All around on the outside they [the stones of the furnace] were supported by clay.[10]

Between two of these stones, numbered 1 and 7, there was an opening about 18 inches wide which served as an aperture for the entrance of air. "There had been a flue leading into the furnace through to the opening between #1 and #7 which had been an intake for the air draft. The blast could not have been driven by water because no watercourse was in the neighborhood."[11]

Nihlen describes the slag as brown and heavy and of different forms and shapes, including cup-shaped. About the furnace he states, "It has been a simple built-up masonry furnace, completely or partly sunk into a heap of soil, supported, masoned and lined by clay and finally, probably with an opening for the blast."[12]

In 1890, archaeologists of the Peabody Museum of Harvard University cut trenches through a mound at Foster's Crossing in Ohio. Almost the same size as the Helgesgarden II mound, it was about 50 feet in diameter and was probably originally 8 or 9 feet high. The builders of this mound had covered a furnace, apparently, in the same manner as the Swedish mound had been built over a furnace: that is, by piling scraped-up ashes, cinders, clinker, refuse, and unused bog ore over the furnace after its walls had been broken down.

Swank describes the discovery of two hearthpits in Belgium resembling the Nordic-type pit on Spruce Hill in Ohio. It is believed that these Belgium furnaces date back to the beginning of the Christian era. Of special interest in the comparison are the stone-covered flues (channels) excavated in the clay.

At Lustine, in Belgium, two ancient furnaces or bloomeries were discovered in 1870 on the top of a hill with iron yet remaining within them. They consisted of simple oval excavations with rounded bottoms in a bed of clay, each twelve feet long and nine feet wide with a depth of three feet, the top being level with the surrounding soil. A channel excavated in the clay but covered over with stones conducted the wind into the lower part of the furnace. The opening of this channel was turned in the direction of the prevailing winds so that the iron could only have been made on windy days. These bloomeries contained lumps of crude wrought iron.[13]

In the Norse ruins at Austmannadal, Greenland, Danish archaeologists discovered a Nordic-type smelter with a complex feature like the unusual arrangement in the first furnace we uncovered in the Arledge mound in Ohio. This feature was a flue passing through loose stones to the extreme rear end of the pit. This flue, which might have been for the purpose of preventing chilling of the molten iron flowing out or of warming the air coming in, shows that the furnace was designed by highly skilled metallurgists. Aage Rousselle describes the furnace excavated in Greenland:

> A curious form of smithy was found at Austmannadal. It stands by itself at the end of the house but inside the home field. . . . A large sloping stone formed the bottom of the forge. There was a narrow channel dug into the bottom gravel, commencing a little way in front of the forge and ending in the middle of it at the end of the large oblique stone. This was undoubtedly an air duct. Small stones were apparently placed upon the forge, filling the space between the slanting stone and the back wall and thus forming a grid capable of bearing fire but not stopping the draft.[14]

Austmannadal was in the West Settlement of Greenland, which was abandoned by the Norse about 1350. The unusual features which the Arledge furnace and the Greenland smithy had in common—an underground flue passing through a cobblestone base under a furnace floor sloping to the rear and a grate of loose stones—point to the Norse of Greenland as builders of the Deer Creek furnaces in the Ohio Valley.

In the earliest iron-smelting operations, much labor was required to carry iron ore up to the hilltop furnaces. Eventually an ingenious method of getting sufficient draft without placing the hearthpits on hilltops was evolved. The hearthpit was made practical for operation on the plains near the settlement by running a flue from it to a second pit dug in the ground at the side, thus creating a two-pit furnace. The winding flue of the two-pit furnace produced the slow fire that is necessary to permit the molten slag and iron from bog ore to seep to the bottom of the pit. The draft could be controlled by manipulation of a loose cover over one of the pits.

Archaeologists from the Peabody Museum found a variety of flues and pits which, it now appears, were furnaces of different types with a flue leading to a small second pit. Two-pit furnaces like those found by Peabody archaeologists in Mound Number 3 of the Turner group in Ohio were used in ancient Germany. One with a cover is shown in a sketch of three *Schmelzoven* furnaces by Ludwig Beck.[15]

Some two-pit furnaces have been found on hilltops in Sweden. Dating probably from Viking days—A.D. 700 to 800—hilltop furnaces of the two-pit type found in Gastrikland were Nordic furnaces like the Spruce Hill furnace and those found in Belgium, except that they were round and much smaller. A large square Nordic two-pit furnace appeared later in Swedish plains.

So far I have not found any two-pit furnaces on hilltops in America, but some will probably be discovered on the hilltops in the Waverly sandstones (a geological formation in the mideastern part of this country), particularly in the Berea Grits.

In his account of the iron furnaces in Germany from the earliest days to A.D. 1500, Ludwig Beck describes many *Schmelzovens*. My identification of several furnaces in Ohio near Deer Creek as *Schmelzovens* is supported by Beck's descriptions of these ancient German furnaces, which are much like the Deer Creek furnaces.

> The construction of the *Schmelzoven,* which are all alike, though differing in size, was as follows: They are on the natural soil without a special foundation. The bottom of the furnace was built of fire-resistant clay six to eight inches thick. The walls were formed in part from the same clay and supported in part from the outside by rough stones which are backed up by ordinary earth. Less than two inches above the floor of the furnace a flue hole was left open which was the full width of the hearth, was flatly arched, and became wider toward the outside. It was made of fire-hardened clay. . . . The working platform was protected by stone retaining walls which were covered by stone lintels. The Roman *hypokausten* were somewhat like the above-described furnace.[16]

The arch and the retaining walls of the Deer Creek furnaces were made of hard-burned bog ore.

Beck's description of the *Schmelzoven* continues:

> The walls of the hearth were twelve to eighteen inches thick; the shaft was cylindrical, and the throat of the furnace was about half the diameter. The shaft height was between eight and nine feet. Coal and ore can be dumped in from above on the front side, while the air was free to flow through. . . . The air draft, in the opinion of Von Quiqueren, was by induced draft only through the tuyere (vent) by natural suction and not by bellows. The single hearth opening, therefore, served as a form for a slag dam and a draft hole for the

air. One could clean out the slag and pull out the billet with an iron bar or hook. Iron ore which has been glazed has been found.[17]

Glazed iron ore is also found around the Deer Creek mounds and the Howe sites in Virginia. The inside surface of the walls directly above the flue openings in the Deer Creek furnaces was very hard-burned, indicating that the hottest part of the furnace was at that point, as it was in the *Schmelzoven,* according to Beck.

> The main heat was directly above the tap hole. Here the walls showed always clinkered, while the clay of the back wall only appeared burned. The author is also presuming that the work done there had been continuous. The slag heaps around every furnace were very considerable and indicate a long continued operation. It seems doubtful whether it was possible to make an artificial draft to reduce the iron in these furnaces . . . the author, who has investigated so many (230) well-preserved furnaces, has never seen any signs of artificial air. . . . The billets could not have weighed more than thirty-three to fifty-five pounds.[18]

The iron bars found in the Deer Creek furnaces were about the same weight as the billets in the German furnaces. The Deer Creek furnaces appear to be a slightly later design than the *Schmelzoven.* In the latter, the bottom of the furnace was about 2 inches below the flue opening, and the billet was formed in a mold inside the pit. At Deer Creek, the furnace floor was in line with the floor of the flue so that the molten iron could flow out on the platform.

In 1732 the English Royal Board of Iron Trade became curious about an ancient furnace which was then still in use in a county in Sweden. Apparently of Celtic origin, the name of this primitive type of smelter was *Enkieling.* Except in a few areas, the *Enkieling,* like the other direct reduction hearthpits, was probably rendered obsolete when the blast furnace came into general use in the fourteenth century. Even the name *Enkieling* had not been heard often during several centuries thereafter. Interested in the ancient process of producing iron without melting it, the Board of Trade sent a mining surveyor to Sweden to examine the still-extant *Enkielings* and to prepare an exact description of the furnace and of the almost extinct process of direct reduction of iron. The illustrations of the furnace produced by the surveyor were reproduced by Emanuel Swedenborg, and his reproductions are the only extant accurate record of the *Enkieling.*

The furnaces recently found in America which were constructed on the *Enkieling* principles are hearthpits backed up by stone work or by earth embankments. Two of them—the Overly and one of the Deer Creek group—were found buried in the banks of a small brook and a creek, respectively. A third *Enkieling* uncovered in this country, though not until recently identified as an iron furnace, is shown in a drawing in the Peabody Museum Field Notes (1890) of an excavation of Clark's mound in the Miami Valley, Ohio. And a fourth *Enkieling* found so far, also in Ohio, is the second Haskins furnace. (See pp. 22–23 for accounts of the findings of these American furnaces.)

In 1652, Gerard Boate wrote a complete description of the operation of the forced-draft furnaces of his time in Ireland. The furnaces in use in the colonial period in America were like these Irish furnaces. About one hundred times as large as the ancient natural-draft furnaces, they had the added virtue of being operable continuously without the interruptions which had been necessary in cleaning out the ancient natural-draft furnaces after each charge. Boate reported:

> These [Irish] ovens are kindled with charcoal and never allowed to go out. It is blown by two pair of vast bellows driven by water power. . . . Within the barn at the bottom of the furnace stand constantly two men with long iron hooks who . . . draw out the unburned ashes, cinders, and coals. . . . On the floor of the barn is a bed of sand in which a furrow is made of sufficient breadth and depth the full length of the barn. Into this furrow, the molten iron runs very suddenly and forcibly. When cooled, it is called *sowe*.[19]

Two hundred and ten men worked on the operation of this furnace. The cost of making iron in this type of furnace and delivering it by water to London was about 2¾ cents per pound. This iron sold in London for 4½ cents per pound, including import duties.

It required five runs of an ancient hilltop furnace to produce from a ton of ore as much iron as a colonial furnace of the same size equipped with bellows could produce in one run. The ancient furnace completed a run in four days, while the forced-draft furnace required only one day to complete a run. Several days of labor were required to rework the slag ball from an ancient furnace into iron like that produced in a forced-draft furnace.

If an American colonist produced iron by the primitive and long-forgotten process used in the obsolete hearthpits recently discovered in

Ohio, it cost him at least one dollar per pound instead of four cents, the probable price on the market. It is very unlikely that he could have made iron in the hearthpit, for, though such a furnace was simple in construction, only an ironworker of long experience could smelt iron in it.

Appendix C:

Old Norse Words
in
Iroquoian Language

English	Old Norse	Iroquoian	Tribe	Authority	Year
accuse	kaera	*kera*wis	Mohawk	Marcoux	1850
	ákaera	en*kerase*	"	"	"
		*gara*wi	"	Bruyas	1700
also	ok	n*eok*	"	Hale	1880
	auk	n*ok*	"	"	"
	og	*och*ni	Onondaga	Zeisberger	1770
and	auk	*ok*	Mohawk	Hale	1880
	ok	n*oke*	"	Long	1770
	og	n*ok*	"	Deserontyon	1782
basin	ker	a*ke*rat	"	Marcoux	1850
		*kar*so	"	"	"
bone	ostéo (Greek)	*osti*endo	Cayuga	Elliott	"
	ásthi (Sanskrit)	*ohstee*uh	Mohawk	Dwight	1800
	os (Latin)	*osti*ea	"	Elliott	1850
	asht (Albanian)	*osti*a	Oneida	Skenando	"
direction	att	*ati*	Mohawk	Bruyas	1700
eat	eta	*at, ate*	"	"	"
end	endi	*enta*on	"	"	"
enter	inni	*inni*on	"	"	"
eye	auga	*oga*te	"	"	"

English	Old Norse	Iroquoian	Tribe	Authority	Year
		o-ga-reh	"	Mallery	1941
		*oka*hra	"	Hale	1850
		*oga*h	Onondaga	Schoolcraft	"
		*oga*hah	"	LeFort	"
		*oga*h	Oneida	Skenando	"
finish	enda	*onde*	Huron	Chaumonot	1635
forehead	enni	*etgeny*	Canada	Cartier	1536
		hetgu*eny*	"	"	"
		ok*enne*h	Tuscarora	Mallery	1941
girl	ekkja (older poetic	*eksaa*	Mohawk	Hewitt	1880
	usage)	*eksaa*h	"	Jones	1831
		exaa	Cayuga	Elliott	1850
god	njǫrðr	*nio*h	Onondaga	Zeisberger	1770
		*niyo*h	Mohawk	Jones	1831
		*neeyoo*h	Oneida	Barton	1800
		*nioo*h	Tuscarora	Mallery	1941
he	hann	*onn*e	Huron	Sagard	1625
I	ek	*ik*	Seneca	Wright	1800
		n*ik*	"	"	"
		d*ick*	Huron	Sagard	1625
ice	iss	o*is*e	Mohawk	Elliott	1850
		ow*iss*a	Onondaga	Zeisberger	1770
		gaw*is*a	Mohawk	Bruyas	1700
		ow*iss*eh	Seneca	Mallery	1941
if	tokko (Finn.)	*toka*	Onondaga	Shea	1700
		taka	Mohawk	Hale	1880
		*taka*t	"	Marcoux	1850
kettle	kanna	*kanna*ken	"	"	"
		*kanne*no	Wyandot	Potier	1743
		*anna*o	Huron	Chaumonot	1635
		*kana*dsia	Onondaga	Shea	1700
		*kanna*dsia	Cayuga	Elliott	1850
		*ganna*tsia	Mohawk	Bruyas	1700
moon	ný	wen*nit*a	Onondaga	Jones	1831
	(nith) nið	en*nit*a	Mohawk	Bruyas	1700
no	ne	*ne*	Huron	Brebeuf	1635
	neita (to deny)	*neto*	Onondaga	Zeisberger	1770
		te	Huron	Chaumonot	1635
nose	nǫs	o*nius*ah	Onondaga	LeFort	1850
		o*nuh*sa	Mohawk	Barton	1800
		o*neuhs*	Oneida	Skenando	1850
now	nú	ho*nuh*	Mohawk	Dwight	1800
	núna	o*na*	Seneca	Morgan	1850
		o*na*m	Cayuga	Hewitt	1880
perceive	kaga (to gaze, to	ken*kago*n	Mohawk	Marcoux	1850
	peep)	*kago*nra	Huron	Chaumonot	1635

English	Old Norse	Iroquoian	Tribe	Authority	Year
relate,	geta	wa*gate*	Onondaga	Zeisberger	1770
say,	kveða	*quadd*adia	Canada	Cartier	1536
speak,	seggja	wa*saga*wenhas	Mohawk	Bruyas	1700
tell	inna	*en, ihen, en*t	Huron	Chaumonot	1636
	senna	i*sen*	Mohawk	Bruyas	1700
	gegna	*gen*	Huron	Chaumonot	1635
sing	renna raustum	ka*renna*	Mohawk	Marcoux	1850
		ka*renna*	Onondaga	Shea	1700
		ren	Wyandot	Barbeau	1930
		ga*ren*da	Mohawk	Bruyas	1700
		at*ren*	"	"	"
	gala	ta*li*	"	"	"
smoke	reykja	ga*rokea*	Onondaga	Shea	"
son	ungr	*yungh*	Oneida	Jefferson	1770
stand	standa	ka*tanda*	Huron	Chaumonot	1635
		tesa*tanda*	"	"	"
		*sta*tsi	"	Sagard	1625
stone	steinn	o*sten*ra	Mohawk	Bruyas	1700
		o*stain*ra	Tuscarora	Mallery	1941
	eista	ar*iesta*	Huron	Sagard	1625
		ar*iesta*	Wyandot	Johnston	1819
testicle	eista	x*ista*	Canada	Cartier	1536
		ar*iesta*	Huron	Sagard	1625
		on*eschta*	Onondaga	Zeisberger	1770
that	sá	*ca*	Huron	Brebeuf	1635
		xa	"	Chaumonot	"
the	inn	*na*	Mohawk	Hewitt	1881
		na	"	Marcoux	1850
wait	hara (Ger. *harren*)	ker*hare*	Mohawk	Marcoux	1850
		jir*hare*	Onondaga	Zeisberger	1770
when	en	*wen*to	"	"	"
	hvénaer	*wen*niyoh	Mohawk	Marcoux	1850
		nen	"	Hewitt	1881
		wen-don	Seneca	Mallery	1941
wife	ekkja	*ech*ro	Onondaga	Zeisberger	1770
	aekkia	*ick*sae	Tionontati	Lahontan	1700
woman	kona	wa*konn*yh	Mohawk	Hale	1880
		a*kon*kwa	Huron	Potier	1745
		*kon*heghtie	Cayuga	Elliott	1850
	kvenna	is*kwen*	Nascapi	Gatschet	1880
word	inna (see "tell")	o-*wenno*	Mohawk	Marcoux	1850
		ka-*wenna*	Onondaga	Shea	1700

(Note: Italics indicate roots.)

European Sources: Richard Cleasby and Gudbrand Vigfusson, *An Icelandic-English Dictionary* (1874); Alois Walde, *Vergleichendes Wörterbuch der Indogermanischen Sprachen* (1930).

Iroquoian Sources: James Adair, A. Boudinot, S. E. Dwight, J. Johnston, J. Parish, *Archaeologia Americana,* Vol. 2 (1836). A. S. Gatschet, J. B. N. Hewitt, Père Marcoux, Father Potier, publications and manuscripts of the Smithsonian Bureau of American Ethnology; J. Wood and Thomas Jefferson, manuscripts of the American Philosophical Society; Rev. Asher Wright, Adam Elliott, Abraham Le Fort, the miscellaneous works of H. R. Schoolcraft; A. H. Mallery, personal collections. All others are from the published works of the authorities cited.

Appendix D:

Confirmation
of
Arlington Mallery's Claim to Have Discovered the Coast of Antarctica
on the
Piri Re'is Map

The following statement was received from Charles H. Hapgood, author of *Maps of the Ancient Sea Kings: Evidence of Advanced Civilization in the Ice Age,* [1] in a letter to Mary Roberts Harrison dated June 23, 1978.

Arlington Mallery's claim to have found the coast of Antarctica on the Piri Re'is map drawn in 1513, three hundred years before the modern discovery of Antarctica, has been fully confirmed. When I read the text of the Georgetown University Forum of the Air (1956) program in which Mallery discussed the map with two distinguished astronomers and with a map expert of the Navy Hydrographic Office, I was fascinated, for the map came as supporting evidence for a proposition I had advanced in my book, *Earth's Shifting Crust*. This proposition, or theory, contained a corollary: the assumption that there must have been a warm period in Antarctica during the last Ice Age in North America. I had been looking for evidence of this, and here was the evidence!

I was determined, then, to investigate this question, to see if Captain Mallery's claim could be proved. I made this a class project at Keene State College, and many students worked on the map, and made important contributions to its solution.

Very early in the study of the map, I saw that the lines on it suggested a geometrical design. There were five centers in the Atlantic Ocean that appeared to lie on the perimeter of a circle that had been erased, but which had been used in laying out the map projection. There were radiating lines at 22½, 45, and 90° angles. These lines at their intersections created rectangles similar to the grid of modern maps of the Mercator type. There appeared to be a center for the whole map somewhere to the east of the torn edge of the map. The whole thing suggested geometry.

We saw that the projection had been based on a circle with a center in eastern Africa. To solve it, we had to find the center and the length of the radius. After five years of work, we did locate the center at the intersection of the Tropic of Cancer and the meridian of Alexandria. We determined the length of the radius and found that the ancient geographers had a more accurate knowledge of the circumference of the earth than Eratosthenes or the astronomers of the Renaissance. That is, they apparently knew it exactly. Calling upon a friend who was a mathematician, I obtained the information necessary for the drawing of a scientifically accurate grid of latitude and longitude with which to test the accuracy of the map. We found that the ancient geographers had placed the Queen Maud coastline in correct latitude and longitude. This was the confirmation of Mallery's claim. These conclusions were checked and accepted by the cartographic staff of the U.S. Strategic Air Command who drew all the maps for the Air Force.

But this was only the beginning. The Piri Re'is map turned out to be a new Rosetta Stone, a key to the understanding of hundreds of maps of the Middle Ages and the Renaissance. Our projection could be used, with various modifications, to check the accuracy of the medieval portolan charts, which we discovered derived from a very remote antiquity, reaching back to the Ice Age. As a group, these maps show us the extent of the scientific achievements of an ancient civilization unknown to us, which, but for these maps, might always have remained the subject of unproved speculations.

The most amazing of all these maps, not excepting the Piri Re'is map, is a world map drawn by a French geographer, Oronce Finé, in 1531, and called the Oronteus Finaeus map. In compiling this map, Finé used some ancient source map of Antarctica, now apparently lost. This is a map of the entire continent, showing all or most of the coasts ice-free, and interior features close to the Pole itself. When we solved the grid of this map, which was based on spherical trigonometry, we found we could locate over fifty geographical points to within two degrees of accuracy in latitude or longitude. The proof of this map of the whole continent serves, of course, as confirmation of Mallery's claim for the Piri Re'is map. From this it seems clear that his work represents an important turning point in our understanding of the past.

Appendix E:

The Ancient Worldwide Signary

I. Authorities Consulted *on* Ancient Signaries

Chadwick, John, *The Decipherment of Linear B,* Cambridge University Press, 1958.

Diringer, David, *The Alphabet,* 2nd ed., Funk and Wagnalls, 1953.

Evans, Sir Arthur J., "Primitive Pictographs and Script from Crete and the Peloponnesos," *Journal of Hellenic Studies,* Vol. 14, 1894; and "Further Discoveries of Cretan and Hellenic Script," *Journal of Hellenic Studies,* Vol. 17, 1897.

Gardiner, A. H., "Egyptian Origin of the Semitic Alphabet," *Journal of Egyptian Archaeology,* Vol. 3, 1916.

Gesinius, W., *Hebrew Lexicon,* 28th ed., 1910.

Hubner, E., *Monumenta Linguae Ibericae,* Berlin, 1893.

Larfeld, Wilhelm, *Handbuch der Grieschen Epigraphik,* O. R. Reisland, Leipzig, 1907.

Myers, J. L., "The Minoan Signary," *Journal of Hellenic Studies,* Vol. 66–67, 1946–1947.

Petrie, Sir W. M. Flinders, *The Formation of the Alphabet,* British School of Archaeology in Egypt, Study Series III, 1912.

Taylor, Isaac, *The History of the Alphabet,* New York, 1899.

Velazquez, Luis Joseph, *Ensayo Sobre Los Alphabetos de Las Lettras Desconocidas,* Spanish Historical Society, Madrid, 1752.

Ventris, Michael and Chadwick, John, *Documents in Mycenaean Greek,* Cambridge University Press, 1956.

II.
Ancient Signaries

Aegean	Lydian
Cretan	Lykian
Cypriote	Minoan
Egyptian, early prehistoric	Mycenaean
Egyptian, late prehistoric	Nabathaean
Egyptian, 1st Dynasty	Oscan
Egyptian, XIIth Dynasty	Pelasgic
Egyptian, XIXth Dynasty	Phoenician
Egyptian, Roman	Runic
Etruscan	Sabaean
Greek	Semitic (North)
Iberian	Semitic (South)
Latin (Ancient)	Spain (North)
Libyan	Spain (South)

III.
Publications
in which
Ancient Inscriptions Are Reproduced

1. *Publications in American Archaeology and Ethnology,* University of California Press, Vol. 24, 1929, No. 2, pp. 47–238, plates 22–94.

2. *Tenth Annual Report of the Bureau of Ethnology,* 1888–89, Government Printing Office, 1893, pp. 61–70, plates 1–11.

3. *Twelfth Biannual Report of State Historical Society of Idaho,* 1929–30, pp. 35–111.

4. Henry Rowe Schoolcraft, *Historical and Statistical Information Respecting the History, Condition and Prospects of the Indian Tribes of the United States,* 1851–57, Vol. 2, p. 88, plate 41; Vol. 4, plates 34c, 34d, and 35; Vol. 6., pp. 112, 606, 610.

5. *U.S. Senate Document 562,* U.S. Engineers, #64, plates 23–73.

6. T. J. Hutchinson, *Two Years in Peru,* S. Low, Marston, Low, and Searle, London, 1873.

7. Adan Quiroga, *Petrografiàs y Epictografiàs de Calchaqui,* Impr. de la Universidad, Buenos Aires, 1931.

8. *American Naturalist,* Vol. 19, 1885, plate 9; Vol. 18, 1894, p. 1190.

9. E. B. Renard, *Archaeological Survey of Eastern Colorado,* Archaeological Survey Series, 3rd Report, Denver University, Department of Anthropology, 1931.

10. Olaf Strandwold, *Norse Inscriptions on American Stones,* Magnus Bjorndal, Weehauken, N.J., 1948.

Notes

Chapter 1
Spruce Hill,
pages 1–10

1. The Foster letter was published in the *American Philosophical Journal* (1814), now in the Ross County Historical Society Library, Columbus, Ohio.
2. H. G. Shetrone, *Primer of Ohio Archeology,* The Ohio State Archeological and Historical Society, Columbus (1938), 3rd ed., pp. 24–26.
3. *Encyclopedia of Archaeology,* ed. by Glyn Daniel (New York: Thomas Y. Crowell Company, 1977), pp. 156–157. (Reference added by editor, after Mallery's death.)
4. Shetrone, *op. cit.*
5. John Percy, *Metallurgy, Iron and Steel* (London, 1864), p. 873.
6. Penniman and Brown, Inc., Baltimore, Md., Report, Aug. 23, 1949.
7. J. M. Swank, *History of the Manufacture of Iron in All Ages* (1884), p. 76.

Chapter 2
The Pre-Columbian
Iron Industry in Ohio,
pages 11–28

1. Aage Rousselle, *Farm and Churches in the Medieval Settlements of Greenland* (1941), p. 215.
2. Ludwig Beck, *Geschichte des Eisens* (1891), Vol. 1, p. 619; Peabody Museum, Harvard University, *Papers in Archaeology and Ethnology* (1911), Vol. 8, No. 3.
3. In 1962 the National Bureau of Standards tested the so-called quicklime and found that it was dolomitic clay containing 36 percent or more iron. The Battelle Memorial Institute also analyzed the "lime" and reported it was clay.
4. Beck, *op. cit.,* pp. 617ff.
5. Letter and report to author from Dr. A. M. Hall, Battelle Memorial Institute, Sept. 25, 1949.

6. Letter to author from R. R. Adams, Battelle Memorial Institute, Jan. 18, 1950.

Chapter 3
The Pre-Columbian
Iron Industry in Virginia,
pages 29–36

1. Frank H. H. Roberts as quoted in the Richmond *Times-Dispatch,* Nov. 12, 1949. Dr. Roberts was then director of River Basin Archeological Surveys, Smithsonian Institution.
2. *Journal of the Washington Academy of Sciences* (Dec. 15, 1948), Vol. 38, No. 12.
3. Richmond *Times-Dispatch,* Nov. 6, 1949.
4. Letter to author from R. R. Adams, Battelle Memorial Institute, Jan. 18, 1950.
5. Letter to author from R. W. Breckenridge, Iowa State College, Ames, Iowa, Nov. 24, 1957.

Chapter 4
The Clash of Theories,
pages 37–49

1. The Foster letter was published in the *American Philosophical Journal* (1814), now in the Ross County Historical Society Library, Columbus, Ohio.
2. Caleb Atwater, *Archaeologia Americana,* 1820, p. 149.
3. E. G. Squier, *Transactions of the American Ethnological Society,* 1848, Vol. 2.
4. E. G. Squier and E. H. Davis, *Ancient Monuments of the Mississippi Valley, Smithsonian Contributions to Knowledge,* No. 1, 1848, pp. 11, 12. Italics added.
5. *Ibid.*
6. *Ibid.,* p. 196.
7. *Ibid.,* p. 208.
8. Atwater, *op. cit.,* pp. 162, 172, 178.
9. Robert Silverberg, *Mound Builders of Ancient America,* New York Graphic Society, 1968, p. 129. (Reference added by editor after Mallery's death.)
10. Atwater, *op. cit.,* p. 140.

11. Silverberg, *op. cit.,* p. 110.

12. Henry Howe, *Ohio Archeological and Historical Quarterly,* Vol. 2, No. 4, March, 1889.

13. *Ibid.*

14. In the E. G. Squier Papers, Manuscript Division, Library of Congress, arranged chronologically.

15. In the Joseph Henry Papers in the Smithsonian Institution Archives, arranged chronologically.

16. E. G. Squier Papers, *op. cit.*

17. E. G. Squier, *Aboriginal Monuments of the State of New York, Smithsonian Contributions to Knowledge,* No. 2, 1850, p. 187.

18. E. G. Squier, *The Primeval Monuments of Peru Compared with Those in Other Parts of the World,* written in 1868 and published in *The American Naturalist,* Vol. IV, 1870, Essex Institute Press, pp. 136, 140.

Chapter 5
An Iron Curtain on
America's Past,
pages 50–52

1. See Chapter 3 for description of Deer Creek furnaces.

2. John Nihlen, *Studier Rorande Aldre Svensk Jarntill Verkning* (1932).

3. *Ibid.*

4. Peabody Museum, Harvard University, *Papers in Archeology and Ethnology* (1911), Vol. #8, No. 3.

5. For sketches of German two-pit furnaces, see Ludwig Beck, *Geschichte des Eisens* (1891), Vol. 1.

6. Samuel F. Haven, "Archeology of the United States," *Smithsonian Contributions to Knowledge,* No. 8, 1856, p. 154.

Chapter 6
Pre-Columbian
Viking and Celtic Migrations to America,
pages 53–59

1. Emil Schurmacher, "It's North Again for Macmillan," *Parade* (Washington *Post*) (July 31, 1949), p. 9.

2. August Demin, *Illustrated History of Arms* (1877), pp. 20, 134.

Chapter 7
The Adventurous Vikings,
pages 60–63

1. *Biskupa Sogur, Hongrvaka* (1856), p. 64. Certain scholars discount this statement because in some documents, Vinland is spelled *Vindland* and a Bishop Jon is reported to have been martyred in *Wendland*.

Chapter 8
Stepping Stones to America,
pages 64–72

1. Polybius, Geminus of Rhodes, Diodorus Siculus, Timaeus, Eratosthenes, Isidorus of Charax, Hipparchus, Crates of Mallus, Strabo, et al.

2. Dicuil, *Liber de Mensura Orbis Terrae* (1807), Chap. 7.

3. Ari Thorgillsson, *Landnamabok* (ca. 1076), I.1.

4. Julius Caesar, *Commentaries on the Gallic Wars,* Book 3.

5. *Ibid.*

6. Bede the Venerable, *Ecclesiastical History of the English Nation* (1840), p. xiv.

7. Dicuil, *op. cit.*

8. P. de Roo, *History of America Before Columbus* (1900), Vol. 2, Chap. 3.

9. Thorgillsson, *op. cit.,* Prologus.

10. Thorgillsson, *Islendinga-bok* (ca. 1080), I,3.

11. Patricksfiord, situated in northwestern Iceland, is one of the nearest to Greenland of the Iceland fiords. Among the more than forty Irish and Gallic names of Icelandic mountains, rivers, fiords, ridges, and islets are Kadalstadir, Brjansloekr, Dugfusdalr, Kalmansa, Kjaransvik, Kylan, Kolkan, Irskileid, and Irskiholl.

12. Thorgillsson, *Islendinga-bok,* VI,2.

13. Letter to author from Dr. N. C. Nelson of the American Museum of Natural History.

14. Also known as the Gaell-Gaedthill, these people were a product of interbreeding between Gallic and Celtic Irish and peripatetic Norse seamen, with a language seemingly related to that of the Gallic Celts of Brittany. The Gall-Gael had their own fleets and armies, maintained an independent political status, and, during the Viking incursions, served as mercenaries for both the Vikings and the Irish. It was probably the Gall-Gael, with their seagoing ships, who carried on the exchange between Christian Ireland and the Celts in Iceland, Greenland, and Vitramannaland on the American continent.

Chapter 9
Vitramannaland:
Refuge of the Celts,
pages 73–81

1. *Eyrbyggia Saga,* Chap. 47.
2. *Codex 770,* Arne Magnean Collection, University of Copenhagen Library.
3. *Book of the Chiefs of Iceland,* 1.37.
4. Ari Thorgillsson, *Landnamabok,* II, 19.2.
5. *Hauksbók Saga of Thorfinn Karlsefni* (ca. 1320), Vol. 10.
6. P. de Roo, *History of America Before Columbus* (1900), p. 32.

Chapter 10
New Horizons for the Norse,
pages 82–93

1. U.S. Hydrographic Office, *Chart H.O. 5784.*
2. Poul Norlund, *Viking Settlers* (1924), p. 171; Lauge Koch, *East Greenland Ice* (1945), p. 263.
3. Norlund, *op. cit.,* p. 27.
4. *Ibid.,* p. 20.
5. A. M. Reeves, *The Finding of Wineland the Good* (1895), p. 36; see also the Friseo chart in Chapter 16, showing the Atlantic Current west of its present location. `
6. Paul Herrman, *Grettis Saga* (1922), Chap. 15.
7. Norlund, *op. cit.,* pp. 75ff.

Chapter 11
The Norse Discover a Continent,
pages 94–99

1. *The Flatey Sagas of the Vinland Voyages* are accepted here as authentic. *The Hauksbók Saga of Thorfinn Karlsefni* is considered to be a historical novel based on a lost Icelandic saga. Where Hauk's version conflicts with the *Flatey Sagas,* the records given in the latter are used. In general, quotations from sagas in this book are based on the translation in the *Flateyjarbok,* published by the Royal Danish general staff in May, 1893. Quotations from the *Saga of Thorfinn Karlsefni* are based on *The Finding of Wineland the Good* by Arthur M. Reeves.
2. Wilfred Grenfell, *Romance of Labrador* (1914), p. 110.

Chapter 12
Leif the Lucky
and Vinland the Good,
pages 100–114

1. N. L. Beamish, *The Norse Discovery of America* (1906), p. 150.
2. David Putnam, *David Goes to Baffinland* (1927), pp. 43ff.
3. Statement of D. B. MacMillan to the author.
4. Junius B. Bird, *Archeology of the Hopedale Area, Labrador* (1945), pp. 140, 141.
5. Lauge Koch, *East Greenland Ice* (1945), p. 263.
6. Adam of Bremen, *Gesta Hammaburgensis* (ca. 1076), Vol. 4, p. 38.
7. Vaino Tanner, *Outlines of the Geography, Life, and Customs of Newfoundland-Labrador* (1944), p. 43.
8. R. H. Bonneycastle, Newfoundland (1842), p. 256.

Chapter 14
The First Settlement in Vinland,
pages 120–134

1. Vaino Tanner, *Newfoundland-Labrador* (1944), p. 479.
2. H. P. Biggar, *The Voyages of Jacques Cartier,* Public Archives of Canada (1924), p. 222.
3. Sir John Richardson, *Narrative of a Second Expedition to the Shores of the Polar Sea in the Years 1825, 1826, and 1827* (1828), p. 189.
4. Diamond Jenness, *Life of the Copper Eskimo* (1913–1918), p. 148.

Chapter 15
Later Viking Migrations to Vinland
and the American Mainland,
pages 135–142

1. *Biskupa Sogur, Hongrvaka* (1856), p. 64.
2. Cladding is the welding at less than normal temperature of thin sheets of steel or carburized iron to a softer metal. A lost art for many centuries, this process has been revived recently in the manufature of jet planes, etc.
3. H. P. Biggar, *The Voyages of Jacques Cartier* (1924), p. 154; *S. de Champlain Works,* Champlain Society (1922), Vol. 3, p. 123; Baron de Lahontan, *New Voyages to North America* (1905), Vol. 2, p. 454; G. W. Dasent, *Iceland* (1861), pp. XCIX, CLff; Poul Norlund, *Viking Settlers,* Med. o. Gronland (1924), pp. 57, 77.

4. Gisle Oddsson, *Annalium in Islandia Farrago, and De Mirabilius Islandiae* (1917), Vol. 10, p. 2.

Chapter 16
Pre-Columbian Charts
and Maps of the New World,
pages 143–153

1. Transcript of "Old and New Discoveries in Antarctica," Georgetown University Radio Forum, Washington, D.C., Aug. 26, 1956, p. 2.

2. N. L. Beamish, *The Norse Discovery of America* (1906), p. 150.

3. Sir John Richardson, *Narratives of a Second Expedition to the Shores of the Polar Sea in the Years 1825, 1826, and 1827* (1828), p. 189; and Diamond Jenness, *Life of the Copper Eskimo* (1913–1918), p. 148.

4. Gerard Mercator, *Map of Iceland 1607.*

5. Gisle Oddsson, *Annalium in Islandia Farrago,* Islendica (1917), Vol. 10, p. 2.

6. Frithiof Nansen, *Bathymetrical Features of the North Polar Seas,* Norwegian North Polar Expedition Report, Vol. 4, p. 173.

7. *Arctic Geography and Ethnology,* Royal Geographic Society (1874), pp. 50ff.

Chapter 17
The Long-Lost Gunnbiorn's Skerries,
pages 154–159

1. Ivar Bardasson, *Description of Greenland,* Hakluyt Society (1873), Vol. 50, pp. 17ff.

2. U.S. Hydrographic Office, *Chart H.O. 5773.*

3. R. B. Flint, *Glacial Geology* (1947), pp. 487ff.

4. Lauge Koch, *East Greenland Ice* (1945), pp. 121ff.

5. Bardasson, *op. cit.*

6. Poul Norlund, *Viking Settlers* (1924), p. 141; Paul DuChaillu, *Viking Age* (1889), Vol. 2, p. 346; G. W. Dasent, *Iceland* (1861), p. cx.

7. R. G. Daly, *Changing World of the Ice Age* (1934), p. 142.

8. *Arctic Geography and Ethnology,* Royal Geographic Society (1874), pp. 52ff.; Aage Rousselle, *Farms and Churches in the Mediaeval Norse Settlements of Greenland* (1941), p. 15.

9. T. Thoroddsen, *Oversigt Over de Islendski Vulkaners Historie* (1882).

10. Cornelius Wolford, *Floods and Inundations,* Statistical Society of London (1875–79).

11. Johann Ruysch, *Map of the World, Ptolemy 1507.*

12. Olaus Magnus, *Di Pygmaeis Gruntland* (1658), p. lccii; Magnus, *Marine Map* (1539).

13. Jan Van Keulen, *Pascaert van Groenlandt* (1700).

14. U.S. Hydrographic Office, *Chart H.O. 5784.*

15. T. Thoroddsen, *op. cit.;* Wolford, *op. cit.*

16. Yves Joseph de Kerguelen-Tremarec, "Relation of a Voyage to the North Sea" in *Pinkerton's Voyages* (1808), Vol. 1, pp. 754ff. Italics added.

Chapter 18
The Black Death:
Return to the Stone Age,
pages 160–167

1. J. P. Papon, *De la Peste* (1740), Vol. 2, p. 270.

2. *Report Plague Control Conference,* U.S. Public Health Service (1941), p. 59.

3. Gisle Oddsson, *Annalium in Islandia Farrago,* Islendica (1917), Vol. 10, p. 2.

4. Knut Gjerset, *History of Iceland* (1924), p. 277.

5. D. G. Brinton, *Annals of the Cakchiquels,* p. 171.

6. J. Brebeuf, *Jesuit Relations,* ed. by R. G. Thwaite (1896–1901), Vol. 11, p. 13; P. Le Mercier, *ibid.,* Vol. 13, p. 119.

7. Martin, Quimby, and Collier, *Indians Before Columbus* (1947), pp. 513ff.

Chapter 19
The Rise of the Iroquois,
pages 168–175

1. L. H. Morgan, *League of the Hodenosaunee* (1904), p. 63; David Cusick, *Sketches of the Ancient History of the Six Nations* (1825); Peter D. Clark, *Origin and Traditional History of the Wyandottes* (1870), Chap. 1; Henry Schoolcraft, *Notes on the Iroquois* (1846), p. 65.

2. Diamond Jenness, *Prehistoric Culture Waves* (1940), pp. 392ff.

3. H. P. Biggar, *The Voyages of Jacques Cartier* (1924), p. 268.

4. *Samuel de Champlain's Works,* The Champlain Society, Toronto (1922), Plates I and LXXXI; Biggar, *op. cit.,* Plates 12 and 14.

5. *Ibid.,* p. 60.
6. H. P. Biggar, *Early Trading Companies of New France* (1930), p. 32.
7. *Samuel de Champlain's Works, op. cit.,* Vol. 1, p. 249.

Chapter 20
The Links of Culture,
pages 176–188

1. W. H. Holmes, *Twentieth Annual Report,* Bureau of American Ethnology (1898–1899), Smithsonian Institution, p. 163.
2. W. J. Wintemberg, *Uren Prehistoric Site,* National Museum of Canada Bulletin (1928), p. 47.
3. *Ibid.,* p. 43.
4. W. M. Beauchamp, *Earthenware of the New York Aborigines* (1898), p. 1.
5. Poul Norlund, *Gardar Meddelelser om Gronland* (1924), Bind 76, Nr. 1.
6. Junius B. Bird, *Archaeology of the Hopedale Area, Labrador* (1945), pp. 140, 141.
7. L. M. Larsen, *Earliest Norwegian Laws* (1935), pp. 11–14ff.
8. *Jesuit Relations,* ed. by R. G. Thwaite (1896–1901), Vol. 28, p. 49.
9. *Ibid.,* Vol. 11, p. 205.
10. *Ibid.,* Vol. 33, p. 246.
11. J. B. N. Hewitt, *Smithsonian Explorations* (1932), p. 84.
12. H. P. Biggar, *The Voyages of Jacques Cartier* (1924), p. 154.
13. Poul Norlund, *Viking Settlers,* Med. o. Gronland (1924), Bd. 67, pp. 77ff; Aage Rousselle, *Norse Building Customs in the Scottish Isles* (1934), pp. 34ff.; G. W. Dasent, *Iceland* (1861), p. XCVIII.
14. Adrien Vanderdonck, *N.Y. Historical Society Collections, 2nd Series* (1849), Vol. 2, p. 195; John Bartram, *Travels to Onondaga* (1743), pp. 40ff.
15. Rousselle, *op. cit.,* pp. 102ff.; Sagard-Theodat, *Grand Voyages des Hurons* (1632), p. 79; *S. de Champlain's Works,* Champlain Society (1922), Vol. 3, p. 123; Dasent, *op. cit.,* p. CL; Bartram, *op. cit.*
16. Sagard-Theodat, *op. cit.;* F. de Peron, *Jesuit Relations,* ed. by R. G. Thwaite (1896–1901), Vol. 15, p. 237; *S. de Champlain's Works, op. cit.;* Francis Parkman, *The Jesuits in North America* (1897), p. 137; Knut Gjerset, *History of Iceland* (1924), p. 327.
17. Anonymous, *Iceland, Greenland, and Faroes* (1840), p. 206; Norlund, *op. cit.;* Vanderdonck, *op. cit.;* Rousselle, *op. cit.;* Bartram, *op. cit.*

18. Dasent, *op. cit.*, pp. CLff.; Jan Petersen, *Gamli gardsamleggi i Rogaland* (1933); Norlund, *op. cit.*

19. Vanderdonck, *op. cit.;* L. H. Morgan, *Houses and House Life of American Aborigines* (1881), p. 64; Parkman, *op. cit;* Bartram, *op. cit.*

20. Sagard-Theodat, *op. cit.;* De Peron, *op. cit.;* S. de Champlain's Works, *op. cit.*

21. *Ibid.*, Vol. 3, plate X.

22. Baron de Lahontan, *New Voyages to North America* (1905), Vol. 2, p. 454.

23. *S. de Champlain's Works, op. cit.;* Rousselle, *op. cit.*

24. Dasent, *op. cit.*, p. CL.

25. Biggar, *op. cit.*, p. 154.

26. Rouselle, *op. cit.*, pp. 34ff.; Sagard-Theodat, *op. cit.; S. de Champlain's Works, op. cit.*, Vol. 3, p. 125; Vanderdonck, *op. cit.;* Parkman, *op. cit.*, pp. 11ff.

27. Rousselle, *op. cit.*, pp. 102ff; *S. de Champlain's Works, op. cit.*

28. Vanderdonck, *op. cit.;* Rousselle, *op. cit.*, p. 34; Norlund, *op. cit.*, p. 77.

29. Biggar, *op. cit.*, p. 154; *S. de Champlain's Works, op. cit.*, Vol. 3, p. 123; Baron de Lahontan, *op. cit.;* Dasent, *op. cit.*, pp. XCIX, CLff; Norlund, *op. cit.* p. 77.

30. Otto Jespersen, *Encyclopaedia Britannica* (1947), Vol. 13, p. 702.

31. Freeman and Stenton, *ibid.* (1946), Vol. 22.

32. H. C. Wyld, *ibid.*, Vol. 8, p. 557.

33. S. G. Morley, *The Ancient Maya* (1947), p. 20.

34. Wintemberg, *op. cit.*, pp. 43ff.

Chapter 21
The Kensington Rune Stone,
pages 189–193

1. Hjalmar Herrmansson, *Islendica* (1936), Vol. 25, p. 50.

2. M. W. Stirling, "The Kensington Stone," Washington *Times-Herald*, March 12, 1948.

Chapter 23
My "Discovery"
of the Piri Re'is Map
pages 199–207

1. For a detailed history of the Piri Re'is map, see P. Kahle, *Geographical Review* (1933), Vol. 23, pp. 621–638.

2. For a method for determining longitude believed by some scholars to have been available to scholars of any age, including antiquity, see Alan R. Gillespie and Rollin W. Gillespie, "Stonehenge and the Piri Re'is Map," *Navigation, Journal of the Institute of Navigation,* Vol. 17, No. 2, pp. 122, 123.

3. J. L. Hough, "Pleistocene Lithology of Antarctic Ocean-Bottom Sediments," *Journal of Geology* (1950), Vol. 58, pp. 254–260.

Chapter 24
The Ancient Worldwide Signary,
pages 208–219

1. Garrick Mallery, "Picture Writing of the American Indians," *Tenth Annual Report,* 1888–89, Bureau of Ethnology, Smithsonian Institution (New York: Dover Publications, 1972), p. 77.

2. For an account of Strong's life, see Joseph Corey Ayoob, *Ancient Inscriptions in the New World,* Vol. I, 2d ed. (Pittsburgh, Pa.: 1964).

3. Arlington H. Mallery, *Lost America* (Washington, D.C.: The Overlook Company, 1951), p. ix.

4. Memorandum (Oct. 19, 1961) to Dr. Fred Kinsey, Chief Curator, Pennsylvania State Museum, from Alan R. Geyer, Topographic and Geologic Survey Department, Internal Affairs, State of Pennsylvania, on "Phoenician Writing on Rock Samples Loaned by Mr. Strong."

5. Sir W. M. Flinders Petrie, *Formation of the Alphabet,* p. 4.

Appendix A
Great Lakes Copper Culture,
pages 223–227

1. National Bureau of Standards, *Letter-Circular LC-444* (July 13, 1935), p. 2.

2. Proc. Wisconsin State Historical Society, Vol. 7 (1876), p. 101.

3. Comment by Dr. George A. Ellinger, National Bureau of Standards, on the results of his examination of submitted specimens.

4. *Discovery and Conquest of Florida,* Hakluyt Society, Vol. 9 (1851), p. 64.

5. *Samuel de Champlain Voyages,* Prince Society, Vol. 2 (1878), p. 236.

Appendix B
Ancient Iron Production,
pages 228–238

1. Henri Hubert, *The Rise of the Celts* (Alfred A. Knopf, 1934), p. 131.

2. In 1920, archaeologist Greenman reported to the Ohio State Archaeological and Historical Society that there was an iron-smelting furnace on Spruce Hill and sent specimens to the Museum of the Society. As stated earlier, James Foster in 1811 also reported the existence of iron-smelting furnaces on Spruce Hill.

3. J. S. Gardner, *Ironwork,* (London: Victoria and Albert Museum, NK 8204. G3).

4. J. M. Swank, *History of the Manufacture of Iron in All Ages* (1884), p. 25.

5. John Nihlen, *Studier Rorande Aldre Svensk Jarntill Verkning* (1932), p. 60.

6. *Ibid.,* pp. 57, 58.

7. Swank, *op. cit.,* p. 76.

8. Nihlen, *op. cit.,* pp. 57, 58.

9. *Ibid.*

10. *Ibid.*

11. *Ibid.*

12. *Ibid.*

13. Swank, *op. cit.,* p. 72.

14. Aage Rousselle, *Farms and Churches in the Mediaeval Settlements of Greenland* (1941), p. 215.

15. Ludwig Beck, *Geschichte des Eisens* (1891), Vol. 1, p. 619.

16. *Ibid.,* pp. 617ff.

17. *Ibid.*

18. *Ibid.*

19. Gerard Boate, *Ireland's Natural History* (1652), pp. 108ff.

Appendix D
Confirmation of Arlington Mallery's Claim to Have Discovered the Coast of Antarctica on the Piri Re'is Map, *pages 243–244*

1. Charles H. Hapgood, *Maps of the Ancient Sea Kings: Evidence of Advanced Civilization in the Ice Age* (Philadelphia and New York: Chilton Company, 1966).

Index

About the Authors

The late **Arlington H. Mallery** was a civil and structural engineer, a navigator, and a cartographer. After graduating from Union College in New York, his native state, he became a structural engineer for the Long Island Railroad. Later, as owner and operator of the Owego Bridge Company, he followed the profession for which his family had been noted for several generations in northern New York. He was a pioneer in the construction of all-steel riveted bridges and was granted patents on structural and mechanical inventions. During World War I, he served in the Army Engineer Corps as a structural engineer, and during World War II as a captain in the Army Transportation Service. He then devoted himself until his death in 1968 to his lifelong avocation, research in pre-Columbian history.

Mr. Mallery has been acclaimed around the world for his research findings. In November, 1948, Dr. Johannes Brondsted, director of the Danish Museum and professor of prehistory at Copenhagen University, came to this country to interview him, and after the interview declared that he was "the world's authority on ancient iron." In his publications, Paul-Emile Victor, the French polar explorer, has often referred to Mallery's "remarkable discoveries in prehistory." As early as 1960, Mallery received from the Soviet Academy of Sciences a letter of commendation for his "discovery" of the Piri Re'is map, describing "the great interest of our scientists and broad public." Mr. Mallery was married to Marta Wittkowska, the internationally famous opera star.

Mary Roberts Harrison collaborated with Arlington Mallery for longer than a decade, assembling from his voluminous notes material for his book, *Lost America,* advising him on sociological factors, and working with him in the writing of that book. Since Mr. Mallery's death in 1968, she has rewritten much of *Lost America* and added six new chapters based on Mallery's notes, his conversations with her, and extensive research of her own.

Mrs. Harrison is a graduate of the University of Minnesota, her native state, where she taught in the Sociology Department while holding a fellowship in anthropology. She completed her graduate studies at the University of California and The American University. In the 1930s, she founded *Freelance,* one of the nationally circulated "little" magazines of fiction and social issues of that era. Since then she has contributed articles on social issues to national publications and worked as a writer for the government and the Bureau of National Affairs. For several years, while working as a free-lance writer, she taught English, sociology, and humanities at colleges and universities. For the past fifteen years, she has been the director of the Cooperative Forum, a private discussion group in Washington founded in the 1930s by government economic and social policymakers.

Dutton Paperbacks
of
Related Interest